The Oblate Assault
on Canada's Northwest

RELIGIONS AND BELIEFS SERIES

The series includes books bearing on the religions of the Americas, the Bible in its relationship to cultures, and on ethics in relation to religion. The series welcomes manuscripts written in either English or French.

Editorial Committee

Robert Choquette, Director
Margaret Dufour-McDonald
David Jeffrey
Pierre Savard

In the same series

Pauline Côté, *Les transactions politiques des croyants,* 1993

Adolf Ens, *Subjects or Citizens?: The Mennonite Experience in Canada, 1870-1925,* 1994

RELIGIONS AND BELIEFS SERIES, NO. 3

The Oblate Assault on Canada's Northwest

ROBERT CHOQUETTE

University of Ottawa Press

This book has been published with the help of a grant from the Canadian Federation for the Humanities, using funds provided by the Social Sciences and Humanities Research Council of Canada.

University of Ottawa Press gratefully acknowledges the support extended to its publishing program by the Canada Council, the Department of Canadian Heritage, and the University of Ottawa.

CANADIAN CATALOGUING IN PUBLICATION DATA

Choquette, Robert, 1938–
    The Oblate Assault on Canada's Northwest
(Religions and Beliefs series; no. 3)

Includes bibliographical references and index
ISBN 0-7766-0402-3

    1. Oblate Missionaries of Mary Immaculate—History—19th century. 2. Catholic Church—Missions—Northwest, Canadian—History—19th century. 3. Missions—Northwest, Canadian History—19th century. I. Title. II. Series: Collection Religions et croyances; no. 3.

BX3821.Z5C3 1995   266'.271   C95-900269-3

Photo credits: All photos, other than those listed below, are taken from the Deschâtelets Archives in Ottawa.

P. 31: R.P. Morice, *Histoire de l'Église catholique dans l'ouest canadien*, vol. 1 (Saint-Boniface and Montreal: Author and Granger Frères, 1921).

P. 36 (George-Antoine Bellecourt): Ibid.

P. 41: Ibid.

P. 63 (Joseph Patrick Kearney): Paul-Émile Breton, *Au Pays des Peaux-de-Lièvres* (Saint-Hyacinthe: N.p., 1962).

P. 82: Provincial Archives of Manitoba.

Cover: Robert Dolbec

Typesetting: Infographie G.L.

CONTENTS

TABLES

ABBREVIATIONS

AACFO Archives of the Association Canadienne-française de l'Ontario, Ottawa

AASB Archives of the Archdiocese of St. Boniface

ACAM Archives de la chancellerie de l'archevêché de Montréal

AD Archives Deschatelets, Ottawa

AG Archives Grandin, St. Albert

APA Archives of the Province of Alberta

AY Archives of Diocese of Yellowknife, NWT

CMS Church Missionary Society

DCB *Dictionary of Canadian Biography*

HBC Hudson's Bay Company

NAC National Archives of Canada, Ottawa

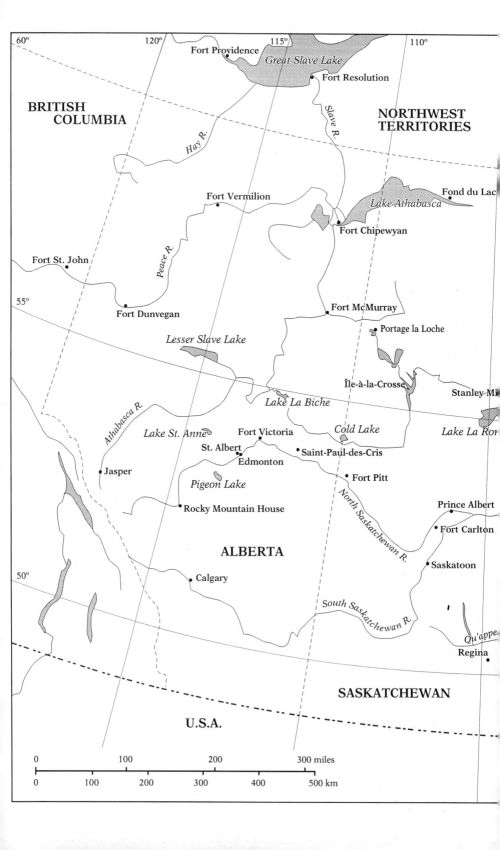

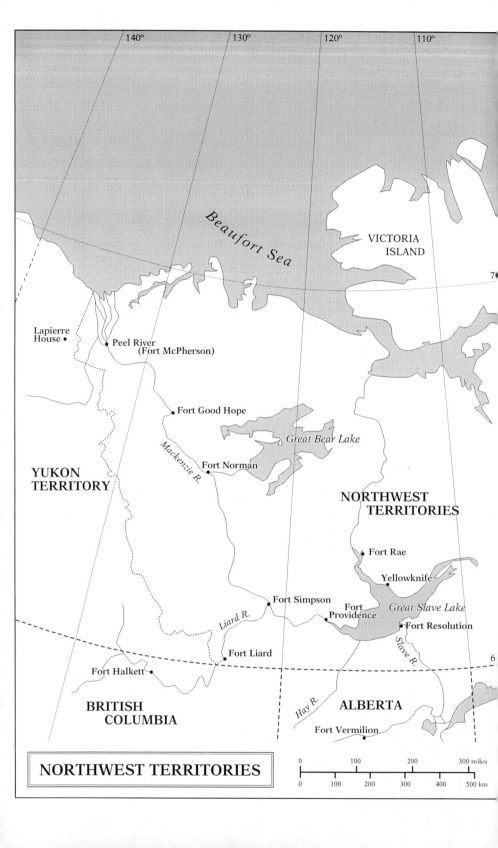

140°　　　　　130°　　　　　120°　　　　　110°

Beaufort Sea

VICTORIA
ISLAND

7

Lapierre
House •

• Peel River
(Fort McPherson)

• Fort Good Hope

Great Bear Lake

Mackenzie R.

• Fort Norman

YUKON
TERRITORY

NORTHWEST
TERRITORIES

• Fort Rae

• Yellowknife

• Fort Simpson

Liard R.

Fort
Providence

Great Slave Lake

• Fort Resolution

Slave R.

6

• Fort Liard

Fort Halkett •

BRITISH
COLUMBIA

Hay R.

ALBERTA

Fort Vermilion •

NORTHWEST TERRITORIES

0 　　　　100　　　　　200　　　　300 miles

0　　　100　　　200　　　300　　　400　　　500 km

PREFACE

I have undertaken this study in order to better understand the historical dynamics of the extremely rapid expansion of the Roman Catholic
Oblate missions in Canada's North and West in the nineteenth century, a chapter in our history that is not well understood. It has entailed
the simultaneous study of the love–hate relationship between Catholic
and Protestant Christians in Canada, since both were vying for control
of the Northwest. Given the fact that the Catholics were French and
the Protestants English, it is hoped that the book will also shed some
light on French–English relations in the Northwest, and on the relationship between religion and cultures in a conflictual setting.

The research for this book was conducted under the auspices of
Western Canadian Publishers, which is owned and operated by the
Missionary Oblates of Mary Immaculate. I am grateful for a research
grant from Western Canadian Publishers, which paid for extensive
research at the various archival centres of western Canada, as well as
for the kind and generous support of the late Guy Lacombe, that
company's director general. The research assistance of Jennifer Reid,
Maureen Korp, and Robert Prudhomme was also helpful. In addition, I
am grateful to the many archivists across Canada, in both civil and
ecclesiastical archives, who always welcomed me and provided their
usual outstanding services.

Thanks to the several Oblate missionaries who shared their views
and recollections with me, particularly those who provided the shelter
and hospitality of their homes in Edmonton, Yellowknife, McLelland,
and elsewhere.

Last but not least, thanks to the University of Ottawa, where my
professorial appointment allows me to indulge in such fascinating
work as researching and writing on the history of religions in Canada.

CHAPTER I

CATHOLICISM
IN THE NINETEENTH CENTURY

IN the course of a mere thirty-five years beginning in the second quarter of the nineteenth century, the Oblate missionaries, a Roman Catholic congregation,[1] were founded in southern France (1826), established a Canadian headquarters in Montreal (1841), founded their first mission in Red River (1845), and proceeded to insert their men into the farthest reaches of Canada's North and West, from the Columbia River (1847) and Vancouver Island (1858), to Lake Athabasca (1856), the Mackenzie River (1858), and the Yukon River (1861). They also put down roots across much of southern, central and western Canada, becoming, by the end of the century, Canada's largest male religious congregation. The six men who had landed in Montreal in December 1841 had become a rapidly expanding regiment of Catholic conquerors intent on winning Canada's North and West over to Catholicism. They founded missions to native people at a dizzying pace, established schools in bush and town, recruited Catholic religious women to staff hospitals and boarding schools, and carved colonies out of the wilderness for both immigrants and Métis; they even built roads, railroads, steamships, and sawmills to better serve their missions. The Oblates then proceeded to staff new ecclesiastical offices, and they challenged the governments of Canada and the West on issues as diverse as Indian rights, Métis rights, French-language rights, and confessional schools, while founding newspapers and colleges.

Who were these men whose arrival and presence would have such far-reaching consequences for the history of Canada, particularly western and northern Canada?

Oblate missionaries were to the nineteenth century what Jesuits had been to the sixteenth and seventeenth. They were the quintessential product of a new mood in Catholicism, a new militancy, a new urge to conquer the world for Christ and his Church. This new Catholic Church included more determined and aggressive popes and bishops, great revitalization or religious re-awakening movements in Catholic countries like Ireland and Canada, a conservative and reactionary theology, a strong movement for centralization of Church power in the Vatican, and a veritable epidemic of vocations to the religious life, by women in particular. By the middle of the nineteenth century, this growing Catholic clerical army understood the world in simple categories. The world and society was the devil's playground, liberalism was virtue's hearse, and the duty of true Catholics was to become Christ's soldiers—troops dedicated to conquering a world being driven to Hell on the accelerating bobsled of Western liberalism and secularism.

This revitalized Catholic Church was a reaction to the mess it was in in 1815, arguably the nadir of the Europe-centred Roman Catholic Church in modern times. Indeed, the defeat of Napoleon at Waterloo on 15 June of that year also signified the replacement of Catholic France by Protestant Britain at the centre of the world's stage. Although France had been acknowledged for two centuries as a bastion of Catholicism, a decade of revolution, followed by fifteen years of Napoleonic rule, had left the Church of France anemic, unsophisticated, poorly led, divided on the issue of republicanism versus monarchy, and dependent upon the favours and the support of the French State. The governments of France, that of Napoleon before 1815 and those of the restored monarchy afterwards, held the Church on a tight leash, strongly influencing, and frequently controlling, the recruiting and training of clergy, the development of Catholic schools and religious orders and congregations, and the extent of Catholic outreach in France.

A handful of French Catholics undertook to liberate their Church from both crippling government control and the mediocre leadership of the bishops. Led by Father Félicité de Lamennais, they sought a wide range of freedoms for all: freedom of religion, freedom of conscience, freedom of the press, freedom of teaching, and separation of Church and State. In sum, Lamennais embraced the new values of freedom and equality for all that were at the core of the French Revolution. He challenged his Church to rediscover the Gospels and its values of liberty, poverty, equality, and love. The Catholic hierarchy, however, did not accept the challenge in the spirit in which it was offered. Lamennais was denounced by the bishops of France, while his ideas were condemned in a papal encyclical in 1832; he was excommunicated, two years later, by Pope Gregory XVI. The crushing of the French Catholic liberals marked the beginning of the Roman Catholic ultramontane theology that would dominate Catholicism for more than a century.[2]

While the Vatican struggled with Lamennais and his followers, the Roman Catholic Church in Canada had problems of its own. The British Conquest of 1760 and the subsequent Treaty of Paris of 1763 had crippled Canada's Catholic Church. Many Church buildings in Quebec had been destroyed in the bombardment and a third of Canada's clergy had either died or returned to France. The Séminaire de Québec was closed for several years, which prevented the training of new priests, and at any rate the British conqueror forbade the recruitment of members for male religious orders. Furthermore, the bishop of Quebec, Canada's only diocese, had died in the summer of 1760. Although a new bishop was appointed in 1766, for more than half a century the leader of Canada's Catholic Church would be required to struggle, make compromises, and negotiate with a British colonial government whose policy was to replace it with the established Church of England, albeit faced with the practical difficulties of implementing such a policy in an overwhelmingly French-speaking and Catholic country.

The political loyalty of the successive bishops of Quebec to their new British sovereign was demonstrated once again during the War of 1812 and finally won over the British government. Indeed, 1815 saw not only the defeat of Napoleon, but also the emancipation of Canada's Catholic Church. The Church had obtained important concessions in the Quebec Act of 1774, but had nevertheless continued to be the object of discrimination by the British government. After 1815, the Catholic Church was allowed to greatly increase the number of its bishops and dioceses in Canada, and to gradually break free of the ties that bound it to its political masters. By the 1850s, government supervision of Church affairs had largely ceased, as had the supply of government money to the clergy. Simultaneously, the Catholic Church in Canada was caught in a whirlwind of growth and expansion. More than half of present-day Canada's land mass was penetrated and its people converted by Catholic missionaries, mostly Oblates.

The theology that supported, drove, and justified this new Catholic imperialism, ultramontanism, was not new in the Catholic Church but would know its finest hour from the mid-nineteenth century to the mid-twentieth. As is the case with all large institutions, the Catholic Church was and is frequently torn between divergent views as to how it should be governed. Over the two thousand years of its history, its polity has ranged from an extreme congregational form of government wherein local communities are largely independent, through regional groupings of churches, to an extremely centralized polity wherein the Pope is a sovereign and absolute ruler. During the five centuries preceding the evangelization of Canada's Northwest, the prevalent form of Catholic government was Gallicanism, or Church nationalism. The civil ruler, whether king or emperor, had a determining voice in matters ecclesiastical within his realm. In France, therefore, as well as in Spain and England, Church incomes, appointments, and policy were all subject to the approval of the monarch. In France, this Gallicanism prevailed under the monarchs of the ancien régime, under Napoleon, and under the restoration monarchy after 1815.

When a group of French liberal-minded Catholics were led by Lamennais to challenge the conspiratorial structure of the French Church and State, therefore, they were crushed by the Vatican in the 1830s. Pope Gregory XVI (1831–46) thereby took over the helm of a Catholic Church that had long been decentralized and had functioned as a loose confederation of national churches. He and his immediate successors, Pius IX (1846–78) and Leo XIII (1878–1903), transformed Rome into the headquarters of the international Catholic Church, a role it has maintained to this day.

The papal iron hand steered the Church on a course set by the ultramontane theology, which meant a profound and sweeping transformation not only of Catholic polity, but of Catholic theology and all that it entailed, including worship, moral teaching, Church–State relations, and missions.

The ultramontane mindset is characterized by a profound distrust of the modern, liberal, secular societies that were the products of the French Revolution. The ultramontane Catholic sees Satan and his minions everywhere—always on the prowl, laying snares for the elect of the Lord. The world is a vale of tears, a battlefield; liberalism is the fount of all heresies; human nature is weak and cannot be trusted; women are the devil's amazons, with their tresses, their bare arms, and their seductive wiles; the forces of evil are consolidated in worldwide conspiracy movements such as the Freemasons. In sum, for an ultramontane Catholic, human beings cannot be trusted; they must be protected from themselves. Moreover, things have reached such a state that there is no room for negotiating with the enemy. Whoever is not with the Church is against it.

The Roman Catholic Church has been entrusted with providing this protection. So it was that as the second half of the nineteenth century wore on, the Vatican became more strident, restrictive, arbitrary, and autocratic in issuing a series of disciplinary, moral, and doctrinal rulings. The most important of these were the proclamation of the dogma of the Immaculate Conception (1854); the encyclical *Quanta Cura* (1864) with its companion *Syllabus Errorum*, which stands as the charter of ultramontane Catholicism; and the proclamation of the twin doctrines of papal primacy and papal infallibility at Vatican Council I in 1870.

Less sensational but no less revealing of ultramontane thinking were a wide range of Church rulings, both Roman and Canadian, on clerical dress (the cassock at all times) and on beards and toupees. Public non-denominational schools were outlawed, women were forbidden to be seen on stage, and there was to be no dancing in Church buildings (dancing was seen as proximate to sin). One of the first acts of Pope Leo XIII upon assuming office in 1878 was to decree the thirteenth-century philosophy and theology of Thomas Aquinas as the *only* philosophy and theology to be taught in Catholic institutions. Ultramontane Catholics sought to return to a Christendom that they considered preferable to the world of the late nineteenth century. This reactionary process was completed by Pope Pius X in 1907 when he published the encyclical *Pascendi* and the decree *Lamentabili*, condemning the modernists—those Catholic intellectuals who sought to reconcile Catholic doctrinal teaching with the scholarship of their day.

This new autocracy depended upon strict discipline among Catholics. In the eyes of the bishops, obedience was the foremost virtue for themselves *vis-à-vis* Rome, for priests *vis-à-vis* their bishops, and for the faithful *vis-à-vis* their priests. While "pay, pray, and obey" became the watchword for the Catholic laity, most Catholic bishops would have endorsed the words spoken by Bishop Michael Fallon in his sermon at the consecration of a new bishop in Alexandria, Ontario, in August 1921:

> The Bishop is placed here to rule. My Lord, the whole church of God is an army. The G.H.Q. [General Headquarters] is at Rome... the commander-in-chief is there. But... every diocese in the whole universal church is an army and there is a commander there, and he alone has the right under the commander-in-chief to govern and rule his diocese.[3]

So it was that by the middle of the nineteenth century, and for a hundred years thereafter, the Roman Catholic Church was a highly structured, authoritarian, centralized, and disciplined international movement bent upon saving humanity from the spiritual perils that threatened from every quarter. A new crusade got underway.[4]

The Catholic Clergy

A *sine qua non* condition for the revitalization of the Church in the nineteenth century was the renewal of its clergy,[5] a renewal that included exponential growth, renewed theological training, stronger discipline, and more rigorous moral teachings. As commitment and numbers grew, so did the clergy's control over the consciences of Catholics. Missionary outreach grew apace, building a Church that in the twentieth century would for the first time become truly universal. Although they were technically not clerics, women played a major role in this renewal of the Catholic clergy, as did religious congregations of men, the majority of whose members were ordained clergymen.[6]

Women who took religious vows and joined one of the scores of Catholic congregations were the indispensable, albeit frequently uncelebrated, assistants of clergymen in the evangelization of Canada. Any work on the Oblate missionaries must take into account the religious women who staffed many of the social service agencies founded or run by Oblates.

Religious women are usually classified as either nuns or sisters. The chief difference between a nun and a sister, or between an order and a congregation, was the clear and exclusive social service orientation of the congregations of sisters. Whereas the traditional nun fled the world in order to seek sanctification in a cloister, the modern sister went out into the world in order to transform it.[7] In nineteenth-century France, their numbers grew by leaps and bounds; they did in Canada as well, sisters soon becoming twice, sometimes three times, as numerous as religious men.

While the seventeenth and eighteenth centuries had not been very fruitful in producing new religious orders or congregations, the reverse was true of the nineteenth century. As the Western world reeled from a series of social, intellectual, economic, and political revolutions, religious life was, surprisingly, born again within the Catholic Church. A record-setting ninety-one religious congregations of men were founded worldwide, several traditional groups such as Jesuits and Dominicans were revitalized, and more than 400 congregations of women were founded in France alone. Indeed France produced more than 200,000 sisters in the nineteenth century, or one sister for every hundred French women. Several of these worked in Canada's Northwest.

Most of the sisters working in the West and North were, however, of Canadian origin, of Quebec origin in particular. The Canadian phenomenon of exponential growth in the number of sisters started later

Table 1
Religious Women in France

1790	55,000
1861	100,000
1880	130,000
1900	135,000

Source: Claude Langlois, *Le catholicisme au féminin.*

than that of France, but once it was under way in the mid-nineteenth century it kept pace with that of the mother country.

Between the Conquest of 1760 and the year 1850, the population of French Canada doubled every twenty-five years, growing from a mere 60,000 people to nearly 900,000. The sisters managed only to triple their numbers, from 190 to 673, during the same period; in the second half of the century, however, their numbers skyrocketed, a phenomenon that would continue until 1960. They were the primary source of cheap labour for the Catholic schools, hospitals, and orphanages of Canada's Northwest.

Table 2
Religious Women in Quebec

1764	190
1800	304
1850	650
1900	6,628

Source: Bernard Denault and Benoît Lévesque, *Éléments pour une sociologie des communautés religieuses au Québec.*

The number of Quebec religious congregations of women grew over the years from the initial five founded during the French regime to fifteen in 1850, and thirty-six in 1900. Many of these would be at work in the Northwest, but it was the Sisters of Charity of the Montreal General Hospital, the Sisters of Providence, and the Sisters of St. Anne who would provide the most women dedicated to serving the Catholic missions.

Male clergy have always controlled the Catholic Church; their numbers and their quality have been determining factors in any revitalization of the Church. In Canada, one of the ways in which the British conqueror tried to cripple Catholicism after 1760 was to ban

Sister of Charity feeding the chickens at Fort Providence farm.

recruitment by male religious congregations and to restrict the freedom of all priests, secular or regular.[8] When added to the temporary closing of the Séminaire de Québec, the lack of a bishop, and the death of some priests and the return of others to France, this led to a reduction in the number of priests in Canada, both secular and regular—from 196 in 1759 to 137 in 1764. Although the seminary reopened in 1765, and a new bishop was in place by 1766, regular clergy disappeared with the death of the last Jesuit in 1800, and the death of the last Recollet in 1813. The only male religious group that managed to survive were the Sulpicians due to an unforeseen influx of new members—refugees from revolutionary France after 1791.

While Canada's regular clergy, Sulpicians excepted,[9] disappeared during the eighty years following 1760, the country's secular clergy barely survived as well, in a society that was doubling in population every twenty-five years. The ratio of faithful to priests grew rapidly, passing from 350 to one in 1759, to 1,800 to one in 1830. On the eve of the revitalization of Canadian Catholicism in 1840, no new regular clergy having entered Canada since the Conquest,[10] the Canadian Church had some 300 priests serving half a million faithful. Montreal's 22,000 Catholics were ministered to by nineteen Sulpician priests and two secular priests.[11]

Thereafter, the decline in the numbers of secular priests would be dramatically reversed. In the half century from 1830 to 1880, their

Sister of Charity visiting parishioners at Fort Providence at turn of the century.

numbers grew from 225 to 2,102. Indeed, as early as 1850, the ratio of priests to faithful was one to 1,000, and by 1880 a healthy one to 500, a ratio that would remain steady until 1960.[12]

The swelling numbers of secular priests would be accompanied by an escalation in the numbers of regular clergy, both foreign and Canadian, working in Canada. These men in religious congregations in Quebec numbered a mere 243 (including thirty-nine Sulpicians) in 1850 and just under 2,000 in 1901. Men and women taken together come to an impressive 8,612 people in 1901,[13] a time when there were four women to one man in congregations in Quebec. Canada's North and West served as spillways for the growing number of Quebec clergy after 1840.

While the Sulpicians were the only group of priests in Quebec in 1840, by 1850 there were six congregations of men, the result of Montreal Bishop Ignace Bourget's recruiting during the 1840s.[14] One of these congregations was the Missionary Oblates of Mary Immaculate, the first of many congregations recruited in post-revolutionary France by Canada's ultramontane bishops.

The missionaries of Provence, founded in the Department of Provence in southern France in 1816, were one of several communities of French secular priests dedicated to preaching and holding parish retreats in their area. Having received papal approval in 1826 under the name Missionary Oblates of Mary Immaculate, the new congregation of priests was intended to conduct local missions. The founder, Eugène de Mazenod, became Bishop of Marseilles in 1837, his uncle Fortuné having preceded him as bishop since 1823. Eugène held the office of both bishop and superior general of the Oblates until his death in 1861. He required that all members of his organization take vows of poverty, chastity, and obedience.

The Oblates had considerable difficulty, however, expanding in France during the 1830s. In a trio of restrictive government regulations adopted in 1828, the university replaced the bishops as the overseer of elementary education in France, the administration of colleges was restricted to those congregations authorized by the government, and institutions classified as seminaries were required to restrict their enrolment to aspiring clergymen. These and other restrictions kept the

Bishop Eugène de Mazenod (1782–1861)

budding Oblate congregation confined to southeastern France, with a total membership of only fifty-five men in 1840. So it was that Bishop de Mazenod looked beyond the borders of France for potential areas of evangelization and expansion. When Montreal's Bishop Bourget landed on his doorstep in 1840 seeking priests for his expanding diocese of Montreal, it seemed like an act of Providence. God had spoken!

Training the Catholic Soldiers

The Catholic Church's Vatican Council II (1962–65) declared that it would promote the laity within the Church, and transform the clergy from a hierarchy of domination to one of service of God's people. For most of Christian history, however, and particularly during the nineteenth century, the clergy, religious women included, has provided not only the shock troops of Catholic conquest, but also the troops of occupation and the officer corps of the Catholic army, from the lowest levels to the highest. Since the fourth century AD, the laity has rarely played any part in decision making or in the staffing of Church offices. Its role has usually been to "pay, pray, and obey."

In the nineteenth century, three groups of clergy were the decisive players in conquering the Canadian North and West for the Catholic Church. They were the secular priests, who were the sole missionaries in the quarter century preceding 1845; the sisters, who began arriving in 1844; and the Oblates, whose mission of two in 1845 had grown to nearly 100 by 1870 and to 273 by the end of the century.

The priest, both regular and secular, while remaining the primary agent of Catholic missions and government, was himself undergoing significant change within the Church of the nineteenth century. As had been the case in earlier times, Church leaders realized that any significant renewal and reform of the Christian Church hinged on reform of the clergy. It was secular clergy from Quebec who initially evangelized the West, both at Red River (1818) and on the Pacific slope (1838), a clergy whose type of training was changing in the nineteenth century.

Until the Grand Séminaire[15] was opened in Montreal in 1840, the only significant institution for the training of Catholic secular clergy in Canada was the Séminaire de Québec.[16] Until its closing during the Seven Years' War, this institution had been primarily a residence and house of spiritual training, the seminarians attending the Jesuits' Collège de Québec for their schooling. When the seminary reopened in 1765, the college was no more; the Séminaire de Québec[17] therefore took on the entire training of prospective priests, providing academic curriculum to replace that offered by the Jesuit college. As was the case in France and in Europe generally, in the latter part of the eighteenth century the seminary became self-sufficient. Philosophy, theology, spiritual training, and clerical studies were all provided under one roof.

The preferred method of teaching was dictation from a textbook, a method that would endure in Quebec until the second half of the nineteenth century. As required by the Council of Trent, the objective was the acquisition not of knowledge, but rather of Christian virtue, piety, and discipline. Primary attention was paid to instilling the virtues of humility, poverty, obedience, mortification, and zeal for the conversion of souls. The means of training were group meditation, lectures on piety, exhortations, spiritual retreats, and devotional readings. Until the early nineteenth century, seminarians spent several years—usually four—in residence at the Séminaire de Québec, under close observation by faculty and the bishop.[18]

During the first decades of the nineteenth century, however, the shortage of priests led many bishops to shorten the stay of students in the seminary, to the point where a growing number spent only two years in residence, many only one year, and some almost no time at all. One of the contributing factors to this phenomenon in Canada was the establishment by the Catholic bishops of an increasing number of classical colleges, which required staffing; the priests in training seem to have been the best source of cheap and able-bodied labour. Although bishops tried to compensate for the lack of training by requiring that these hastily ordained priests devote time to the personal study of theology, the circumstances of the ministry were such that few managed to do so. The result was a poorly educated secular clergy, who were largely ignorant in matters of theology, Catholic or otherwise. In Canada, significant improvements in the seminary training of Catholic priests would have to wait until the twentieth century.

In France, the land of origin of most of the Oblates, the situation was no better, ecclesiastical studies remaining in a poor state throughout the nineteenth century. While Canada was strapped for clergy in the wake of the British Conquest, in France it was the French Revolution that caused the shortage. Desperately short of clergy, French bishops curtailed the training of seminarians in order to get them ordained and into the ministry. Theological studies were reduced to a minimum. Church leaders justified their actions by arguing that what mattered was a priest's saintliness and virtue, not his knowledge.

Moreover, the limited academic training that the seminarians did receive left much to be desired. French seminaries were desperately short of qualified staff, who, like the seminarians, were chosen for their piety and virtue. Scholarliness was a secondary criterion. Since university theology faculties were closed down during the Revolution, many seminary professors were self-taught men who had never acquired scientific method. Lamennais's group had tried to remedy this state of clerical intellectual stagnation, only to be condemned in 1834. A similar fate awaited another intellectual reformer, Father Louis Bautain, who was excommunicated in 1840. A number of efforts were made to renew Catholic studies, such as publication of a series of texts by the fathers of the Church, by Father Migne (1836), renewal of the Dominican Order by Father Lacordaire (1843), return to the study of Thomas Aquinas, and adoption of the moral theology of Alphonsus Liguori. Nevertheless, any significant intellectual renewal of Catholic studies in France would have to wait until the last quarter of the century, when Catholic Faculties of Theology were founded.

During most of the nineteenth century, in both France and Canada, therefore, a teaching position in a Catholic seminary was a pastoral appointment, like an appointment to head a parish, only of lesser importance. Frequently, a newly ordained priest would be given a teaching post for a few years, in order to acquire experience before being promoted to the parish ministry. He could be appointed teacher before finishing his studies, so that seminarians were frequently taught by a faculty composed primarily of men in their twenties. This new professor needed no academic qualifications; he taught a wide range of subjects, from arithmetic through astronomy and chemistry at the college level, and from philosophy and Holy Scripture through moral and dogmatic theology at the seminary level, always reading from an officially approved textbook; in his spare time, such as it was, he supervised dormitories and skating rinks, and performed parish ministry. In sum, anybody could teach anything in most French and Canadian seminaries during much of the nineteenth century.

The theological textbooks used by seminarians in France left much to be desired. During the first half of the century, the traditional Gallican, or French nationalist, view permeated the texts. The ultramontane view, which became more prominent after 1850, was accompanied by the rapid acceptance in French seminaries of Thomist philosophy and theology, alongside Liguorian moral theology; the latter supplanted the previous rigid, Jansenist moral theology in the second half of the century.

The academic programme in a typical French seminary was supposed to last four years, but many of the Oblates who came to Canada had been in residence only one or two years, in some cases not at all. Indeed, the Oblate General Chapter of 1850 stipulated that Oblates who were sent directly to mission lands would not have to spend the required two years in a seminary before ordination. It was felt that they could study on-site in their country of destination, under the supervision of the local missionary.

The four-year programme was divided into two years each of philosophy and theology. There were two one-hour classes per day, one in the morning and one in the afternoon. After 1850, in some seminaries, a second hour was added in the morning. The student was expected to spend another six hours in personal study, usually memorizing the contents of the lessons based on the approved Latin textbooks, and on the lectures, which repeated the textbooks.

The theological programme consisted primarily of courses in moral theology and dogmatic theology, each taught five days a week; Biblical study was added as a course of secondary importance, the Bible being considered useful as an arsenal of arguments to be used in apologetical discourse. Some schools gradually added limited teaching of Church history, canon law, liturgy, and chant in the latter half of the century.

While the philosophy programme consisted in a kind of simplified Cartesian rationalism, the dogmatic theology programme evolved through authors such as J.-B. Bouvier and Louis Bailly, who reflected the ancien régime, to the textbooks of the second half of the century that reflected the ultramontane concern with reinforcing papal authority by focusing almost exclusively on matters such as papal infallibility, Catholic hierarchy, and the magisterium of the Church. The increasing apologetic tone of these texts presented Protestants as heretical adversaries and infidels as fair game for Catholic missionaries. After 1850, the writings of Thomas Aquinas dominated Catholic dogmatic theology textbooks. In the area of moral theology, Alphonsus Liguori became the dominant author. The poverty of the teaching of the history of Christianity in French seminaries is illustrated by Montalembert's noting in 1837 that probably not more than five of the eighty seminaries in France taught the history of the Christian Church,[19] a subject that the Council of Trent had not prescribed as part of the curriculum.

In Canada, the programme, teaching methods, and authors largely mirrored those of French seminaries. One novel textbook was Bishop Saint-Vallier's *Rituel du diocèse de Québec*, published in 1703, which served as a kind of pastoral, theological, and moral summary of Catholic teaching. Catholic pastors constantly referred to the *Rituel* until the 1830s. There were not many other significant differences in the theological training, or lack thereof, of Catholic priests in France and

Canada. This was true for both the Séminaire de Québec and Montreal's Grand Séminaire, many of whose professors were Sulpician priests from France. The French Oblates who worked in the Northwest were trained in Marseilles, France, while their Canadian colleagues studied in Ottawa, at Canada's Oblate seminary.

Making an Oblate

In 1823 Eugène de Mazenod was appointed Vicar General, or second in command, of the diocese of Marseilles, by his uncle, Bishop Fortuné de Mazenod. Four years later—and one year after the Missionary Oblates of Mary Immaculate had been given official Roman approval—the fledgling congregation of fewer than thirty men was entrusted with the staffing and management of the diocesan seminary of Marseilles. Oblates would continue to run the seminary until 1862, a year after the death of their founder. Eugène de Mazenod had been made Bishop of Marseilles in 1837 and remained so until his death in 1861. This total Oblate control over the Marseilles seminary offers a prime example of Oblate training in France.

The regulations of the seminary were written in 1829. They were modelled on those of the Sulpicians, and tended to put the priest on a pedestal, underlining his dignity as well as his responsibilities. The Marseilles regulations were very much Rome-centred, each Oblate himself having sworn a vow of obedience to the Pope upon entering the congregation. Alphonsus Liguori inspired the seminary's moral outlook, which made more allowance for human weakness, mercy, and kindness than did traditional Gallican–Jansenist moral theology. The director of the seminary was second only to the bishop, having full authority over his staff, the selection of textbooks, and the instruction of seminarians. His staff had received no special training, many being young men in their twenties who were themselves studying for the priesthood; today, they would be called teaching assistants. The number of staff varied from four to seven during this period, the student body ranging from thirty-five in the 1830s to eighty in the 1850s. The theology, textbooks, and curriculum were typical for French seminaries. If the Oblates distinguished themselves in any way, it was in their early adoption of the moral theology of Liguori, and in their early insistence on Roman authority; in other words, they were among the first ultramontane Catholic clergy.

All Oblates received the same training. In fact, as we have seen, foreign missionaries could be excused from part or all of their theological training because it was felt that little or no instruction was required for missionary work. After administering the Church of the Northwest for thirty-two years, Bishop Provencher wrote:

> For a long time, the assistants sent to me were young clergymen without any seminary or theological training... Their arrival meant the departure of their predecessor who had become useful, and we fell back into the situation that prevailed upon the latter's arrival. The superiors of the Oblates have sent us three or four young men without any seminary, theology, orders, or experience in the ministry... What is one to do here with such a young man?[20]

Respect for other cultures was not included in the training of a nineteenth-century missionary. The missionary did not set out to adapt his Church to indigenous cultures; he set out to convert any and all to the Roman Catholic way, the only true way, for outside the Church there was no salvation—whether for pagan, infidel, Protestant heretic, or Eastern schismatic. And given the total ignorance of these people about Roman Catholicism, a rudimentary knowledge of Catholic doctrine was sufficient for the missionary.

Shortly after the arrival of the Oblates in Canada, their superior in Canada, Father Joseph-Eugène-Bruno Guigues, was appointed first bishop of the new diocese of Ottawa. Within weeks of his arrival in his new episcopal see in the summer of 1848, Guigues founded a college; shortly thereafter he entrusted the college to his congregation and decided that it would also serve as a training house for Oblates in Canada. For a quarter of a century thereafter, until 1885, Canadian Oblates would be educated at the College of Ottawa, along with candidates for the secular priesthood in the diocese of Ottawa. In 1885, the Canadian Oblates moved into a separate seminary in the neighbourhood of the college.

In Ottawa, seminary or scholastic life was much as it was in Europe. Candidates for the priesthood, whether secular or Oblate, made up most of the teaching personnel of the College of Ottawa, while they also pursued their studies at the same institution. Until 1870, the theological programme consisted primarily of dogmatic and moral theology; then courses on the Bible, the history of Christianity, and canon law were added. After 1889, other courses were added, in biblical languages and homiletics. Textbooks were imported from Europe, and they reflected the scholarly mediocrity of those used in France.

The Oblates came to Canada as a result of a discovery by Bishop Ignace Bourget of Montreal. On a recruiting journey to Europe in the summer of 1841, Bourget happened to stop overnight at the bishop's palace in Marseilles. Learning of the existence of the young congregation, the enterprising Bourget had soon obtained from Bishop de Mazenod the promise of at least four men to assist him in his apostolic endeavours in Canada.

Six Oblates, four priests and two brothers, arrived in Montreal on 2 December 1841.[21] Within days, Bourget entrusted them with the parish of St. Hilaire on the Richelieu River, a parish that included an adjoining shrine on Mount Belœil. They immediately began to preach missions in other parishes as well as their own, frequently leaving the host parishes with newly established temperance societies and confraternities of Marian devotion. The Oblates also undertook itinerant missionary work in the Eastern Townships of Quebec and in the vast Ottawa Valley, one of their number, Father Telmon, promoting the establishment of a congregation of teaching sisters at Longueuil, under the leadership of Eulalie Durocher.[22] Eager to get closer to Montreal, in August 1842 the Oblates moved their principal residence to Longueuil, across the river from Montreal, thanks to property from a benefactor. Six years later, they were entrusted by Bishop Bourget with the parish of Saint-Pierre-Apôtre in Montreal, thus penetrating the heart of the city that would soon become Canada's metropolis. Throughout the nineteenth century, this would remain their headquarters in eastern Canada. Meanwhile, their missionary journeys had expanded to include James Bay, the St. Maurice River, the Saguenay River, the North Shore of the Lower St. Lawrence, and the Canadian Northwest. They would soon extend their apostolate to Labrador, the Pacific, the Arctic, the northeastern United States, and Texas.

The arrival of the Oblates in Canada and the rapid expansion of their apostolic field during the 1840s was part of a broader movement of religious awakening in Canadian Catholicism. This awakening included the founding of Bourget's weekly journal, *Les Mélanges Religieux* (December 1840), and the fifteen-month preaching tour (September 1840 to December 1841) of the fiery Bishop Forbin-Janson from France. Forbin-Janson, a revivalist preacher, packed the churches of French Canada, particularly Montreal, with Catholics who longed for a message of forgiveness, hope, and salvation in the wake of the crushing of the rebellions of 1837–38, the publication of Lord Durham's Report, and the union of the Canadas. The revival was sustained by the arrival of a series of French religious congregations that were imported into Canada in the following years—not only the six congregations of men already noted,[23] but two congregations of women, the Society of the Sacred Heart, six of whose sisters arrived in December 1842, and the sisters of the Good Shepherd, from Angers, four of whom arrived in June 1844. To these were added congregations of women founded in Canada: the Sisters of Charity of Providence (1843), founded by the widow Émilie Gamelin; the teaching Sisters of the Holy Names of Jesus and Mary (1844), founded by Eulalie Durocher; the Sisters of Mercy (1848), founded by the widow Rosalie Cadron Jetté; and the teaching Sisters of St. Anne (1850), founded by Marie-Esther Blondin. Add to these the five established female congregations,[24] and in 1850 the Canadian Church had eleven congregations of women, rather than the five of 1840. Moreover, the long-established Sulpicians were now joined by Brothers of Christian Schools, the Jesuits, the Holy Cross congregation, the Viatorians, and, last but not least, the Oblates. The Oblates would soon become the largest and most widespread male congregation in Canada.

The Field of Battle

Within four years of landing in Montreal, two Oblates would be beaching their canoes in Red River, launching an epic of evangelization of Canada's North and West.

The land they would penetrate so rapidly was immense, covering more than half of present-day Canada's ten million square kilometres. It was divided into three huge territories: Rupert's Land, the Northwest Territories, and the Pacific slope territory that drained into the Pacific Ocean, a region corresponding to today's British Columbia extended to include the States of Oregon and Washington. While the Northwest Territories included all the land draining into the Arctic Sea, Rupert's Land embraced all the land draining into Hudson Bay and James Bay, and therefore all of the northern portion of central Canada.

All of this land was under the exclusive control of the Hudson's Bay Company (HBC), a commercial monopoly created by English royal charter in 1670 and bent on profiting from the fur trade throughout British North America. By the time the Oblates arrived in 1845, the HBC had absorbed its chief trading rival, the North West Company of Montreal (1821), and had bought back from the heirs of Lord Selkirk the colony he had founded and run for a quarter of a century (1835).[25] It was also busy fending off the forays of American whiskey and fur traders from south of the 49th parallel, a boundary established by treaties between Great Britain and the United States in 1818 and 1848.

This huge land mass was inhabited by several nations of Indians. Between Lake Superior and the Rocky Mountains, tribes of Algonkian, Siouan, and Athapaskan language stocks occupied distinct regions. From northwestern Ontario through the southern half of Manitoba were found the Ojibwa, or Saulteux, of Algonkian language stock. To the southwest, in the southern portion of Saskatchewan, resided the

Assiniboine of Siouan linguistic extraction, while much of northern Ontario, Manitoba, and Saskatchewan belonged to the Cree, of Algonkian language stock. Alberta was the land of the Blackfoot Confederacy, another Algonkian group, while the vast lands of the northern country stretching from northern Saskatchewan and Alberta to Alaska belonged to the Athapaskan or Dene groups, which included the Chipewyans at their southernmost perimeter. The far northern shores of the Arctic Ocean belonged to the Inuit. However, nations of the same language stock did not necessarily speak the same language, although there could be similarities. In 1868, Bishop Taché estimated that the population of the Saulteux, or Ojibwa, was 30,000, the Chipewyan 15,000, the Assiniboine 4,000, the Blackfoot

Blackfoot chief in Alberta.

6,000, and the Inuit 5,000.[26] Oblates would work with each of these nations in their diverse languages.

British Columbia's native population was much more diverse. Anthropologists classify it by language, each major linguistic group containing several dialects. At least seven distinct Indian nations inhabited the coast and islands of British Columbia,[27] while another four could be found in the interior.[28] Most of these nations would become the permanent object of Oblate ministrations.

Finally, it should be noted that the Canadian North and West that the Oblates invaded in 1845 changed profoundly during the first half century of their missionary campaigns. The two-month canoe journey from Montreal, one that the first Sisters of Charity and Alexandre Taché would make in 1844 and 1845, would soon be replaced by a journey via the United States, by means of a combination of riverboat, ox cart, train, and steamship. The fur trade monopoly of the HBC was effectively ended in 1849; thereafter, various free traders vied with the company for the spoils of the trade. Sweeping political changes began in the late 1860s, resulting in the takeover of the Northwest by the Dominion of Canada and the Riel insurrection at Red River (1869–70), the creation of the province of Manitoba (1870), and the entry of the colony of British Columbia into the Canadian federation (1871). The unjust handling of the Métis people led to the Northwest Rebellion and the hanging of Louis Riel (1885).

Meanwhile, the population of the region was changing apace. Until the Northwest, British Columbia included, became part of Canada, white people were but a tiny minority among Indian and Métis people. Indeed, in 1868 Bishop Taché estimated that the Indians of the Northwest, east of the Rockies, numbered some 60,000, alongside 15,000 Métis, and only 4,000 white people mainly centred in Red River. Whether in the prairies, the North, or British Columbia, the land was Indian. Until the 1880s, white people were in the minority in all of the North and West. It was the large immigration following completion of the Canadian Pacific Railroad in the 1880s that transformed the Indian majorities into minorities who became more and more negligible in the eyes of the white man. The Oblates frequently stood at the point of

Unidentified Indian woman and child in their native habitat in the Northwest.

contact between the white juggernaut and the proud Indian who was becoming, more often than not, a victim.

This Book

The primary objective of our study is to present the history of Oblate missionary work in the North and West during the nineteenth century. That saga is presented as a conquest of liberation of Canada's aboriginal population, but frequently resulting in their subjugation to white Euro-Canadian society. Protestants, particularly the Church of England and its Church Missionary Society (CMS), opposed the Oblates' every move.

The book will be couched in a military analogy of conquest. This approach will illustrate the aggressive stance of the Oblates in their efforts not only to occupy every strategic position in the land and to convert the Indians, but also to regiment themselves with a view to defeating an ever-threatening enemy. The ongoing battle with their Protestant adversaries will be dealt with in detail.

The basic orientation of a society—its world-view, values, myths, symbols, and networks of symbols—are found in its religion, a term designating a people's relationship with reality and with one another. Given that (1) religious myth is the overriding determinant in the nature of the relationship among peoples, (2) that the Oblates were the primary Catholic religious agency in the region, and (3) between 1845 and 1991 the Indian people of the North and West were in fact conquered religiously and were largely assimilated,[29] it is argued that the Oblates were at the cutting edge of a conquest whose objectives and battle strategy were set by Euro-Canadian ultramontane Catholicism. The natives were to be converted to the true religion, that of Jesus Christ, in its nineteenth-century Roman Catholic incarnation, an incarnation that just happened to be almost exclusively French or French-Canadian.

While seeking to analyze the Oblate assault on the Northwest, the study is set in the context of the usually latent and sometimes open conflict between Catholic priest and Protestant minister. A primary objective of the book is to explore the extent and nature of the relationship between Catholic and Protestant missionaries in the North and the West. While the natives were being converted, the heretical and misguided Protestant rivals had to be defeated, or at least held in check, in order for a new Christian Church to emerge, a Church built along ultramontane Catholic lines.

A second thematic thread that runs throughout the study is that of ethnicity, or cultures. The Indians referred to the Catholic Church as the religion of the French and to the Church of England as the religion of the English, for the obvious reason that all Anglican ministers were English, while just about all Catholic clergy, Oblates in particular, were either French or French Canadian.

Religion and culture are two webs of symbols, meanings, and values, two foci that are simultaneously distinct and overlapping in a given society. Their order of priority changes from one society to another, and within a given society over time, but regardless of whether a religion or a culture is perceived as dominant at any given time, it usually drags the other along in its wake. In Canada, until the middle of the nineteenth century, religion was perceived as the dominant web of meaning, dragging cultures along in its wake. This is why legislation of the period was careful to protect religious minority rights, linguistic and cultural rights getting short shrift.

Since the formation of the nations of France and England in the late Middle Ages, the countries had been rivals, frequently enemies, in Europe. They continued to be such in their North American colonies beginning in the seventeenth century. When Britain definitively broke France's North American political stranglehold in 1760, the former colonial, political, and military rivalry turned into a usually latent, sometimes open, hostility between Canadians of French and those of British allegiance. This hostility was carried over to the Northwest.

For half a millennium preceding the settlement of the Canadian Northwest, both France and England had State churches that were intimately bound to the nation's political and cultural agendas. The Church of England was one side of the English coin, the other being the Crown, and the typical Englishman was loyal to both. In France, the French Revolution hardly changed anything in the strong relationship of the Catholic Church to the nation, although Frenchmen were divided about which form of government was preferable. Given that France stood at the heart of European civilization and culture in the eighteenth century, and given that the nineteenth-century revitalization of world Catholicism was in many respects driven by French Catholics, it is not surprising that Catholic missionary activity in the Northwest was French, while Protestant, particularly Anglican, missionary activity was English.

Secondary sources of the history of the Catholic Church in the Northwest tell us a great deal about dates, events, and people, but very little about the role and meaning of Catholic and Oblate history in the broader contexts of nineteenth-century Catholic, Christian, and Western Canadian history.

One part of that history that is central to our concern, Catholic–Protestant relations, is largely ignored in the literature. Nineteenth-century publications that deal with these relations may be placed in two distinct categories, both of which rest on a profound ignorance of one of the parties in question. The first category is partisan, bigoted treatises that assume that "their" denomination is the only valid one, the "other"'s existence being the handiwork of the devil. In the second category are travel accounts by various tourists or visitors to the Northwest in the nineteenth century. The reader is sometimes surprised to find high praise for francophone Catholic missions and missionaries by anglophone Protestant writers. Such writings stand in contrast to the venomous and spiteful words of many clergymen.

Another secondary source is the writings of twentieth-century historians and scholars. Here the reader will find very little that is useful, at least before 1970. These twentieth-century authors either remain ignorant of any relations between Catholics and Protestants or choose to be silent on the subject. W.L. Morton briefly discusses the role of the clergy in the political events leading to the 1869–70 insurrection at Red River, noting that these clergymen greatly contributed to the maintenance of civilization in the Northwest. For his part, the Oblate historian Adrien-Gabriel Morice revels in denouncing the injustices against Catholics and francophones, sometimes demonstrating reprehensible partisanship. In sum, until the centennial of Canadian Confederation in 1967, the few publications of professional historians tell us little or nothing about the relationships of Catholics and Protestants in Canada's nineteenth-century Northwest missions.

In the past twenty-five years, the situation has improved somewhat. John Webster Grant reminds us in his general works on Canadian religious history of the continual competition and sustained animosity between Catholic and Protestant missionaries. Grant goes no further, however, having chosen not to develop this theme. In a book published in 1957, however, the late Oblate historian Gaston Carrière cites a series of archival documents that illustrate mutual

Adrien-Gabriel Morice
(1859–1938)

assistance and even warm friendships between Oblate missionaries and HBC officers in Canada's Northeast—that is, around James Bay, in Labrador, and on the north shore of the St. Lawrence River.[30] These HBC officers were usually anglophone and Protestant.

Since 1970, research has intensified in various aspects of the history of Canada's North and West. A growing number of books, articles, and dissertations underline the weaknesses of the northwestern missions. While various studies noted the virulent anti-Catholicism of several Protestant ministers in the nineteenth-century Northwest, the historian Frits Pannekoek goes so far as to flatly condemn the Anglican clergy in Red River during the half century preceding the first Riel insurrection. Pannekoek casts a wide net, accusing the Anglican clergymen of just about every sin under the sun; they are charged with being the primary agents of the disintegration of the Red River community on the eve of Riel's insurrection.

The least that can be said is that such a sweeping indictment stands in stark contrast to the honeyed statements of former partisan writers, at least when they wrote about their own denomination. In fact, Pannekoek takes aim at the Anglicans only, leaving aside the Catholic clergy, who would have had little contact with the anglophone white people of Red River. This author settles the question of Catholic–Protestant relations by declaring that they were non-existent, a rather cursory argument when one considers that for French Catholic historian Morice it was precisely the bigotry of the Anglo-Protestant "Canadian" party from Ontario that was at the root of the Riel insurrection of 1869–70.

In spite of the growing list of studies, and their increasingly improved quality, a basic understanding of the history of Christianity in Canada's North and West has still to find its way into the writings of some Canadian historians.[31] This phenomenon is possibly a result of a combination of factors: contemporary historians of religion and church historians have not done their share in the scholarly study of Canada's North and West; most primary material on the Catholic Church in the North and West is written in French, a language that remains foreign to some historians; many historians dismiss religion as irrelevant, and therefore have not given it serious attention; the religious illiteracy of many Canadians, scholars included, which means that even those who sense the importance of religion do not know how to study it; and the politically correct popular attitudes in this late twentieth century that take comfort in blaming Christian missionaries for the destruction of aboriginal cultures, choosing to overlook the fact that eighty-five percent of today's Canadian Indian people freely consider themselves Christian.

Although not exhaustive, the research for this book was extensive. In addition to consulting the considerable secondary literature on the history of the Canadian West, the role of religion in particular, the author delved into several collections of primary sources, including the archival collections of the CMS and of the HBC found in the National Archives of Canada in Ottawa. He also explored in depth the extensive archival collections of the Oblates of Mary Immaculate held in the Deschatelets Archives in Ottawa, in the Grandin Archives in St. Albert, Alberta, and in the Provincial Archives of Alberta in Edmonton. The archives of the Archdiocese of Grouard-MacLennan, Alberta, and of the Diocese of Mackenzie-Fort Smith in Yellowknife, NWT, were also explored.

Notes

1. In Roman Catholicism, groups of men or women who live in a community bound by vows of poverty, chastity, and obedience are members of either religious orders or religious congregations. The difference between orders and congregations is a technical, canonical one, "order" designating those groups bound by solemn vows, "congregation" designating those bound by more simple, temporary vows. The Oblates of Mary Immaculate were technically a congregation.

2. The word "ultramontane," meaning literally beyond the mountains, was coined in southern France at this time. It designates those Catholics who looked beyond the Alps—that is, towards Rome—for their salvation.

3. AACFO.

4. For an overview of the history of the Roman Catholic Church in the nineteenth century see Roger Aubert, *L'Église dans le monde moderne*, vol. 5 of R. Aubert et al., *Nouvelle histoire de l'Église* (Paris: Seuil, 1975). Good general studies of nineteenth-century Catholicism in Canada are Lucien Lemieux, *Les années difficiles (1760–1839)*, and Philippe Sylvain and Nive Voisine, *Réveil et consolidation... 1840–1898*, tomes 1 and 2 of Nive Voisine (ed.), *Histoire du catholicisme québécois*, vol. 2, *Les XVIIIe et XIXe siècles* (Montreal: Boréal, 1989, 1991). On ultramontanism see Nive Voisine and Jean Hamelin, *Les ultramontains canadiens-français*.

5. From the early Middle Ages to the year 1972, the rite of admission into the ranks of the Catholic clergy involved the ritual ceremony of the tonsure. This practice was abandoned in 1972, to be replaced by an episcopal blessing given during a special Mass.

6. In Catholic theology, the clerical state is an office, intended for the ministry and structured by the sacrament of Holy Orders. The religious life is a state of being, usually defined by vows and communal living and not necessarily entailing ordination. Thus nuns and sisters are "religious"—that is, members of religious orders and congregations—but are not ordained, and therefore are not members of the clergy in the strict sense of the word. However, male "religious," other than monks and brothers, are more often than not ordained, thus becoming simultaneously clergymen as well. Since such fine distinctions are lost on most readers, in this book "clergy" will designate all of the people noted above, male and female.

7. As was the case for men, women in the "religious" state of life were canonically divided into *nuns* and *sisters*. Nuns were members of traditional, frequently medieval, groups, who took formal and permanent vows of religion—the Carmelites or Benedictines, for example. Few nuns worked in the Canadian North and West. Sisters were members of religious congregations—that is, a type of religious grouping that had become typical in the sixteenth century. Their vows of poverty, chastity, and obedience were canonically considered simple or temporary. Just about all religious women who worked in the West and North belonged to this latter category.

8. In 1760, the ban affected the Society of Jesus (Jesuits), the Recollets, and the Gentlemen of Saint-Sulpice (Sulpicians).

9. Although the Gentlemen of Saint-Sulpice are technically secular priests who happen to live in community, for all practical purposes they live like other regular clergy. Therefore, for ease of reference, the author here considers them to be part of the regular clergy.

10. One exception to this was the arrival of the Brothers of Christian Schools in Montreal in 1837, men who are never ordained clergymen.

11. Pierre Savard, *Aspects du catholicisme canadien-français au xixe siècle* (Montreal: Fides, 1980), p. 26. This text was initially published in *Recherches sociographiques 8*, 3, September–December 1967.

12. Louis-Edmond Hamelin, "L'évolution numérique séculaire du clergé catholique dans le Québec."

13. Bernard Denault and Benoît Lévesque, p. 48.

14. In addition to the Oblates, the six congregations included the Society of Jesus, the Clercs de Saint-Viateur, the Fathers of the Holy Cross, the Gentlemen of Saint-Sulpice, and the Brothers of Christian Schools.

15. See Rolland Litalien (ed.), *Le Grand Séminaire de Montréal de 1840 à 1990: 150 ans au service de la formation des prêtres* (Montreal: Éditions du Grand Séminaire, 1990).

16. In addition, beginning in 1825, Bishop Lartigue of Montreal founded the Séminaire Saint-Jacques, an institution that would receive a handful of aspiring priests until it closed upon the opening of the Grand Séminaire in 1840.

17. For the history of this institution see Noël Baillargeon, *Le Séminaire de Québec de 1685 à 1760* and *Le Séminaire de Québec de 1760 à 1800* (Quebec: Les Presses de l'Université Laval, 1972 and 1981).

18. Bishop Hubert (1784–97), for one, resided in the seminary.

19. Alfred Baudrillart, p. 9.

20. Provencher to Bourget, St. Boniface, 5 August 1850. ACAM copy, 71.220, 1007, APA.

21. Fathers Jean-Baptiste Honorat (superior), Adrien Telmon, Jean Baudrand, and Lucien Lagier; Brothers Basile Fastray and Louis Roux.

22. Sisters of the Holy Names of Jesus and Mary, established in 1844.

23. The Brothers of Christian Schools, the Oblates, the Jesuits, the Clercs de Saint-Viateur, the Congregation of the Holy Cross, and the Sulpicians.

24. The Ursulines, the Sisters of Notre Dame, the Grey Nuns, and the nursing sisters of both Quebec and Montreal.

25. Lord Selkirk's Assiniboia colony, centred at the junction of the Red and Assiniboine rivers, existed from 1811 to 1835.

26. A. Taché, *Esquisse sur le Nord-Ouest de l'Amérique* (Montreal: n.p., 1869).

27. The Tlingit, Tsimshian, Bella Coola, Kwakiutl, Coast Salish, Haida, and Nootka.

28. The Carrier, Chilcotin, Interior Salish, and Kootenay.

29. The Census of Canada of 1991 (Catalogue 93–319) shows that fully eighty-five percent, or 401,000 of Canada's 471,000 aboriginal people, consider themselves Christian, whereas only three percent, or 11,000, claim "native Indian or Inuit religion" as their primary religious affiliation. Only 173,000 Canadians claim that their mother tongue is one of the aboriginal languages.

30. *Les missions catholiques dans l'est du Canada et l'Honorable compagnie de la Baie d'Hudson (1844–1900)*.

31. For example, in an otherwise fine study, the historian J.R. Miller wrote in 1989 that the Oblates had a continuous presence in the Canadian West as of 1821, when in fact their congregation was created only in 1826 (in France), did not come to Canada until December 1841 (to Montreal), and sent its first two men to the West in 1845. (See *Skyscrapers Hide the Heavens*, revised edition [Toronto: University of Toronto Press, 1989], p. 130.)

CHAPTER II

THE PATHFINDERS

THE spearhead of Catholic evangelization in the vast Canadian West would initially be made up of secular priests, the sole Catholic missionaries in the area between 1818 and 1845. Then, beginning in 1845, these men would be joined by a growing legion of Oblate missionaries who in the fifteen years between 1845 and 1860 began the evangelization of the territory encompassed by today's prairie provinces, Northwest Territories, British Columbia, and Yukon.

The first phase of this evangelical spearhead, that of the secular clergy, was three-pronged, aimed in turn at Red River, the Pacific slope, and the upper Saskatchewan River.

The Red River Mission[1]

Although the odd Jesuit missionary had passed through parts of the Northwest in the eighteenth century,[2] it was not until the Scottish philanthropist Thomas, Earl of Selkirk, founded his Red River colony in 1811 that any sustained and consistent effort was made to maintain missionaries in the region. The Irish priest Charles Bourke accompanied the first shipload of settlers in 1811, but Bourke's strange behaviour led to his being returned to England after having wintered in York Factory on Hudson Bay, the port of disembarkation. The colony of Red River, located at the junction of the Assiniboine and Red rivers, was therefore without clerical ministrations for the first seven years of its existence.

In the context of the ongoing struggle between the rival Hudson's Bay Company (HBC) and the North West Company for control of the fur trade, and in the wake of a tragic armed confrontation between the two camps (the Battle of Seven Oaks) that left twenty-two men dead, in 1816, Selkirk and his local governor, Miles Macdonell, asked Bishop Plessis of Quebec to send Catholic priests to Red River. Selkirk considered that the priests could only help appease the largely French-speaking Métis people, who made up the bulk of the manpower of the rival North West Company.

Bishop Plessis sent Father Pierre-Antoine Tabeau on a voyage of exploration to the Northwest. The priest had gotten as far as Rainy Lake when he heard about the Battle of Seven Oaks; he immediately returned to Quebec and recommended that a permanent mission not be established, because the situation was too conflictual. However, Tabeau's report was countered by petitions and pleas from the residents of Red River, and they won the day.

Travelling at the expense of their hosts, in the summer of 1818 Father Joseph-Norbert Provencher, formerly pastor of Kamouraska, Father Sévère Dumoulin, and the seminarian Guillaume Edge journeyed to Red River. They were the first resident clergymen to set foot in the colony. The new missionaries enjoyed the support not only of Governor General Lord Sherbrooke of Canada, but also of Selkirk's wife. In fact, the earl had given the Catholic mission some twenty square miles on the right bank of the Red River, across from the mouth of the Assiniboine. The land would become the nucleus of the town of St. Boniface—a Catholic colony, therefore, founded with the support of the Protestant gentlemen Selkirk and Sherbrooke.

Not only did Governor General Sherbrooke chair the fundraising drive for the Red River mission, but Bishop Plessis instructed his missionaries to show unwavering loyalty to the British governors. Indeed, on 20 April 1818, the bishop asked fathers Provencher and Dumoulin to make known to the Indian people the advantages of living under the government of His Majesty; the priests were to teach, by word and deed, respect for and loyalty to the sovereign.[3]

Promoted bishop in 1820 and consecrated in 1822, Provencher continued to benefit from the good offices of the HBC. Governor George Simpson of the HBC wrote in 1824 that the conduct of the Catholic missionaries was above reproach; not only did they abstain from meddling in the colony's political and commercial affairs, but

Joseph-Norbert Provencher (1787–1853)

they avoided any controversy with the Protestants.[4] Simpson congratulated Provencher for his exemplary conduct, for his indefatigable zeal,
and for his missionaries' exceptional perseverance.[5] In a resolution of
22 August 1825, the Council of the company's Northern Department
endorsed the view of its governor and, as a gesture of gratitude, decided
to make an annual grant of £50 to the Catholic mission. Bishop
Provencher had equal respect and esteem for Simpson and the HBC
officers, and frequently bore witness to their generosity and good will.[6]

As the tiny colony of Red River struggled to survive through periodic floods, grasshopper infestations, famines, and fires, Bishop Provencher had considerable difficulty maintaining enough clergy for his flock. Provencher included, sixteen secular priests worked in the greater Northwest, British Columbia included, between 1818 and 1845, but the length of their stays varied from the five weeks of Father Blanchet, who was only passing through on his way to the Pacific, to the lifetime service of others. Two seminarians also went West, but left without being ordained.

Until 1844 Provencher never had more than four priests at his disposal at any one time in Red River. That year the number rose to five. Then, the arrival of two Oblates in 1845 marked the beginning of a new era.

There are several reasons for this modest number of clergymen in Red River. One is the shortage of clergy in Canada itself,[7] which made it difficult to find the required number of personnel. Another is the fact that many of these priests were just out of seminary, where their train-

Table 3
Secular Clergy in the Northwest, 1818–45

NAME	ORDAINED	ARRIVED	DEPARTED	DIED
J.-N. Provencher	1811	1818	–	1853
S. Dumoulin	1817	1818	1823	1853
W. Edge	NO	1818	1820	–
T. Destroismaisons	1819	1820	1827	1866
J. Sauvé	NO	1820	1822	–
J. Harper	1824	1822	1831	1869
F. Boucher	1829	1827	1833	–
G.-A. Bellecourt	1827	1831	1847	1874
C.-E. Poiré	1833	1832	1838	–
J.-B. Thibault	1833	1833	1879	1879
M. Demers	1836	1837	1838	1869
J.-A. Mayrand	1838	1838	1845	1895
F.-N. Blanchet	1819	1838	1838	1881
J.-E. Darveau	1841	1841	–	1844
L.-F. Laflèche	1844	1844	1856	1896
J.-B. Bolduc	–	1843	1843	1867
A. Langlois	–	1843	–	–
J. Bourassa	–	1844	1855	–

Sources: A. Taché, *Vingt années de missions*; David Roy, "Monseigneur Provencher et son clergé séculier"; Émilien Lamirande, "L'implantation de l'Église catholique en Colombie-Britannique, 1838–1848," p. 360; various archival sources.

ing had been less than thorough. They were all young men in their twenties when they went West, only Bishop Provencher having crossed the threshold into his thirties.[8] Having been prevailed upon to serve in the distant Northwest, usually by Provencher through his episcopal colleagues, these young men arrived in the Northwest only to discover that under the best of circumstances life was hard. To the hardships that everybody shared, such as insufficient finances and the difficulties of mere survival, was added the excruciating loneliness that was the lot of most Catholic clergymen who found themselves entrusted with the ministry in places isolated from any meaningful relations with their fellow priests. The result was profound disappointment, at times moral depression, and the firm resolve to leave the country at the earliest opportunity. As soon as a new clergyman disembarked from the canoes arriving from Canada, a forlorn young priest usually boarded for the return voyage. Some justified their action on the grounds that they had given a few years to Provencher's missions; after all, most priests had not done that much.

Taking into account the fact that when they arrived some of these men were yet to be trained and ordained, in the end Bishop Provencher could count on the services of a priest for an average of five years. He felt that he was always starting over, despite his every effort to recruit more clergy and to improve the quality of their training.

The British Columbia Mission

The second prong of this first phase of the Catholic evangelical spearhead in the Northwest was led by fathers Modeste Demers and François-Norbert Blanchet.[9] Their story resembles that of the Red River missionaries in many respects, although Father Blanchet was exceptional in that he went West in 1838 at the ripe old age of forty-three. Like their Red River colleagues, they were recruited by Provencher and found life very difficult in their new mission territory.[10]

Priests had been sought by the French-Canadian and Métis inhabitants of two settlements on the Willamette and Cowlitz rivers, tributaries of the Columbia River, in the area of the HBC's Fort Vancouver in today's Oregon. These former and current voyageurs of the North West and Hudson's Bay companies had petitioned Bishop Provencher in 1834 and again in 1835 for priests. He responded with pastoral concern and promises; he then undertook to find suitable clergy. Provencher was particularly concerned because since 1834 a total of five Methodist missionaries had come from the United States and were active in the area of the lower Columbia, among the Flathead or Nez Percés Indians, in the present-day states of Idaho and Washington.

Having obtained the moral support of bishops Signay of Quebec and Lartigue of Montreal, Provencher went to Rome in the early months of 1836; there he obtained the support of the Vatican for his Oregon project, as well as the extension of his episcopal jurisdiction over the area. Back in Montreal, during the winter of 1836–37, Bishop Provencher sought the desired missionaries. Father François-Norbert Blanchet, pastor of the parish of Les Cèdres in the diocese of Montreal, accepted the mission. His companion would be the newly ordained Modeste Demers, then curate in Trois-Pistoles. Although the bishop had hoped to implement his plan as early as 1837, the HBC refused to authorize the mission at the time, forcing a delay until the following year. Governor Simpson wrote in April 1837 that his company feared the eruption of religious controversies in the area if both Catholic and Protestant missionaries were present. Bishop Provencher, in the meantime, took Father Demers with him to Red River.

Faced with Provencher's appeals, by the autumn of 1837 Governor Simpson relented and agreed to a Catholic mission in Oregon. He stipulated, however, that it be located on the Cowlitz River, a northern tributary of the Columbia, 100 kilometres from Fort Vancouver, and not on the Willamette, a southern tributary that lay in territory claimed by the expanding United States of America. Provencher readily agreed. The way was clear for fathers Blanchet and Demers to travel to the Pacific in 1838. Both were pious and zealous, although unexceptional, priests. They travelled as passengers on board the HBC summer fur brigade, leaving Red River on 10 July 1838 and travelling via the North Saskatchewan and Athabasca rivers and Jasper House; a packhorse journey took them to the British Columbia river system that brought them to Fort Vancouver on the Columbia on 24 November. They were the first Catholic priests in the territory since the departure of the Spanish friars half a century earlier.

So it was that the northern portion of the Oregon mission, today's British Columbia, was initially evangelized by these two priests, by Demers in particular. From his base on the Cowlitz, Father Demers was entrusted with the northern portion of the mission, visiting the lower Fraser River as far as Fort Langley in 1841. The Canadian priests soon learned of an adjacent Jesuit mission established in 1840 among the Flathead Indians, a territory under the jurisdiction of the Catholic bishop of St. Louis. Jesuit Father de Smet met Demers and Blanchet in the summer of 1842, and the three priests undertook joint planning for the evangelization of the region.

It was decided that Demers would pre-empt the likely Protestant penetration of New Caledonia, or the British Columbia mainland, by taking an extended missionary journey up the Fraser River. He left Fort Vancouver with an HBC brigade on 30 June 1842, journeyed hundreds of kilometres up the Columbia River as far as Stuart Lake, wintered at Fort Alexander, and was back home in late April 1843. Along the way he baptized 280 people, mostly Indians. Except for the earlier Spanish mission, his was the first sustained missionary endeavour on the west coast of today's Canada.

However, the Catholic missionary enterprise in British Columbia (New Caledonia) operated by fits and starts for several years. One reason for this was the reluctance of the HBC, under Simpson's orders, to provide transport and lodging for missionaries; another was Demers's reluctance to relive the difficulties of his voyages of 1841 and 1842. Although Father J.-B. Bolduc evangelized some Indians on Vancouver Island in the spring of 1843, baptizing a number of them, he soon pulled up stakes and returned to the Columbia River; no follow-up occurred.

The only significant missionary activities on mainland British Columbia during the next few years were those of the Jesuit missionaries, fathers Pierre-Jean de Smet and John Nobili in particular. Father de Smet crossed the Rockies in the latter part of 1845, wintered at Fort Edmonton,[11] and then recrossed the mountains via Jasper in the spring of 1846, baptizing and evangelizing along the way. Later that year, it was the newly arrived Father Nobili's turn to go up the Fraser as far as Stuart Lake; he would continue to work in the region until late 1848, baptizing hundreds of Indians and building chapels here and there. Father Nobili's religious superior then ordered him to concentrate on the more southerly missions. The interior of British Columbia would be without a missionary for a decade, until the arrival of the Oblates in the area in 1859.

The Upper Saskatchewan Mission

The third prong of the first phase of the Catholic missionary spearhead into the Northwest, that of the secular priests, was led by Father Jean-Baptiste Thibault (1810–79), a man who had been working in Red River since 1833 and who would devote the lion's share of his career as a priest to his ministry in the Northwest. A native of Lévis, Quebec, Thibault had studied at the Séminaire de Québec until his departure for Red River in the spring of 1833. Arriving in June, he was ordained at Red River in September. His ministry in the Red River area made him fluent in the language of the Ojibwa and Cree people.

Jean-Baptiste Thibault
(1810–79)

Thibault's historic importance results from Bishop Provencher's difficulties in securing permission from the HBC to transport a Catholic missionary to posts on the upper Saskatchewan River. With the exception of the founding of the Oregon mission in 1838, from its outset in 1818 the Catholic mission at Red River had not spread its tentacles very far. The few priests were usually busy evangelizing the Métis and French-speaking population of the Red River area. Father George Bellecourt travelled further afield to evangelize the Indians at Rainy Lake and on the Winnipeg River. Then in one fell swoop, in 1840, the HBC imported six Methodist missionaries into the Northwest and stationed them in areas that had heretofore remained closed to clergymen of all persuasions. Fort Edmonton was one of these areas. Simultaneously, the Church of England's Church Missionary Society (CMS) parachuted the native catechist Henry Budd into The Pas on the Saskatchewan River. Needless to say, Bishop Provencher became concerned. When he sought permission to send a priest on the HBC brigades up the Saskatchewan to Fort Edmonton, Governor Simpson repeatedly refused to grant it. Provencher thereupon decided to send his missionary overland, across the prairies on horseback.

The chosen missionary was Jean-Baptiste Thibault, who, in spite of his mere thirty-two years, was one of the most experienced missionaries in the West. Beginning in Red River in the spring of 1842, his six-month journey on horseback marked the beginning of the Catholic evangelization of the northwestern prairies. Thibault

George-Antoine Bellecourt
(1803-74)

toured various Indian and HBC stations before returning to Red River in October. He reported to Bishop Provencher that all the Métis and most of the Indians he had met had abandoned the Protestant minister and flocked to the Catholic priest. This moved the Reverend Robert Rundle, the Methodist missionary, to curse denounce, defame, and lie about the Catholic Church; meanwhile, Thibault baptized 353 people and solemnized twenty marriages.[12]

Father Thibault returned to the upper Saskatchewan in 1843, continuing his itinerant missions in the area. In 1844, after wintering at Frog Lake, he established permanent residence at Lake St. Anne, the name he gave to the Crees' Devil's Lake, located some seventy-five kilometres west of Edmonton; this mission would remain his base of operations until his return to Red River in 1852. During all of those years in Alberta, beginning in 1844, Father Thibault was assisted by a secular priest, Father Joseph Bourassa. Back in Red River, he devoted a further sixteen years to the ministry, until his return to Canada in 1868. He would thereafter remain in the East, except for a two-year stay in Red River in 1870–72 as a member of a negotiating team sent by Ottawa to deal with Louis Riel. One reason for Father Thibault's spectacular success in the region that would become Alberta is the fact that most of the HBC employees were Métis and readily reverted to the faith of their fathers when the priest appeared among them. Thibault and succeeding Catholic missionaries therefore had a ready-made constituency in most of the HBC trading posts throughout the North and the West; the fact that both the priests and the Métis were French-speaking only reinforced this tendency.

Interior of the first chapel in Lake St. Anne.

An Oblate Beachhead

The second phase of the Catholic evangelical spearhead into the Northwest was led by the Oblates of Mary Immaculate. Their pathfinders can be divided into four platoons, each entrusted with establishing an Oblate beachhead in vast territories: Red River, northern Saskatchewan and Alberta, Alberta itself, and British Columbia.

The Red River beachhead was the first. In his perpetual search for new priests, Bishop Provencher had soon secured the support of Bishop Ignace Bourget of Montreal, the man who had personally obtained the services of the first Oblates in 1841 and who was rapidly becoming the most powerful churchman in Canadian Catholicism. Not only was Montreal growing into the metropolis of Canada, but the diocese of Montreal was outdistancing all others in number of priests, religious congregations, and sisters, and in amounts of money it sheltered. Moreover, in 1844 the Montreal Church was already three years into a full-scale revival. All of these factors gave growing power to its bishop. It would be foolhardy for the head of a religious congregation like the Oblates, a congregation not only desiring, but needing, overseas expansion, to dismiss or ignore a Bourget appeal. Besides, Mazenod was as determined to expand his congregation's apostolate in North America as Bourget and Provencher had been to obtain Oblate services. Not only did Mazenod enjoy the full support of his men in his North American adventure, but he thought that it was the heaven-sent opportunity to crack open the door to the evangelization of several nations. It was the will of God![13]

So it was that when Bourget wrote to Bishop de Mazenod on 10 October 1844, urging him to accede to Provencher's urgent appeal for help, the superior general of the Oblates did not hesitate. Mazenod had been aware of Provencher's desire for the Oblates since the early months of 1844; it had been one of the reasons for his appointing Father Guigues plenipotentiary representative of the superior general in Canada.[14] Within weeks of his arrival in Canada in 1844, Father Guigues had waxed eloquent about the Red River mission, as did the bishops of Montreal and Quebec. At its meeting of 16 December 1844, therefore, the Oblate General Council agreed with their founder: two Oblates would be sent to Red River in 1845. Father Guigues was entrusted with executing the decision; when he hesitated, then wrote that he could not implement the directive due to a shortage of personnel, Mazenod fired a broadside at his lieutenant, telling him in no uncertain terms that his was not to reason why; he had only to obey orders.

> Do not invoke the difficulties of your position in America due to the numerous appeals for assistance and the shortage of priests...

I find that you are very unreasonable to continually complain of your limited numbers... I order you to write to... [Provencher] that we agree to his request for assistance in his vicariate, and that you have two missionaries available for him. I designate for this interesting mission Father Pierre Aubert, for whom you will name a Canadian associate.[15]

Father Guigues assigned the young Alexandre-Antonin Taché[16] to accompany Father Aubert. Born in Rivière-du-Loup and raised in Boucherville near Montreal, Taché (1823–94) had ancestral ties to the

Alexandre-Antonin Taché (1823–94)

seventeenth-century explorer Louis Jolliet and to the eighteenth-century western pathfinder Pierre Gaultier de Varennes et de La Vérendrye. Imbued with a sense of destiny, he was conscious of the fact that Jolliet's companion, Father Marquette, had embarked on his journeys from Boucherville; in addition, Taché himself lived for a time in the Manor of Sabrevois where he cohabited with the ghost of Marguerite Bourgeois—who had also lived there. He was a nephew of the noted physician Sir Étienne-Pascal Taché (1795–1865), Prime Minister of the United Canadas in 1855–56, and the brother of Joseph-Charles Taché, who would become a noted physician, parliamentarian, and author, and one of the fathers of the Canadian Confederation of 1867.

In 1833, at the age of ten, the boy entered the seminary-college of St. Hyacinthe, decided to become a priest, and enrolled in the Grand Séminaire in Montreal in September 1841. He received the clerical tonsure in May 1842. Shortly thereafter he was appointed regent at Chambly College, then professor of mathematics at the St. Hyacinthe College in January 1844. Having been attracted to the Oblates since their arrival in Montreal in December 1841, Taché entered their novitiate at Longueuil at the end of 1844 and soon informed Father Guigues of his longing to evangelize the mysterious Northwest. Compelled by Mazenod to find a companion for Father Aubert, Guigues chose the twenty-one-year-old subdeacon.

Departing Montreal on 25 June 1845 aboard HBC canoes, the two Oblates covered the more than 2,300 kilometres to Red River in sixty days, Taché doing his share of the paddling and portaging duties, in addition to directing the voyageurs in prayer and chant, while Father Aubert heard some confessions and celebrated Mass. On 31 August, six days after his arrival, Taché was ordained a deacon. Six weeks later, on 12 October 1845, he was ordained in the priesthood at the age of twenty-two; the next day he took his religious vows of poverty, chastity, and obedience as a full-fledged member of the Missionary Oblates of Mary Immaculate. By 1 September 1845, therefore, the Oblate pathfinders were in place. There remained only to construct a beachhead.

Fathers Aubert and Taché spent the winter of 1845–46 at the bishop's house in St. Boniface or in the company of Father George-Antoine Bellecourt at his neighbouring parish, learning the language of the Ojibwa while assisting in the local ministry to the Métis. Then, in 1846, they set out on their first missionary journeys to the Indians, Aubert visiting Ojibwa gathering places around HBC trading posts to the east and north of St. Boniface, on the Winnipeg River and at Rainy Lake, stations previously visited by Father Bellecourt. Although the Ojibwa would prove very difficult to evangelize, the Oblates had secured a footing in the Northwest.

The second Oblate platoon would range almost as far from Red River as Red River was from Montreal. Along with a secular priest, Louis-François Laflèche, Father Taché was charged with founding a new Catholic mission station at Île-à-la-Crosse, an HBC trading hub some 1,500 kilometres northwest of Red River on the main route of the brigades crossing the height of land between the upper Saskatchewan River and the basins of the Athabasca, Slave, and Mackenzie rivers. It was there that the fur trade brigades that came up the Saskatchewan from Hudson Bay and Red River met the barges from the broader Mackenzie basin to exchange furs for supplies.

Louis-François Laflèche
(1818–98)

Father Laflèche[17] had first set foot in Red River in June 1844 and thereafter worked at learning the Ojibwa language and at evangelizing some of the area's Indian villages. Rarely had two more competent and talented missionaries been sent out as a team. The men soon became fast friends, and the friendship would outlast not only three years of dogged and painful missionary work in northern Saskatchewan, but also the subsequent half century of eventful, at times explosive, situations that would both bless and bedevil the lives of the two men in the West and in central Canada. They were destined to become pivotal figures in the unfolding ecclesiastico-political events that shaped the history of Canada in the second half of the nineteenth century. The pairing of the secular priest Laflèche and the Oblate Taché can be taken as representative of the best that both groups of missionaries had to offer, the passing of command of the Northwest missions from devoted but hamstrung secular priests to equally devoted but better-equipped Oblate missionaries.

Departing on 8 July 1846, Taché and Laflèche travelled on HBC barges, with the blessing of Governor George Simpson, who recommended them to Roderick McKenzie, commanding officer of the fort at Île-à-la-Crosse. McKenzie welcomed them into his trading post, where they spent the winter learning the Cree and Chipewyan languages, and he saw to the construction of their first mission station near the fort, a combination house and chapel that would become the model for many other mission stations.

It was from this base of operations that the two priests undertook the consolidation of the tenuous Catholic position in the northwestern woodlands. Crippled as Laflèche proved to be by rheumatism, he ministered in the vicinity of the post, while Taché went further afield, in the spring of 1847 to Reindeer Lake (Lac Caribou), more than 500 kilometres to the northeast, and in the autumn of the same year to Lake Athabasca, which stood some 600 kilometres north of Île-à-la-Crosse. There he encountered hundreds of Cree and Chipewyans who had gathered at the HBC trading post of Fort Chipewyan. After wintering at Île-à-la-Crosse, Father Taché returned to Lake Athabasca in the fall of 1848 with renewed hope, given that he had received reinforcements in the person of Oblate Father Henri Faraud, who had arrived at Île-à-la-Crosse in July 1848. Father Faraud was put in charge of the permanent Athabasca mission of La Nativité at Fort Chipewyan in 1849, a base that would serve as a launching pad for Oblate missionaries to the Peace River, Fond du Lac at the eastern end of Lake Athabasca, and Great Slave Lake.

Meanwhile, Father Taché continued his itinerant ministry in the area of Île-à-la-Crosse, until he was recalled to St. Boniface in the summer of 1851. He had been appointed coadjutor bishop to Provencher, and was destined to succeed him. As bishop-elect, Taché was replacing his friend and colleague, the twenty-nine-year-old Laflèche, who had

Fish being hauled to La Nativité mission at Fort Chipewyan during autumn.

been the first choice. That is why Provencher had recalled Laflèche to St. Boniface in 1849; however, Laflèche adamantly refused to consider the appointment, managing in the process to become more ill. Provencher could not win. In 1850 he turned to Taché, one of the two leaders of the second platoon of Oblate pathfinders that was now in place in northern Saskatchewan.

Father Taché was appointed by Rome in 1850, at the insistence of his superior general, and was ordained bishop in the cathedral of Viviers, France, in late November 1851. Upon his return to the Northwest in 1852, he again took up residence in Île-à-la-Crosse, now empowered not only as coadjutor bishop of the diocese of St. Boniface,[18] but also as superior of the Oblates in the Northwest, a missionary group that was since 1851 administratively independent of the Oblates of Canada. Bishop Taché remained at Île-à-la-Crosse for another two years—until November 1854, more than a year after the death of Bishop Provencher in June 1853 and his own automatic accession to the governance of the diocese of St. Boniface.

The third platoon of Oblate pathfinders was directed by Father Albert Lacombe, who would become a legend in Alberta. Born in the parish of St. Sulpice near Montreal on 28 February 1827, Albert was the son of Agathe Duhamel, a descendant of a maiden carried off into captivity by the Iroquois in their seventeenth-century wars against the French. After seven years of study at L'Assomption College (1840–47), Albert took up residence in Bishop Bourget's palace in Montreal, in order to prepare for the priesthood under the supervision of Coadjutor-Bishop Prince. Two years later, he left for the West, where he ministered in the Pembina area for two years (1849–51). Having returned to Montreal in 1851, the twenty-five-year-old priest offered his services to the twenty-eight-year-old Taché on Taché's visit to Montreal. Taché welcomed the new recruit, particularly since Father Lacombe intended to join the Oblates.

When he arrived in St. Boniface in 1852, Lacombe met Father Thibault, who had just returned from the Edmonton area where he had left Father Bourassa, his companion of many years. Bishop Taché immediately designated Lacombe to replace Thibault, foregoing Lacombe's intended Oblate novitiate, which he was to have spent in St. Boniface. In fact, Father Lacombe would get around to making his perpetual vows as an Oblate only in 1856. In the meantime, he spent the year 1852–53 ministering to the people of Fort Edmonton, a post commanded by the Catholic John Rowand; most of the 150 inhabitants of the post were Catholics of French-Canadian or Métis stock. In the spring of 1853, Lacombe officially replaced Father Bourassa at the Lake St. Anne mission; the latter returned to Red River.

Albert Lacombe (1827–1916)

It was from this Alberta territory that Albert Lacombe worked during the better part of the next half century of his life, until his death in 1916. Not only did he serve the white and Métis population of Edmonton and Jasper House, and the growing Métis settlements at Lake St. Anne, St. Albert, and Saint-Paul-des-Cris on the Saskatchewan River, but he also itinerated to evangelize the 1,100 aboriginal people of the surrounding area, 700 of whom were baptized by the mid-1860s. Beginning in 1855, he visited the Peace River country and the satellite mission of Lesser Slave Lake, some 260 kilometres away, all the while developing ties of friendship and trust with the Cree, the Blackfoot, and the Chipewyan.[19]

While there may have been a short delay in Lacombe's entry into the Oblate congregation, after 1853 his associates were Oblates to a man. His first companion at Lake St. Anne, Father René Rémas, founded an Oblate mission at Lake La Biche in 1853. Others, like Jean Tissot and Augustin Maisonneuve, came in subsequent years. This third platoon of Oblates led by Lacombe had established their own beachhead in Alberta.

The Oregon Territory was the destination of the fourth platoon of pathfinding Oblates. Until a treaty was signed by the United Kingdom and the United States in 1846, all of the northwestern Pacific territory

Unidentified Indian woman in Alberta.

Sarcee woman in Alberta.

encompassing the Columbia River Valley and present-day British Columbia as far north as Russian Alaska was exploited by the British HBC, under charter from the British Crown. The treaty of 1846 extended the previously agreed-upon international border between Canada and the United States, the 49th parallel, through the Rockies to the sea. Thereupon, the HBC proceeded to move its primary Pacific headquarters from old Fort Vancouver on the Columbia River (U.S. territory) to Victoria on Vancouver Island.

With the new international boundary, the resident Catholic missions of the secular clergy and the Jesuits on the Willamette, the Cowlitz, and among the Flatheads all fell into U.S. territory. While the new border was being put into place, the superior general of the Oblates faced growing demand for his men. In 1845, Archbishop F.-N. Blanchet of Oregon City had vainly sought the services of Oblates; Bishop de Mazenod refused. However, in 1846 the archbishop's brother, Bishop A.-M. Blanchet of Walla Walla, also appealed for Oblate missionaries, but to Canadian Oblate superior Joseph Guigues in Montreal. With Guigues having agreed to help, Bishop de Mazenod relented and promised to staff some Oregon missions. So it was that in February 1847 Father Pascal Ricard, three priests-in-training, or scholastics, and one brother embarked at The Hague for the Oregon mission.[20] They arrived at Walla Walla on 5 September.

The headquarters of the Oblate mission in Oregon was located in the diocese of Oregon City, in the state of Washington. For a decade, the Oblates endeavoured to establish a successful mission in the region, but were frustrated by a series of factors. The Indians did not prove overly receptive to their ministrations, one reason being a bloody war between the Indians and the U.S. government in 1855–58. Moreover, Archbishop F.-N. Blanchet insisted on conducting business with the Oblates as he did with his secular clergy, refusing to recognize their claim to own their own corporate property, distinct from that of the diocese.

After a decade of clerical bickering with Blanchet, the Oblates decided to pull up stakes and start afresh in British Columbia, in the diocese of Bishop Modeste Demers, a territory that included everything north of the 49th parallel. Although some Indian missionary work continued in Oregon for twenty years afterwards, beginning in 1858 the Oblate story on the Pacific slope is limited to British Columbia,[21] where the first resident Oblate mission was founded at Esquimalt on Vancouver Island in 1858, by Father Louis D'Herbomez, regional superior.[22] Close on its heels came the founding of the first Oblate mission on the mainland, at Lake Okanagan in 1859. The fourth Oblate platoon had done its work.

The Oblate beachhead in the greater Northwest was established, with outposts in Red River, northern Saskatchewan and Lake Athabasca, northern Alberta, and British Columbia. Theirs was a somewhat tenuous hold, however. If the missions were to have a lasting effect, they would need to be reinforced with many more missionaries, provided with the various social services that frequently proved to be the lifeblood of a mission station, and given an administrative and institutional infrastructure that would ensure that the missions outlasted the vagaries of some of their personnel.

The pathfinders had done their work. It was time for the invasion by the main Catholic missionary force.

Notes

1. The author first wrote about this early Catholic Church in Red River and its relations with the Church of England in "Les rapports entre catholiques et protestants dans le Nord-Ouest du Canada avant 1840," Raymond Huel (ed.), *Western Oblate Studies 1/Études Oblates de l'Ouest 1*, pp. 129–40. This phase of Western Catholic history, along with the rest of that history until 1915, is dealt with in detail by A.-G. Morice, *Histoire*, 1921.

2. For the history of Christianity in Canada before 1776 see Robert Choquette, "French Catholicism Comes to the Americas," Charles H. Lippy, Robert Choquette, and Stafford Poole, *Christianity Comes to the Americas, 1492–1776* (New York: Paragon House, 1992), part 2, pp. 131–242. Other studies in English include Cornelius Jaenen, *The Role of the Church in New France* (Toronto: McGraw-Hill Ryerson, 1976), and H.H. Walsh, *The Church in the French Era* (Toronto: Ryerson, 1966).

3. J.-O. Plessis, Instructions to Provencher and Dumoulin, Quebec, 20 April 1818, in Grace Lee Nute, p. 59.

4. 5 June 1824. 3M4, D 4/7. HBC papers, NAC.

5. Ibid., 22 August 1825.

6. Provencher to A. Dionne, Saint-Boniface, 17 July 1826 and 1 July 1829, in *Les Cloches de Saint-Boniface* 31, 4 (April 1932): 88–92, 93–94.

7. On the history of the Catholic Church in Quebec between 1760 and 1840, see Lucien Lemieux, *Les années difficiles (1760–1839)*.

8. Upon their arrival in Red River, they were aged as follows: Harper, 20, Poiré, 21, Thibault, 22, Destroismaisons, 24, Boucher, 24, Dumoulin, 25, Darveau, 25, Laflèche, 26, Demers, 27, Bourassa, 27, Bellecourt, 28. See David Roy, "Monseigneur Provencher," pp. 7–8.

9. Some Spanish missionaries had been present on the west coast, from time to time beginning in 1774. See Émilien Lamirande, "Traditions orales du xix^c," 393–412; "L'établissement espagnol de Nootka," 212–231; "L'implantation de l'Église catholique," 213–25, 323–63, 453–89.

10. Provencher remained in charge of the Oregon missions until July 1845, when Blanchet was consecrated first apostolic vicar of Oregon. Provencher himself remained under the jurisdiction of the Bishop of Quebec, at least until his Northwest district was raised to the rank of apostolic vicariate on 16 April 1844; the Oregon mission therefore remained under the sway of the Bishop of Quebec. Oregon was made a distinct apostolic vicariate on 1 December 1843, signalling the severing of its ties to both Quebec and Saint Boniface, as soon as the first apostolic vicar was consecrated. This occurred with Blanchet's consecration in Montreal on 25 July 1845. Blanchet immediately sought to obtain the formation of a new ecclesiastical province of no fewer than eight dioceses in Oregon, with himself as archbishop, and he managed to do so in short order. The treaty between Britain and the U.S. signed on 14 June 1846 assigned all lands below the 49th parallel to the U.S. The following month, on 24 July 1846, Blanchet was appointed first archbishop of the diocese of Oregon City; his colleague Modeste Demers was made first bishop of the new diocese of Vancouver Island, with responsibility for two others, Queen Charlotte Islands and New Caledonia. Simultaneously, Blanchet's brother, Augustin-Magloire, was made bishop of the new diocese of Walla Walla on the American side of the border.

11. He arrived there on 31 December 1845 and departed the following April.

12. J.-N. Provencher to Archbishop J. Signay, St. Boniface, 2 January 1843, in *Bulletin de la Société historique de Saint-Boniface* 3 (1913): 210–13.

13. This and the following paragraphs are largely based on the very revealing correspondence of Eugène de Mazenod, in particular his *Lettres aux correspondants d'Amérique, 1841–1850*, and *Lettres aux correspondants d'Amérique, 1851–1860*. The above collections are hereafter referred to as *Lettres...I*, and *Lettres...II*.

14. Guigues's title was Extraordinary Visitor. Mazenod to Guigues, Marseilles, 10 June 1844, in *Lettres...I*, pp. 97–99.

15. Mazenod to Guigues, Marseilles, 24 May 1845, in *Lettres...I*, pp. 123–5.

16. See Dom Benoît's lengthy if somewhat dated biography of Taché. More recent is Jean Hamelin, "Taché, Alexandre-Antonin," *DCB* 12, pp. 1093–1103.

17. Laflèche (1818–98), who later became famous as Bishop of Trois-Rivières, claimed some western Indian blood in his family, on his mother's side. A graduate of the seminary-college at Nicolet, where he resided without interruption from the day of

admission as a student in October 1831, he had become a trusted and widely read faculty member at Nicolet when he accepted Bishop Provencher's invitation to work in the Northwest. Ordained in January 1844, Father Laflèche arrived at St. Boniface by HBC canoe on 21 June 1844. The journey initiated him in the pain and suffering of rheumatism, a disease that would haunt him for the rest of his life and prevent his appointment as successor to Provencher. He remained in the West until 1856, first as Taché's companion at Île-à-la-Crosse (1846–49), then as a trusted priest, vicar general, and administrator in St. Boniface (1849–56). After his definitive departure from Red River, he remained for the rest of his long and controversial life a devoted and trusted friend of western Catholics. For recent biographies of Laflèche see Nive Voisine, *Louis-François Laflèche, deuxième évêque de Trois-Rivières* (Saint-Hyacinthe: Édisem, 1980), and the same author's article in *DCB* 12, pp. 551–7, which contains a bibliography.

18. While in Europe, Taché had obtained Vatican authority to change the name of the diocese of the Northwest to St. Boniface, the patron saint of the cathedral.

19. See biographies of Lacombe by Katherine Hughes and James C. Macgregor.

20. The three scholastics were Félix Pandosy, Eugène-Casimir Chirouse, and Georges Blanchet. The religious brother was Célestin Verney.

21. British Columbia is here taken to include Vancouver Island, the mainland, and the Queen Charlotte Islands. Things were not so simple in the 1850s and 1860s when the distinct colonies of Vancouver Island and British Columbia existed side by side before they were merged in 1868.

22. The regional Oblate vicar of missions was autonomous under the superior general of the Oblate congregation. The same was true for Taché in the Northwest since 1851, as it had been earlier for Guigues in Canada from his arrival in 1844.

CHAPTER III

DEPLOYMENT IN ATHABASCA–MACKENZIE

Having established their beachheads in each of four regions of the greater Northwest, the Oblate conquerors did not so much as pause before proceeding to deploy their main forces throughout each of these regions.

Throughout the second half of the nineteenth century, driven by the urgency of conquering the pagan and indifferent world of the Northwest for their Church while keeping the Protestant enemy at bay, the Oblate missionaries pursued their objectives aggressively and relentlessly. Their supporters would perceive their work as the heroic saga of a band of men, many of them larger than life, who sacrificed all they had in this world to extend the Kingdom of God. For some of their supporters, theirs was a long-overdue act of revenge of the French against the English. Their adversaries, particularly a number of Protestant ministers, preferred to perceive the rapidly expanding Oblate network of missions as a stain upon the record of a liberty-loving, Rome-hating, blood-bought Protestant country. For some, the French were not keeping their place, the one assigned to them on the Plains of Abraham.

The Athabasca–Mackenzie Campaign: Phase I

When Father Taché crossed Portage la Loche (Methye Portage) above Île-à-la-Crosse to found a mission station at Fort Chipewyan in 1847, and when Henri Faraud hung his hat at the same mission, La Nativité at Fort Chipewyan on Lake Athabasca, in 1849, it marked the beginning of the permanent occupation of the vast Athabasca–Mackenzie basin by the Oblates. The first phase of this Oblate deployment had occurred in the 1850s, when Oblate missionaries such as Taché, Faraud, and Henri Grollier ranged far and wide, establishing a circuit of mission stations at places like Fond du Lac at the eastern extremity of Lake Athabasca, forts Vermilion and Dunvegan on the Peace River, Fort Resolution on Great Slave Lake, and Fort Simpson on the Mackenzie, to name only a few. The second phase of this northern deployment of the Oblates was the subsequent race with the Anglicans down the Mackenzie River, up the Peel River, down the Yukon River to the Arctic Sea, and into every backwater of the vast Canadian North.

For forty years, Henri Faraud (1823–90) remained the leader of the Oblates' northern conquering regiment. Born in Gigondas, Vaucluse, France, the twenty-one-year-old Faraud took his perpetual vows as an Oblate in 1844, studied philosophy for another two years in an Oblate college, and was sent to Canada in 1846 by Bishop de Mazenod, who was pressed by Bishop Provencher to provide more priests. After arriving in St. Boniface in November 1846, he spent the next six months in the company of Father Bellecourt learning the language and customs of the Ojibwa Indians. In the meantime, Provencher catapulted him through Holy Orders, making him a subdeacon in late April, a deacon on 1 May, and a priest on 8 May 1847. For the next year Faraud ministered in the Red River area, visiting the Indians at Whitedog (Wabassimong) on the Winnipeg River. In June 1848, Provencher sent him to Île-à-la-Crosse.

Henri Faraud was a classic case of the missionary whose training was accelerated in order to meet the pressing demands of the missions. When Bishop de Mazenod learned of the man's speedy accession to Holy Orders, he was incensed, declaring to the Oblate superior in Red River, Father Pierre Aubert, that never again would he send to the missions young Oblates with incomplete theological training.

> How could you have had... Faraud ordained priest without his knowing a word of theology? He was sent to you on the understanding that he would study the indispensable science of theology while simultaneously learning the Indian languages. Who would have thought that you would have thrown him into the ministry without his knowing anything?[1]

A year's residence at Île-à-la-Crosse in 1848–49 with the young but outstanding missionaries that both Taché and Laflèche proved to be may have compensated for Faraud's lack of theological training. Be that as it

Henri Faraud (1823–90)

may, the fact was that the man who would manage the Oblates' vast northern missions for forty years had never studied theology.

A year after his arrival in Île-à-la-Crosse, Father Faraud left for Fort Chipweyan, where he resided as sole missionary for a full three years until he was given an assistant in the person of Father Henri Grollier, who arrived in October 1852. Then Father Faraud crossed Lake Athabasca and descended the Slave River to found another mission at Fort Resolution on Great Slave Lake, which would become a resident station only in 1858.

Unidentified missionary on pastoral visitation in Fort Chipewyan area.

Throughout the 1850s, Faraud continued to govern his growing missionary district from Fort Chipewyan. After 1860, he had a new immediate supervisor, Vital Grandin, who had been designated coadjutor bishop of the diocese of St. Boniface in 1857 and entrusted with its northwesterly portion, including the missions of the Athabasca–Mackenzie. By the time Grandin had been informed of his episcopal promotion (1858), consecrated in France (November 1859), and reinstalled in the Northwest (1860), the decade of the 1860s was underway.

Oblate brothers at their lumber shanty near Fort Resolution. The only available fuel being wood, and the heating season lasting just about all year, woodcutting was a major occupation for the early missionaries.

Given concern among the Oblate superiors that the Hudson's Bay Company (HBC) would soon cease to provide transportation for missionaries and their supplies, the mission of Lake La Biche, Alberta, which had been founded in 1853 by Father René Rémas from Île-à-la-Crosse, became, in 1855, a central supply centre for the northern Oblate missions. At Lake La Biche, farm produce and cattle existed alongside warehouses containing supplies transported from further afield. The directors of the mission, fathers Tissot and Maisonneuve, even carved out a road over the 160 kilometres separating the mission from Fort Pitt on the upper Saskatchewan River, in order to ensure the resupply of their missions. North of Lake La Biche, a water route was available.

With this more solid infrastructure and a growing list of missionaries, Father Faraud was able to arrange another leap forward, again to the north. In 1858, Henri Grollier, the man who had been assisting Faraud since 1852, was assigned to Fort Resolution on Great Slave Lake. He was to become the first Catholic missionary to descend the Mackenzie River, he was to found a string of mission stations in the vast Mackenzie wilderness, and he was to be the first Oblate to die in the area. He has long been perceived by many Catholics as a legendary hero.

Henri Grollier

Henri Grollier (1826–64) was born in Montpellier, Hérault, France. He took his vows as an Oblate in 1848, completed his studies at Marseilles, was ordained a priest in June 1851 by Mazenod, and ministered in France for a year before leaving for the Northwest in the spring of 1852. After stopping over for only ten days in St. Boniface, he arrived in Fort Chipewyan in October 1852, the station where he would reside for the next six years (but for the year 1856–57, when he was stationed at Île-à-la-Crosse). Then, only months after having taken up residence at Fort Resolution in 1858, he dogged the heels of newly

Henri Grollier (1826–64)

arrived Anglican clergyman James Hunter on his way to Fort Simpson on the Mackenzie River. In the light of this invasion of the Mackenzie by Church of England forces, in 1859 Grollier was transferred from Fort Resolution. He was ordered to establish a new Catholic mission station at Fort Good Hope on the lower Mackenzie River, beyond the Arctic Circle. It became his base of operations in the following years, until his untimely death in 1864 at the age of thirty-eight.

Henri Grollier is acknowledged as the founder of a long string of missions in the Northwest Territories, including those of Fond du Lac (1853), Fort Simpson (1858), Fort Rea (1859), Fort Norman (1859), and Fort Good Hope (1859). In 1860 he was the first Catholic priest to visit Fort McPherson on the Peel River.

Henri Grollier was the tip of the Catholic Oblate spearhead penetrating the Mackenzie River valley. It was a tarnished and brittle tip, for when his celebrated missionary journeys began with his challenge to the Reverend Hunter in 1858, Grollier was perceived by his superiors and colleagues as a mediocre Oblate. Bishop Taché regretted being unable to send a better-trained missionary into the Mackenzie.[2]

In fact, Henri Grollier was causing no end of grief for his missionary colleagues, quarrelling with chief trader Bernard Rogan Ross of the Mackenzie district, and making enemies of every single clergyman he encountered, not to mention the white, Métis, and Indian populations who crossed his path. When Bishop Taché sent the difficult priest down the Mackenzie River to found the new mission of Good Hope in 1859, he had no illusions that things would go smoothly, but merely hoped to keep the man busy spoiling the missionary efforts of the Protestants.

During his first year of residence at Fort Good Hope in 1859–60, surprisingly enough the priest seemed to be getting along rather well.[3] But it would not last. By the summer of 1860, not only Ross, but also fathers Isidore Clut and Zéphirin Gascon were speaking very disparagingly about their colleague. While Ross attributed his difficulties to Grollier's way of doing things and his conse-

One of Fort Chipewyan missionaries' best friends.

quent unpopularity among HBC staff,[4] young Father Gascon from Fort Resolution elaborated on the reasons why everybody in the region detested Grollier.[5] Father Isidore Clut at Fort Chipewyan asked his bishop for the favour of never being given Grollier as a companion: in spite of the man's extraordinary zeal, his character and way of doing things were altogether incompatible with those of Clut.[6]

Everyone who crossed Grollier's path became the object of his scorn and criticism. Although the Protestants were one of his favourite obsessions,[7] they were not alone by any means. The Indians were "mud,"[8] and every single one of his colleagues suffered his wrath and calumny. Fathers Faraud and Clut were seen as incapable of learning any Indian languages, their writings being "masterpieces of vanity" written with the sole intention of obtaining admiration.[9] Each of Grollier's three colleagues at Good Hope also became a target of the disgruntled priest. The reliable Father Jean Séguin (1833–1902) was described as lacking in piety, devoid of initiative, and useless in the ministry. "To have the least esteem for him is impossible."[10] Grollier also set his sights on the Canadian priest Zéphirin Gascon, appointed director of the Good Hope mission in 1862. He was described as a tyrant and potentate who proved very trying to someone of Grollier's "angelic patience."[11] Brother Patrick Kearney, a saint by everyone else's reckoning, was described by Grollier as an Irishman who always had to have his way and who frequently did not make much sense.

Grollier's colleagues were no more enchanted with him than he was with them. While Father Clut thought that Grollier was obsessed with the Protestant minister, Gascon feared Grollier's reaction to his appointment as director of the mission in 1862. Father Séguin, who arrived at Good Hope in the company of Brother Patrick Kearney in August 1861, noted not only Grollier's severe asthma, but also his universal unpopularity in the area, the staff of the trading post uttering endless grievances against the missionary, while the Indians did not appreciate Grollier because he was always angry. Brother Kearney was the object of Grollier's constant wrath and criticism.

Bishop Grandin was well informed of the painful situation in Good Hope but did not know what to do about it. As early as January 1861 both he and Father Faraud feared that Grollier would go mad. A year later he told Bishop Taché that he was at a loss as to what to do with Grollier, a man who was most zealous but lacking in every other missionary quality: "He will always be a veritable cross for his companion."[12] By 1863, Grandin had upgraded Grollier a notch, qualifying him as a "a veritable source of torture" for his companions. Grandin saw his warped judgement as the source of all his woes, leading to his being detested by everyone—traders, Indians, and Métis. Grandin knew

ICI
repose le R.P. Pierre H. Grollier O.M.I.
décédé le 4 Juin 1864
1826   à l'âge de 38 ans.   1864

R.I.P

Je meurs content, ô Jésus, votre étendard
est élevé jusqu'aux extrémités
de la terre.

Last resting place of Henri Grollier (1826–64),
Canada's first Catholic missionary in the Arctic.

that he would have to remove Grollier from Good Hope, but he had nowhere to send him, all missionaries, himself included, refusing categorically to live with the man. The priest settled the issue by dying in 1864, much to everyone's relief.[13]

The Athabasca–Mackenzie Campaign: Phase II

In spite of his failings, Father Grollier had opened the vast Mackenzie basin to Catholic missions, a necessary initial phase in evangelizing the region. In a second phase, others would nurture the seed he sowed so controversially.

Given the enormous distances involved, the harsh weather conditions, and the scattered and diverse aboriginal population of the Northwest Territories, it was essential that the region's missions be governed by someone who was not thousands of kilometres removed from the scene. On the other hand, these missions relied on outside money, supplies, and personnel, resources that could be marshalled only by someone who was not away in the bush for most of the year.

In fact Father Faraud governed these missions from the outset, first from his residence at La Nativité in Fort Chipewyan (1849–61), then from Île-à-la-Crosse (1861–63). Appointed first apostolic vicar of the new vicariate of Athabasca–Mackenzie in 1863, Faraud was ordained bishop in France in November of the same year, and upon his return to the Northwest in 1865 established his headquarters at Providence on the upper Mackenzie River, a site chosen four years earlier by Bishop Grandin as the central mission for the Mackenzie district; buildings had been constructed on the site beginning in 1862. However, in 1869, after only four years in that distant outpost, Faraud moved his episcopal residence to Lake La Biche, invoking health reasons. He also managed to obtain authorization from Rome to appoint Isidore Clut as his auxiliary bishop, entrusted with the more northerly portion of his vicariate. Bishop Faraud rarely stirred from his house in Lake La Biche from that time until his death twenty-one years later.[14]

Throughout these years, Henri Faraud supervised a growing number of missionaries based in an increasing number of resident and permanent missions, each of which in turn served several widely scattered satellite stations.

A total of twenty Oblates, thirteen priests, and seven brothers were sent to Athabasca–Mackenzie before 1871. As would be expected, the missionaries included saints and sinners, men whose virtues or vices were perhaps more evident in that region, given their isolation and desolation. Among the reputed saints one must include Father Jean Séguin (1833–1902) and Brother Patrick Kearney (1834–1918). Father Zéphirin Gascon stands out as a loyal and faithful servant who worked in the difficult missions his entire adult life. Henri Grollier was one of the more problematic men; be that as it may, as a cause of anguish he could not hold a candle to Father Émile Petitot, the most celebrated Oblate missionary in the North and the man whose eighteen-year missionary career was an integral part of the Athabasca–Mackenzie campaign.

Émile Petitot

While Grollier was a thorn in the side of his Oblate colleagues and superiors, the man chosen to replace him at Good Hope became their very own nightmare. Émile Petitot (1838–1917) arrived from France in 1862, the year of his ordination to the priesthood, and in the course of his missionary career in the Northwest he earned a reputation as one of the world's leading geographers, linguists, and anthropologists, publishing some twenty books and several articles in scientific journals. He also proved to be a first-class artist, transforming the inside of the small church of Good Hope into the jewel of the northern Church.

In June 1862, Petitot and Father Émile Grouard, another newly ordained priest, who had just joined the Oblate order,[15] travelled from

Red River to Fort Chipewyan on an HBC barge, in the company of the Reverend Robert McDonald who was also heading into the distant Mackenzie district for the first time. Petitot reported to Bishop Taché that McDonald was a gentleman and an excellent travelling companion; it was he who had first approached the Catholic priests, in a friendly manner, and he greeted them every morning in similar fashion. Moreover, the crew of the barge behaved like saints, avoiding all profane and blasphemous language while showing infectious good humour

Émile Petitot (1838–1917)

and helpfulness. Petitot was enchanted. While camped at The Pas on a stopover, Petitot and Grouard had tea with the Reverend Robert Hunt, who invited them to his home and showed them "uncommon courtesy." Like Taché before him, Petitot considered Hunt's home a veritable palace in the wilderness; nothing was lacking: "We dined on jam and cakes, served in porcelain and crystal."[16]

Having arrived in Fort Chipewyan on 2 August, Grouard stayed on to become Father Clut's associate, while Petitot continued on to Providence in the company of Bishop Grandin. After living with Petitot for a year, the coadjutor bishop of St. Boniface told Bishop Taché what he thought of the young man.

The first church in Fort Good Hope. The steeple is a later addition.

> He dreams only of long voyages. He often asks me to send him to the Eskimos... He made things difficult all winter by his fastidiousness, showing disgust at fish or even meat; he needs only to see one hair of an animal or of an Indian woman to lose his appetite. Moreover, he charges carelessly into the greatest dangers... Last fall, I had to invoke religious obedience to prevent him from going skating on ice that was only one inch thick... He is even more careless in a canoe or on a barge. He had to freeze his fingers before agreeing to wear mittens... He has a great facility for learning, and an even greater one for walking, but... he must be made into a good missionary... It will take time. He is a very immature young man; he reasons like a schoolboy, or at best a seminarian.[17]

In the early months of 1863, Bishop Grandin sent Petitot to take over the mission at Fort Resolution. His reasons were twofold. First, Father Germain Eynard needed to be replaced due to his inability to handle the day-to-day administration of the mission. Second, Father Petitot had developed an excessive attachment to the young Indian boy who worked in the Providence mission, an attachment that the bishop wanted to put to an end. Grandin felt that things had gone too far, Petitot

Interior of the church at Fort Good Hope, decorated by Father Petitot.

having committed "indiscretions"; in fact, Grandin had in hand the text of an intimate letter from Petitot to the boy, Baptiste. In short order, the bishop's fears seemed to be confirmed, for one of Petitot's first acts as director of the Fort Resolution mission was to ask Grandin to transfer the boy to his station. The bishop refused, citing Petitot's "fatal attachment to a child."[18]

In 1864, needing to replace the deceased Grollier at Fort Good Hope, Grandin decided that it would be best to send Petitot there to work with Brother Kearney, under the supervision of Father Jean Séguin. Having barely set foot in the region, Petitot proceeded to denounce and demean two of his Oblate colleagues, fathers Grouard and Gascon, only to later offer his excuses for his outbursts. Bishop Grandin was not overly surprised at Petitot's erratic behaviour.

In the final months of 1865, one year after Father Petitot's arrival in Good Hope, it was said among the Indians and traders that Petitot was an active homosexual or a pedophile, his preferred—but not exclusive—partner being a fifteen-year-old Indian boy in the employ of the mission. Upon receiving reports from Father Séguin, Bishop Faraud called the priest to account. In a letter of 15 January 1866, Petitot confessed his wrongs, begged for forgiveness, and promised to correct his ways,[19] whereupon Bishop Faraud allowed the man to stay in office provided he severed all ties with the boy in question; Petitot promised to

Joseph Patrick Kearney
(1834–1918)

Jean Séguin (1833–1902)

do so. However, six months later, the apostolic vicar was stunned to learn that Petitot was travelling throughout his vast mission territory in the company of the same boy, arguing that he had been unsuccessful in dismissing the boy from the mission's employ. Bishop Faraud thereupon pronounced a sentence of excommunication against Petitot. When Father Séguin rejoiced at the fact that the young man had just married and returned to the wilds with his bride, however, Faraud succumbed to Petitot's entreaties and lifted the excommunication order.[20]

It would be more of the same throughout Petitot's years at Good Hope, from 1864 through 1873. In fact, within months of Faraud's lifting his excommunication order of 1866, Father Petitot was travelling with the same young man; when Bishop Faraud or the Oblate superior general, Father Fabre, intervened, Petitot would utter the most sincere confession, beg forgiveness, and promise never to succumb to his sexual instincts again.[21] Given the priest's mastery of Indian languages, his zeal, and his indefatigable labours, his superiors chose to believe him, and nothing changed.[22] However, by the late 1860s Petitot was showing signs of something more serious: a mental illness that would periodically turn him into a violent and dangerous madman.

Beginning in the winter of 1868–69, Petitot's erratic and strange behaviour began to be accompanied by symptoms of serious mental derangement. The testimony of his colleagues, particularly of Séguin who lived with him, speaks of a man more and more driven by the monomaniacal conviction that all the Indians and all the white men, including his associates, spoke against him, ridiculed him behind his back, hated him, and were trying to kill him. This either because of Petitot's homosexual activities, which he had confessed to them, or because the Indians had a secret that they were unwilling to share with Petitot, for then he would be able to fully understand them and convert them. Petitot then convinced himself that he had to undergo circumcision in order to be accepted by the Loucheux Indians and avoid their planned homicide.

Petitot first became violent in the winter of 1868–69, a situation that would recur thereafter twice every winter. Father Séguin noted that his relapses into violent, irrational behaviour usually occurred first between the feast of the Immaculate Conception (8 December) and Christmas, and then again after the feast of the Epiphany (6 January). The crises lasted for between three and fourteen days, during which time the man became stark-raving mad, predicted the end of the world, accused Father Séguin of murdering Jesus Christ and the Virgin Mary, and believed that he was a Mohammedan, Jew, pagan, Antichrist, or angel. During these crises, Petitot was frequently tied down and placed under guard after having run around naked outdoors at temperatures below minus forty degrees Celsius. On two occasions he tried to murder Séguin by strangling him or butchering him with an axe, in order to offer him in sacrifice for the salvation of the world, all the while screaming and howling in a totally demented state. Once the crisis passed, the man would slowly return to his normal state of mind.[23]

Having survived murderous attacks by Petitot in December 1870 and January 1871, in the spring of 1871 Father Séguin was authorized to send Petitot to Providence where Father Victor Nouël de Krangué was in charge. After spending the summer months there and having shown no new mental breakdowns, Petitot was sent back to Good Hope in the company of Bishop Clut, who then spent six months there—from September 1871 to February 1872. During that winter of 1871–72, Clut observed that the monomania still dominated Petitot but that he did not show violent or demented behaviour; Clut felt that he should nevertheless be removed from the territory. However, since Faraud was away in France, nothing was done. When both bishops were absent from the territory during the year 1872–73, Petitot again became violently mad for thirteen days. Father Séguin ordered him out of Fort Good Hope by the spring barges, but succeeded in securing his agreement to leave only by allowing him to be accompanied by his young boyfriend. Petitot journeyed upriver through the various mission stations, ending up at Lake La Biche (1873–74), and eventually at Fort Carlton in the summer of 1874. After another display of his mental disorder at that trading post, he went to France in order to see to the publication of some of his writings.

After spending nearly two years with his Oblate colleagues in France, in March 1876 Father Petitot embarked upon his return journey to Good Hope. His arrival was preceded by the following testimonial by the Oblate superior general, Joseph Fabre:

> What I can affirm in good conscience is that this dear Father, so intelligent and so devoted to the northern missions, has produced in France the best and happiest impression both within our houses and without. Moreover, he has done so during *his entire stay*, and I am not excepting a single day. For my part... I am in admiration of the devotion that this priest has shown in doing the work that he has... Father Petitot left here with the best of dispositions.[24]

In fact, Oblate headquarters felt that Petitot was being persecuted by his superiors in the missionary field because they were jealous of his success and his devotion to duty. They had observed Petitot during two years in France and noted absolutely nothing wrong with the man. Added to the financial and administrative disagreements that plagued Oblate relations at the time,[25] in the eyes of Fabre and his associates Bishop Faraud was emerging as more and more of an ogre.

Petitot spent another two years at Good Hope, still suffering from the mental illness. Father Séguin reported that although he had not become violent again, in the summer of 1878 he had himself circumcised again by the local Indians, always driven by the same strange convictions, the foremost being his belief that the Indians never forgave him his homosexual acts; this was why they wanted to kill him. Séguin escorted Petitot to Providence in September 1878 and left him there, to the shocked surprise of Father Auguste Lecorre, who, after discussing matters with Petitot, convinced him to move on to Lake La Biche in order to consult Bishop Faraud.

Meanwhile, Petitot had sought and obtained from the Oblate superior general a transfer, effective fall 1878, to Bishop Grandin's diocese of St. Albert. He went to work in the missions of Fort Pitt and Cold Lake, the latter becoming his primary base of operations for the next three years (1879–81). Bishop Grandin visited him in July 1880 and reported that while the priest's mental disorder continued, he was mad in only one area and manifested it only in private, all the while remaining very influential with both government agents and Indians.

It was during the subsequent eighteen months that the Petitot question came to a head and was settled by the Oblate congregation. On 11 February 1881, Bishop Grandin informed Archbishop Taché that

Petitot's insanity was now widely known and had to be dealt with. The tormented priest had just arrived in St. Albert, and during the next three weeks gave ample evidence of his mental distress, at times keeping his bishop awake all night with his allegations of plots and conspiracies. Grandin wanted to send him back to Europe, but, giving in to the priest's pleas, authorized him to return temporarily to the Fort Pitt area. On 18 August 1881, Grandin formally ordered Petitot to go to St. Boniface, and then on to France, for henceforth his ministerial faculties were suspended. The priest ignored the order, returned to the bush, and in October 1881, at the Fort Pitt mission, Father Petitot married a Métis woman from Frog Lake and cohabited with her for three months. Considering that the man had lost his senses, Bishop Grandin sent fathers Félix Fafard and Victor Bourgine after him; they forcibly separated Petitot from his wife, but while being taken back to St. Albert Petitot escaped his captors and appeared on Bishop Faraud's doorstep at Lake La Biche on 11 December 1881. Not only did Faraud refuse to receive him, but only hours after his arrival in the dead of winter, another team of Oblates arrived hot on his heels; they had been sent by Bishop Grandin to ensure that Petitot got to St. Albert, in irons if necessary. On 31 December 1881, the group, along with Father Émile Grouard arrived in St. Albert with the delinquent priest.

From St. Albert, on 12 January, Bishop Grandin sent Petitot to Montreal, escorted by Oblate Father Constantine Scollen and by future Oblate Edward Cunningham, a boy who was en route to the Oblate juniorate in Ottawa. The day after their arrival at the Oblate provincial house in Montreal on Shrove Tuesday 1882, Petitot was surreptitiously registered at the Saint-Jean-de-Dieu hospital for the mentally ill. There he spent two years, all the while endeavouring to effect a reunion with his wife and a return to France. Once back in his native land in 1884, he earned his living at various occupations such as proofreader, author, and printer, while trying unsuccessfully to be accepted as a missionary in one of the English Protestant missionary societies.[26] It would seem that his conversion was not motivated by doctrine or theology, but a means of getting back to the Northwest in order to be reunited with his wife.

Having been released from his vows in the Oblate congregation on 19 April 1886, Father Petitot was accepted into the ranks of the diocesan clergy and spent the rest of his life as pastor of the parish of Mareuil-les-Meaux (1886–1917).[27] His eighteen years of missionary work in the Northwest had not been an unmitigated success for the Catholic Church, for Petitot's on-again, off-again mental illness created havoc on a paradoxically both vast and tiny missionary stage.

Isidore Clut

While Bishop Faraud remained officially in charge of the Oblates'
most northerly missions, his associate, Isidore Clut, was the man
who actually led the missionary
contingent in the field during the
last third of the nineteenth century.

Isidore Clut (1832–1903)

The story of Coadjutor Bishop
Isidore Clut (1832–1903) is a simultaneously realistic, eloquent, and
sad commentary on Catholic episcopal leadership in the vast Northwest mission. Responding to the
invitation of Bishop Alexandre
Taché, the young French Oblate
came to Red River to be ordained to
the priesthood in 1857. After his
year of apprenticeship in St. Boniface, Clut was sent to Lake Athabasca
in 1858; he remained at this mission of La Nativité at Fort Chipewyan
until 1869, having become director of the mission in 1861 upon the
transfer of his companion Faraud to Île-à-la-Crosse.

While in Europe (1863–65) for his episcopal consecration, Bishop
Faraud had been authorized to select and ordain a coadjutor bishop for
himself. He chose his former companion, Isidore Clut, whom he consecrated, assisted by two of his priests, at La Nativité mission on 15
August 1867. Clut could not know that he was misguided in choosing
as his motto *Jugum meum suave est* (My burden is light).

The first problem was the way in which Faraud went about choosing Clut. Faraud had in his possession a papal bull dated 3 August 1864
appointing whomever Faraud designated, after due consultation, as
Bishop of Arindel and coadjutor to the apostolic vicar of Athabasca–
Mackenzie. Faraud consulted some, but not all, interested priests and
bishops. He then obtained from the Oblate superior general, Father
Joseph Fabre, an order for Clut to accept the appointment, which he did
at Providence on 3 January 1866.[28] When Bishop Grandin realized that
Bishop Faraud was not even going to ask for his views on the appointment, he complained to Bishop Taché.[29] Fifteen years later, Grandin
bitterly recalled that in order to avoid unwelcome advice, Faraud had
simply not consulted him on Clut's appointment.[30]

Bishop Grandin had never been overly impressed with Clut, from the first days of Clut's stay in the Northwest. When Father Faraud wrote in 1861 that his assistant in La Nativité mission (Father Clut) could be entrusted with running a mission station, but not a diocese, Bishop Grandin was in agreement, noting that while young Father Clut was zealous he appeared incapable of inspiring others, be they colleagues or Indian faithful.[31] Two years later, he added that Clut was inclined to worry and to suffer depression, while not enjoying the best of health.[32]

In fact, Father Clut could handle some situations in surprisingly direct ways. For example, in the spring of 1862 he had to deal with a member of his congregation who was also an Indian prophet at Fort Chipewyan. The prophet spent the winter of 1861–62 hearing the confessions of his Indian colleagues, particularly women. He explained that his manner of hearing the confessions of women was different from that of the priests. The penitents had to discard their clothing and join their confessor in bed. When Clut excommunicated the man and denounced him from the pulpit, the latter's brother attacked the priest with a rifle, whereupon Clut knocked him senseless using his fists and a stick,[33]—a method that apparently settled the problem.

If Faraud's intentions in choosing Clut were to have an assistant who would spend his time visiting the distant mission posts while the apostolic vicar remained at home, his hopes seem to have been more than fulfilled. Indeed no Catholic bishop in the Northwest travelled as extensively, and for as many years, as Isidore Clut. While stationed at Fort Chipewyan (1858–69), he regularly visited the Fond du Lac mission at the eastern end of Lake Athabasca, built the first mission at Fort Vermilion on the Peace River (1868), and travelled to Europe for the First Vatican Council (1869–70). Upon returning to the Northwest, he journeyed to Providence (November 1870), and then returned through forts Resolution and Chipewyan (February 1871) to Lake La Biche (May 1871); he then reversed course, journeying through Fort Chipewyan, Fort Resolution, and Providence to Fort Good Hope (September 1871 to January 1872). Having returned up the Mackenzie River through forts Norman and Simpson in February 1872, Bishop Clut and Father Bruno Roure spent the months of April through June 1872 at Fort Rae, evangelizing the Dog Rib Indians of the area. There he received a letter from the Oblate provincial superior in Montreal, Father Florent Vandenberghe, suggesting that Clut undertake a missionary visit to the Yukon and Alaska, distant territories devoid of Catholic missionaries. In fact one of Vandenberghe's parishioners, François Mercier, who was in the employ of the Alaska Fur Trading Company, was to take over Fort Yukon and all of the fur-trading posts in Alaska in April 1872 and promised every assistance to any Catholic missionaries who appeared. Vandenberghe suggested that the entire territory could become Catholic if Clut could find a way to get there.

Clut was sorely tempted, be it because of apostolic zeal, or wanderlust, or both; and given Bishop Faraud's absence in France, the coadjutor decided to go. On 30 August 1872, he left Providence, picked up young Father Auguste Lecorre as a companion at Fort Norman, stopped at Good Hope where he refused the entreaties of fathers Émile Petitot and Jean Séguin to accompany him, and set off for Fort McPherson and Peel River on 14 September 1872. A week's portage of some 125 kilometres separated Peel River from Lapierre House, the next way station on the route to the Porcupine and Yukon rivers. In his journal, Bishop Clut describes in detail the travel conditions of himself and Father Lecorre, the hospitality or hostility they met in the various trading posts run by the HBC (forts McPherson and Lapierre) or the American trading company based in San Francisco.

Generally speaking, the Catholic missionaries were well received in the trading posts, although they discovered that their work was proving fruitless. Indeed, as fathers Petitot and Séguin had discovered a decade earlier, the Tukudh, or Loucheux, Indians of the area had been won over to the Church of England by the earlier visits of the reverends Kirkby and McDonald, the latter having resided at Fort Yukon for eight years (1862–70) before moving to Fort McPherson. In fact, McDonald continued to minister in the area on a regular basis, supported in 1872–73 by the touring Reverend Bompas. Although Clut and Lecorre regretted the "indifference" of the area's people, turned away from Catholicism by the "superstitions and lies" preached by the Protestants, they acknowledged that there was little to be done. After wintering at Fort Yukon, the two priests journeyed all the way down the Yukon River to its mouth on the Bering Sea, Lecorre remaining on the river and then travelling to Europe, Clut arriving back at Providence on 7 October 1873. There he learned that the Alaska Territory was part of the diocese of Vancouver, and had been so since 1868, thus standing outside his area of jurisdiction.

Upon his return to the Mackenzie district, Bishop Clut continued his constant travelling around Great Slave Lake (Fort Rae, Hay River, Fort Resolution), up the Liard River (Fort Liard, Fort Nelson), on the Mackenzie River (Providence, Fort Simpson, Fort Norman), and as far as Lake Athabasca (Fort Chipewyan, Fond du Lac). Until 1884, he resided at Providence, although he visited Europe in 1877–79 and again in 1882–84. Beginning in 1884 he resided further south at the St. Bernard mission, at Grouard on Lesser Slave Lake, with protracted visits to Montreal for health reasons (1886–90, 1893–94, 1901–2).

Towing barges upstream on unidentified river in Northwest.

Portaging on the Mackenzie.

Indian family at camp in Fort Providence area.

Bishop Clut's first serious clash with his superior, Bishop Faraud, occurred when Faraud discovered that his coadjutor had gone to the Yukon and Alaska territories[34] for the year 1872–73. From Paris, Faraud fired a broadside at Clut, advising him that he should consider staying in place for a while in order to consolidate newly established mission stations. Faraud reprimanded Clut for authorizing an 1873 trip to Europe by Father Lecorre, in order to recruit missionaries for the Alaska Territory that stood outside their jurisdiction. He told him to henceforth mind his own business.[35]

After another year had passed, relations between the two bishops had gone from bad to worse. While continuing to complain about his various aches and pains, Bishop Faraud indicated to Clut that they did not see eye to eye on a host of points. One example was the allegedly contradictory advice Clut gave Faraud on the advisability of publishing Father Petitot's dictionaries of Indian languages, books that were, according to Faraud, only "more or less accurate" and apt to mislead readers. Clut had first praised and then criticized the work, strongly recommended its publication, then recommended against it, causing significant embarassment to Faraud. The latter commented: "Please... avoid contradictions. You seem to write and act on the spur of the moment, and then forget what you previously wrote."[36] Faraud went on to say that he wanted to resign but that Clut's reprehensible behaviour kept him from doing so. He added: "As long as I am in office..., you

The Lafferté family of Fort Providence at turn of the century.

are and can only be an assistant entrusted with executing my orders, and not with making decisions yourself." By this time, Faraud was also incensed at Clut's attitude on the question of his superior's residence at Lake La Biche; for Clut, along with all the other bishops, was urging Faraud to move to Providence and to give the Lake La Biche mission back to Grandin.

Faraud's hostility towards Clut continued unabated until Faraud's death in 1890. While declaring that all the priests in his vicariate supported his judgements on Clut, Bishop Faraud repeatedly accused his coadjutor of imprudence, contradictions, and futile behaviour. He even accused him of being negligent and imprudent in having ordered Oblate Brother Alexis Reynard to journey to Lake La Biche in 1875 in order to build a river barge; given that during the journey Brother Alexis was murdered by his Iroquois travelling companion, Faraud was thereby intimating that Clut was partly to blame for the man's death.[37] To add insult to injury, upon his extended visit to Europe between 1877 and 1879, Isidore Clut found himself criticized by Oblate headquarters for trying to raise funds for his missions.

After returning to his mission field in 1880, Bishop Clut finally decided to voice his grievances to Faraud.

> It is said everywhere that I carry out Confirmations only; that you delegate no powers to me, that I can do nothing, decide nothing,

make no changes... Most of our priests and brothers are of this view... The people, even the traders, say so... The rumour that I have no powers has spread everywhere in the Northwest, even as far as Oblate headquarters in France.[38]

In reply, Faraud told Clut that he had the authority of a vicar, and that he would be given no more, for to invest him with any more authority Faraud would have to relinquish his own position. He reminded Clut that in past years he had abused his authority and had to be reprimanded by Faraud. "As long as it pleases God to leave me at the head of this vicariate, the priests and brothers will always answer to me, and will consider an order only when it comes from me."[39]

Apostolic Vicar Faraud was determined not to allow his coadjutor any room to manoeuvre. During his twenty-four years as coadjutor to Faraud, Clut continued to do his job to the best of his ability, always hamstrung by his lack of authority. Attempting to reason with Faraud, he complained of the difficult situation he was in, admitting to his superior in 1882 that he had indeed made decisions on his own during the three years (1872–75) that Faraud was away in France. The reasons he gave for having made these decisions were Faraud's prolonged absence; instructions by the Oblate superior general, Fabre; and Faraud's own written declarations that he had every intention of resigning his see and never returning to the Northwest. Forced to return to his vicariate in 1875, Faraud never forgave Clut for his independent actions.[40] He carried his grudge to his grave, deliberately withholding Clut's candidacy in 1881, and again in 1888, when the hierarchy was selecting a candidate for new episcopal offices. Archbishop Taché[41] reprimanded Faraud for such unjust and dishonourable behaviour,[42] although it should be noted that Bishop Grandin was no more desirous than Faraud of having Clut appointed head of a diocese.[43]

If medals were given for patience and forbearance, Bishop Isidore Clut would certainly rank high on the list. Although not blessed with the most level-headed judgement, he was an honest and zealous priest, performing a difficult task under the jealous and power-hungry eye of the unreasonable and spiteful Faraud. His attitude towards his Protestant fellow missionaries was typical of the priests of his day—that is, Protestantism was heresy, Protestant rivals were guilty of demeaning and misrepresenting Catholics, and the Catholic Church had to prevail over the "ministers of error." It is ironic that most of Clut's grief was caused not by his Protestant rivals but by his own superior, Bishop Faraud.

Results of the Athabasca–Mackenzie Campaign

By the end of the century, the mission territory of Athabasca–Mackenzie was well in hand. The Oblates had followed up the work of the pathfinders by opening a series of permanent resident mission stations staffed by a growing number of missionaries.

During most of the last twenty years of his life (1870–90), Apostolic Vicar Henri Faraud resided at the mission of Our Lady of Victories at Lake La Biche, a station that was technically part of the diocese of St. Albert but that Bishop Grandin lent to Faraud to serve as a central warehouse and transportation centre for the vicariate of Athabasca–Mackenzie.[44] The fact that it was possible to travel by boat from Lake La Biche to most missions of the vicariate was a prime reason for this temporary transfer of authority. Also, the Oblates at Lake La Biche built roads joining the station to Fort Pitt to the south and down the eighty kilometres of the Little La Biche River, which led to the Athabasca River. These roads served as the main supply route to the northern missions until the HBC opened its Edmonton–Athabasca Landing route in 1887.

Thereafter, there was no more need for the Lake La Biche route. In 1888, therefore, but only after a protracted dispute, Bishop Faraud returned the station to Bishop Grandin of St. Albert, and moved his headquarters to the mission of La Nativité on Lake Athabasca, near Fort Chipewyan. While the apostolic vicar's official residence was at Lake La Biche or at La Nativité, his coadjutor, Isidore Clut, handled the more northerly missions of the vicariate from his residence at Providence on the Mackenzie River. In fact, Faraud's assistant, Father Émile Grouard, moved to La Nativité in 1888, and administered the vicariate while the sickly Faraud retired to St. Boniface, where he died in 1890. Grouard succeeded him.

By the end of the century, Faraud's and Grouard's apostolic vicariate of Athabasca–Mackenzie employed two bishops, thirty priests, and thirty brothers. A quarter century earlier, only half as many priests and brothers had worked in the area.

The vicariate comprised four districts: Peace River, Athabasca, upper Mackenzie, and lower Mackenzie. It also served the mission of St. Bernard on Lesser Slave Lake, although, like Lake La Biche, this was part of the diocese of St. Albert. While Lesser Slave Lake and Fort Chipewyan had been occasionally visited by fathers Bourassa, Thibault, Taché, Faraud, and others after 1844, we have seen that the first resident priests in the area had been at Fort Chipewyan (1849), Lake La Biche (1853), and Fort Resolution (1858).

The Peace River district included two mission stations with resident priests, St. Charles at Fort Dunvegan, as well as St. Henry at Fort Vermilion; from these bases the priests ranged widely up the Peace River to Fort St. John and Hudson's Hope in the Rocky Mountains. The central Athabasca district included the key mission of La Nativité near Fort Chipewyan, and those of Fond du Lac at the eastern end of Lake Athabasca, St. Isidore at Fort Smith on the Slave River, and St. Joseph at Fort Resolution on Great Slave Lake. The upper Mackenzie district was centred in the Providence mission; there were also resident missionaries at Fort Rae on the northern shore of Great Slave Lake and Fort Liard on the Liard River, while posts like Fort Halkett on the upper Liard and Fort Simpson on the upper Mackenzie were visited once or twice a year. Finally, the lower Mackenzie district was centred in Fort Good Hope, the only station with resident Catholic missionaries. The missionaries travelled widely, up the Mackenzie to Great Bear Lake, Fort Norman, and Fort Wrigley, and down to Fort McPherson and the satellite posts of Lapierre House and Fort Yukon on the Porcupine and Yukon rivers in the Yukon Territory.

The stations at Lake La Biche, Fort Chipewyan, Fort Resolution, and Providence usually provided adequate lodging and provisions for the missionaries. In the more remote and isolated posts, however, survival was frequently in question, as fish or game became scarce, or supplies ran out. Supplies were delivered to the various mission posts by annual HBC barges, the company having reassumed responsibility for transporting mission supplies once its road from Edmonton to Athabasca Landing was completed in 1887. Also, in 1888 the HBC built steamers on various sections of the waterway from Lesser Slave Lake to the lower Mackenzie. However, when the company suddenly doubled its fees in 1891, Bishop Grouard arranged to import the required machinery and build his own steamer, the sixty-foot *Saint Joseph*, at Fort Chipewyan. Henceforth, the territory stretching from Fort McMurray in the south to Fort Smith in the north, including Lake Athabasca and the lower Peace River as far as Fort Vermilion, was supplied by the vicariate's own steamer. In 1895, Grouard built a second steamer. The *Saint Alphonsus* plied the waters below Fort Smith, all the way to the lower Mackenzie and Peel rivers.

By the end of the century, the mission of La Nativité on Lake Athabasca had become a relatively prosperous centre. In addition to its sawmill (1891) and printing press (1888), not to mention its steamboat, as of 1874 it boasted of a convent school run by the Sisters of Charity of Montreal, a congregation that operated similar institutions at Île-à-la-Crosse (1860), Lake La Biche (1862), St. Albert (1863), Providence (1867), Prince Albert (1883), Edmonton (1888), Lesser Slave Lake, Fort

For most missionaries as well as their charges in remote mission posts, orphanages, and hospitals, fish was an essential part of their diet. While fishing went on year-round, a major effort was made in the late summer and fall in order to store large quantities of fish that would last until the following summer. Here missionaries and their men set out on a fishing expedition on Great Slave Lake.

Thousands of fish drying at Fort Providence before being stored for winter.

Resolution (1903), and Fort Simpson (1916). At Providence, Fort Simpson, and St. Albert, the Sisters of Charity also directed hospitals.

In the lower Mackenzie, fathers Grollier, Séguin, Petitot, and Giroux, assisted by Brother Kearney, conducted their ministry from Good Hope, Séguin and Kearney staying there for more than thirty years after arriving in the early 1860s. Their limited success at the predominantly Protestant Fort McPherson led them to establish a new mission at Arctic Red River in 1896. By the end of the nineteenth century, the Catholic missionaries had gained the upper hand over their Church of England rivals in the contest for Indian converts in the Athabasca and Mackenzie watersheds. While Church Missionary Society (CMS) missionaries dominated in posts like Fort Simpson, Fort Norman, Fort McPherson, Lapierre House, and Fort Yukon, Oblate missionaries could claim victory in Fort Chipewyan, the Peace River district, Fond du Lac on Lake Athabasca, forts Resolution and Rae on Great Slave Lake, the Liard River district, Great Bear Lake, and Fort Good Hope.

The furthest reaches of the vicariate of Athabasca–Mackenzie were the distant lands of the Yukon Territory, more than 3,000 kilometres from Edmonton. Ever since the visits of CMS missionary William Kirkby in 1860 and 1861, and the residence of his colleague, the Reverend Robert McDonald (1861), in Fort Yukon, the territory had been hostile to Catholic missionaries like Séguin, Petitot, Clut, and Lecorre. It was a Church of England preserve, and it became, during the last quarter of the nineteenth century, the choice mission territory of Church of England Bishop W.C. Bompas.

The Klondike gold rush that prompted the creation of a distinct Yukon Territory (1898) also prompted the sudden emergence of Dawson City (1896), a town that mushroomed to 16,000 inhabitants in 1898 when some 30,000 migrants headed for Dawson City via the American towns of Dyea and Skagway on the Alaskan panhandle. The gold-seekers travelled over the mountains, through Chilcoot and White passes, to the headwaters of the Yukon River. The town of Whitehorse also emerged at the foot of the Whitehorse rapids; with the completion of a railway through White Pass to Whitehorse in 1898, Whitehorse became the centre of navigation on the river. The North West Mounted Police (1894) and a field force of 200 Canadian soldiers (1898) enforced the law.

In spite of its being part of the vicariate of Athabasca–Mackenzie, the Yukon Territory had no resident Catholic missionary. The first priest to work there for any length of time was Father Judge, an American Jesuit, who, in 1896, moved up the Yukon River from Alaska, visited the mining camps of the Klondike, and returned to Forty-Mile for the winter of 1896–97. In the spring of 1897, Judge returned to the budding Dawson City, was given a lot, and began the construction of a small hospital with a residence for sisters and servants. He soon obtained the services of the Sisters of St. Anne, who were already at work in Alaska; by October of the same year, a dozen sisters were caring for 132 patients in the hospital. Meanwhile, in 1898 Judge built his second church at Dawson City, the first having burned to the ground in June. The wealthy Catholic prospector Alexander MacDonald paid the costs.

It was also in 1898 that the Oblates sent their men into the Yukon Territory. While Father Camille Lefebvre travelled overland from Fort McPherson to Fort Selkirk on the Yukon River, Oblate fathers Edmond Gendreau and Alphonse Desmarais, secular priest Corbeil, and Oblate Brother Augustin Dumas left Vancouver on 23 May 1898, travelled via Chilcoot Pass, and met Lefebvre at Fort Selkirk. Having planned the construction of a chapel there, Oblate superior Gendreau proceeded downriver to Dawson City, where he agreed with Judge on the division of labour. As it turned out, Father Judge had only another year to live. His death in 1899 marked the end of Jesuit work in the Yukon Territory. In fact, Gendreau soon stopped work on the proposed Oblate residence at Fort Selkirk and concentrated his men at Dawson City. By the turn of the century, six Oblates were working in the area, under the direction of French Oblate Émile Bunoz, who would become first apostolic vicar of Prince George and the Yukon in 1908.

Simultaneously, similar developments were taking place in the more southerly part of northwestern Canada—in Red River, Alberta, and British Columbia.

Notes

1. Mazenod to Pierre Aubert, Marseilles, 4 March 1849, in *Lettres...I*, p. 220.

2. A. Taché to H. Faraud, Red River, 7 June 1859. Taché papers, AG.

3. HBC archivist Alice Johnson cites both Grollier and Ross to that effect in *Notes on Fort Good Hope* (London: n.p., 1958), booklet, Good Hope papers, AG.

4. B.R. Ross to A. Taché, Portage la Loche, 6 August 1860. Copy from AASB, 71.220, 1010, APA.

5. Z. Gascon to A. Taché, Fort Rae, 1 June 1860. Copy from AASB, 71.220, 1010, APA.

6. I. Clut to A. Taché, Lake Athabasca, 30 June 1860. Copy from AASB, 71.220, 1010, APA.

7. This will be discussed later.

8. H. Grollier to H. Faraud and I. Clut, Peel River, 29 July 1861. Grollier papers, AG.

9. H. Grollier to V. Grandin, Good Hope, 14 February 1862. Copy from AASB, 71.220, 1011, APA.

10. H. Grollier to V. Grandin, Good Hope, 10 September 1862. Copy from AASB, 71.220, 1011, APA.

11. H. Grollier to A. Taché, Good Hope, 18 July 1863. Copy from AASB, 71.220, 1012, APA.

12. V. Grandin to Superior General Fabre, Athabasca, 28 July 1862. Grandin papers, vol. 13, AG.

13. The above paragraphs on Henri Grollier are based on a series of letters scattered throughout various collections of papers in the AG, APA, AD, and AY.

14. The sickly Faraud went on a two-year fundraising tour of Europe in 1872–74, visited his vicariate in 1879–80, and then attended the first provincial council of the Archdiocese of Saint Boniface in July 1889, the year before his death.

15. The secular priest Émile Grouard would make his final vows as a member of the Oblate congregation in 1863.

16. É. Petitot to A. Taché, Lake Cumberland, 23 June 1862. 71.220, 979, APA.

17. V. Grandin to A. Taché, Providence, 3 April 1863. Copy from AASB, 84.400, 911, APA.

18. V. Grandin to A. Taché, Providence, 3 May 1863. Copy from AASB, 84.400, 911, APA.

19. É. Petitot to [H. Faraud], Good Hope, 15 January 1866. Petitot papers, AG.

20. J. Séguin to H. Faraud, Good Hope, 13 September 1866, Séguin papers, AY. É. Petitot to [H. Faraud], Good Hope, 15 September 1866. Petitot papers, AG.

21. A series of revealing letters from Petitot to Faraud, dated from February 1867 to September 1868, are in the Petitot papers, AG.

22. J. Fabre to H. Faraud, Paris, 14 March 1868. Fabre papers, AG. I. Clut to H. Faraud, Athabasca, 15 February 1869. Clut papers, AG.

23. The most explicit descriptions of these attacks are found in J. Séguin to H. Faraud, Good Hope, 25 July 1870. Séguin papers, AY, and J. Séguin to I. Clut, Good Hope, 24 January 1871, cited in I. Clut to J. Fabre, 14 May 1871, G LPP 692, AD.

24. J. Fabre to H. Faraud, Paris, 1 May 1876. Fabre papers, AG.

25. See below in text.

26. É. Petitot to Secretary of Society for the Promotion of Christian Knowledge (SPCK) in London, Paris, [1866]. Copy HEC 6491.E53L 20, AD. W.H. Grove to H.W. Tucker, London, 19 March 1886. Copy, HEC 6491.E53L, AD.

27. The above story of Émile Petitot is based primarily on a series of letters found in the AG and the AD.

28. Much information about Clut is found in his own *Journal*, which can be found in his own handwriting in a series of thirteen small notebooks conserved in the archives of the Archdiocese of Grouard in MacLennan, Alberta. One notebook can be found in the archives of the Archdiocese of Edmonton. In 1988, Janine and Claude Roche transcribed this journal into two typewritten volumes entitled *Journal de Monseigneur Clut Vicariat apostolique Athabasca Mackenzie 1857–1903*. A copy is in the Deschatelets Archives in Ottawa, HE 1721.C63J. A recently published biography of Clut by the same authors makes extensive use of the same journal. See Claude Roche, *Monseigneur du Grand Nord*.

29. V. Grandin to I. Clut, Île-à-la-Crosse, 24 September 1866. Grandin papers, AY.

30. V. Grandin to A. Taché, [St. Albert], February 1881. Copy of AASB, 84.400, 911, APA.

31. V. Grandin to A. Taché, Lake Athabasca, 24 June 1861. Copy of AASB, 84.400, 911, APA.

32. V. Grandin to A. Taché, Providence, 3 April 1863. Copy of AASB, 84.400, 911, APA.

33. I. Clut to H. Faraud, Athabasca, 20 May 1862. Clut papers, AG.

34. Yukon became a distinct Territory within Canada in 1898.

35. H. Faraud to I. Clut, Paris, 5 April 1874. Faraud papers, AG.

36. H. Faraud to I. Clut, St. Boniface, 29 May 1875. Faraud papers, AG.

37. H. Faraud to I. Clut, Lake La Biche, 29 September 1875. Faraud papers, AG.

38. I. Clut to H. Faraud, Athabasca, 18 February 1881. Clut papers, AG.

39. H. Faraud to I. Clut, Lake La Biche, 18 November 1881. Faraud papers, AG.

40. I. Clut to H. Faraud, Dunvegan, 25 April 1882. Clut papers, AG.

41. Taché was promoted archbishop upon the creation of the ecclesiastical province of St. Boniface in 1871.

42. A. Taché to H. Faraud, St. Boniface, 28 March 1881 and 11 October 1888. Taché papers, AG.

43. V. Grandin to A. Taché, Paris, 10 February 1878, and [St. Albert], February 1881. Copy of AASB, 84.400, 911, APA.

44. For a detailed study of the controversy between Grandin and Faraud over the governing of the Lake La Biche mission see Raymond Huel, "La mission Notre-Dame-des-Victoires du lac la Biche et l'approvisionnement des missions du Nord: le conflit entre Mgr V. Grandin et Mgr H. Faraud," in Raymond Huel (ed.), *Western Oblate Studies 1/Études Oblates de l'Ouest 1*, pp. 17–36.

CHAPTER IV

DEPLOYMENT IN RED RIVER, ALBERTA, AND BRITISH COLUMBIA

Even after the Pacific coastal region was separated from it in 1845, the diocese of St. Boniface was immense. It extended from the western shores of Hudson Bay to the Rocky Mountains, and from the United States border at the 49th parallel to the Arctic Ocean, an area embracing today's provinces of Manitoba, Saskatchewan, and Alberta, in addition to the Yukon and Northwest territories. This area of just under six million square kilometres represents more than half of Canada's entire territory. The newcomer was taken aback by the sheer extent of a diocese that was nearly seventeen times the size of France, six times that of Ontario, and four times that of Quebec. Although a series of ecclesiastical subdivisions gradually limited the size of the diocese,[1] the entire area remained part of the ecclesiastical province of St. Boniface (1871) throughout the period under study.

On its western boundary, across the Rocky Mountains, were a handful of clergy directing newly formed dioceses in British Columbia, a land that was also largely evangelized by Oblates. In terms of sheer size, British Columbia measured just under one million square kilometres—nearly ten percent of the Canadian land mass. Clearly, one of the first adjustments required of a newcomer to Canada's Northwest was to appreciate the sheer immensity of that quarter continent.

The Red River Headquarters

The Catholic evangelization of this vast land had from the outset been centred in Red River. By 1855, this headquarters of the Catholic

Cathedral of St. Boniface, built by Bishop Provencher in 1830s and destroyed by fire on 14 December 1860 along with the bishop's adjoining residence. The cathedral's interior measurements were 100' × 45' × 40' and it was considered the finest building in Red River.

Church in the Northwest consisted of the stone cathedral built by Provencher in the 1830s, the bishop's house, the convent of the Sisters of Charity, and various buildings, including a girls' school, a boys' school, barns, warehouses, and sheds for the farming and mission-supply activities of the sisters and priests.

These installations were in the parish of St. Boniface. The only other long-standing permanent parish at Red River was that of St. Francis-Xavier, otherwise known as White Horse Plain, established in 1824 when the Métis population of Pembina was invited to move to British territory, subsequent to the positioning of the U.S. border. In 1855, Father Thibault was pastor of St. Francis-Xavier on the Assiniboine River, assisted by Father Joseph Bourassa, his erstwhile Alberta companion. Bourassa left for Canada that same year. The parish served more than a thousand Métis faithful who were still engaged in the annual buffalo hunt on the prairies. In 1854, a third parish, St. Norbert, began to form on the Red River some ten kilometres above St. Boniface; it received its first resident priest in late 1857. From these bases in Red River Catholic priests made seasonal visits to the surrounding area.[2]

During Bishop Taché's administration, expansion was the order of the day in the Red River colony. In 1856, the region's population of some 3,000 people was equally divided between Catholic and Protestant families, the former being organized into three parishes. A fourth parish, St. Charles, was slowly taking shape on the Assiniboine River, having been served by the clergy of St. Boniface since 1854. In addition, a mission with resident priest was founded at the southern extremity of Lake Manitoba in 1858, serving some thirty families. In these years

Indian hunter after successful hunt near Fort Chipewyan. Caribou was an indispensable part of the diet of many northern Indians.

a priest would periodically accompany the Métis hunters on their annual hunting expeditions across the prairies, and these same hunters founded the settlement of Pointe-de-Chênes at the eastern extremity of the prairie, where it met the forests of the Canadian Shield. The parish of St. Anne would be formed there in the late 1860s, as would another in Saskatchewan's Qu'Appelle Valley.

In 1857, Bishop Taché had a total complement of sixteen priests, fourteen of whom were Oblates; the others were the veteran Father Thibault and a new recruit from Canada, Father Zéphirin Gascon, who would later become an Oblate. In the four years since 1853, Bishop Taché had managed to double the number of Oblate priests from seven to fourteen, but lost three of his five secular priests. On balance, therefore, during the first four years of his episcopal administration Taché had increased the number of his priests by four. By 1858, Sisters of Charity and Brothers of Christian Schools were staffing schools in the parishes outside St. Boniface.

In spite of these promising developments, Taché and his faithful had their share of crosses to bear. Shortly after Father Goiffon, from the neighbouring mission of Pembina in the United States, died from exposure in November 1860, fire destroyed Bishop Taché's cathedral and residence in St. Boniface, on 14 December 1860. Taché, who was visiting his western missions at the time, lost everything. Then another fire on 30 May 1861 destroyed a barn on the St. Boniface farm of the Sisters of Charity before consuming four sheds and warehouses on Taché's neighbouring property. As if this were not enough, major flooding followed the same spring when the Red River overflowed its banks, as it was wont to do periodically.

On the verge of despair, Bishop Taché decided to rebuild. By the fall of 1863 a new cathedral had been erected, although the steeple and the interior would not be completed for several years. In addition, by the spring of 1865 a spacious new episcopal residence had been completed and occupied. Hope was reborn in the diocese, in spite of the fact that since 1864 the country was being plagued annually by grasshoppers. In 1862, when the subsequently famous Father Joseph-Noël Ritchot[3] arrived from Canada to begin forty years of ministry in the parish of St. Norbert, the number of Catholic priests in the diocese of St. Boniface had grown to thirty-six, thirty-three of whom were Oblates.

During the latter third of the nineteenth century, the Catholic archdiocese of St. Boniface encompassed the territory of today's Manitoba, in addition to the western portion of Ontario and southeastern Saskatchewan.[4] The archdiocese's eastern district included missions at Kenora (Rat Portage), Fort Alexander at the mouth of the Winnipeg River, Selkirk at the mouth of the Red River, and St. Boniface. Its central district included parishes at Winnipeg, St. Norbert on the upper Red River, St. Charles on the Assiniboine River, St. Laurent on Lake Manitoba, and Rivière-aux-Épinettes near Duck Bay on Lake Winnipegosis. The western district was centred on Lebret in Saskatchewan's beautiful Qu'Appelle Valley, a mission dedicated to St. Florent

Cathedral of St. Boniface, built by Bishop Taché in 1862–63. The interior was completed several years later. This church served until it was destroyed by fire in 1906.

for some twenty years, but then changed to Sacred Heart in the late 1880s.

In 1891, the parishes of the diocese were reinforced by the founding of a monastery of Regular Canons of the Immaculate Conception when Father Paul Benoît and three other priests arrived from Europe, leading a group of French and Swiss settlers. They settled at Pembina Mountain in the southern part of the diocese, a place that would be given the name Notre-Dame-de-Lourdes. Coincidentally, in 1892 four Cistercians (two priests and two brothers) arrived from France to establish a Trappist monastery at St. Norbert.

Across the Red River from St. Boniface, in the new city of Winnipeg, 1,000 Catholics among the city's 7,000 residents had no church of their own. Between 1869 and 1875, they worshipped in the chapel of the sisters' St. Mary's Academy, ministered to by Oblate Father Joseph McCarthy from St. Boniface. In 1874, Albert Lacombe was appointed pastor of the parish of St. Mary's in Winnipeg. Within a year he was presiding over the construction of a new Oblate residence in Winnipeg, Archbishop Taché having salted away funds to pay for the building located on land donated by the Hudson's Bay Company (HBC). The second storey of the house served as both school and church until St. Mary's Church was blessed on 4 September 1881, the year that witnessed the completion of a new convent for the Sisters of the Holy Names of Jesus and Mary, another convent for the Sisters of Charity across the river in St. Boniface, and a new building for St. Boniface College. The Brothers of Mary had arrived in 1880 to staff Catholic boys' schools.

Most resident stations served several outlying missions. For example, the missionary resident in Kenora in northwestern Ontario travelled to Fort Francis on Rainy Lake, among other places. From 1875 to 1882, the construction of the railway over the more than 600 kilometres separating Selkirk and Kenora added several hundred white workers to the largely Indian population of the area. Archbishop Taché appointed a succession of priests to minister to these gangs. In November 1880, it was Albert Lacombe's turn.

The veteran missionary tells of his two-year apostolate among the 1,500 men, divided into gangs of thirty to sixty workers, spread along the 100 kilometres between Kenora and Eagle River. One third of the workers were French Canadian, the other two thirds a mixture of Irish, English, Scots, Icelanders, and Danes. Fifty percent were Catholic. The moral reformer faced the twin challenges of continual cursing and swearing and the nefarious effects of liquor, in spite of strict regulations aimed at banning the bottle. The missionary to the railroad gangs performed his ministry in the evenings, much like the missionaries to the lumber camps.

The western district of the archdiocese of St. Boniface, an area of some 128,000 square kilometres, was centred on Lebret, or Qu'Appelle, the Oblate mission of the Sacred Heart located 500 kilometres west of Winnipeg. Having chosen the site of the mission in 1865, during the next two years Archbishop Taché sent Father Ritchot from St. Norbert on seasonal visits. In 1868, Oblate Father Jules Decorby was appointed resident pastor. Twenty years later, the Oblates directed not only the parish of Qu'Appelle, but also an 837-hectare farm and an industrial school for Indian children. By 1893, the school enrolled 194 children; five years later, the number had grown to 238. It was supervised by two Oblates and staffed by nine sisters, two teachers, five trade instructors, a bookkeeper, and a handyman. Some 5,000 people, 3,750 of whom were Indian, inhabited this western district, which was served by Oblates in Qu'Appelle and occasionally in a variety of other stations, including Montagne-de-Bois to the west and Fort Ellice in the east.

From the outset, St. Boniface remained the heart of the Catholic Church and the Oblate network in the greater Northwest. Not only was it the archbishop's residence, and simultaneously the headquarters of the Oblates, but it was also the centre of Catholic institutions such as St. Boniface College. Supplies usually came through there, as did resources in money and personnel. It was the gateway to the Catholic Northwest.

The Alberta Campaign

The Oblate missions of the upper Saskatchewan River that had been started by secular priests in 1842 were also undergoing rapid development in the wake of the arrival of Father Lacombe and his colleagues after 1852. The pivotal mission of Lake St. Anne continued to operate, but was replaced as the headquarters of the region's missionaries by the new mission of St. Albert, founded in 1861 by Bishop Taché. Beginning in 1868, Bishop Vital Grandin occupied the role of officer in charge of the region's church, first as coadjutor bishop of St. Boniface and superior of the region's Oblates, then as bishop of the diocese of St. Albert (1871).

Vital Grandin (1829–1902) was born in France, made his vows as an Oblate in 1853, was ordained by Bishop Eugène de Mazenod on 23 April 1854, and left immediately for the Northwest. After spending a

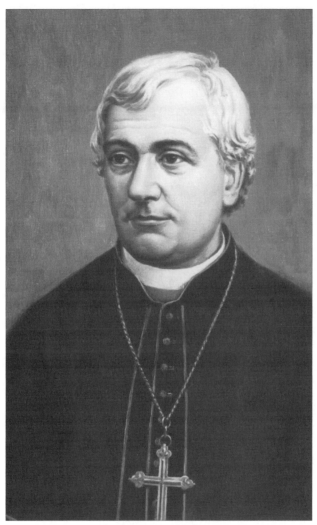

Vital Grandin (1829–1902)

year in St. Boniface learning Indian languages and assisting in the min-istry, he was sent to Fort Chipewyan for two years (1855–57) and then to Île-à-la-Crosse (1857–59), whence he left for Europe to be ordained Coadjutor Bishop of St. Boniface. Returning to Canada in 1860, he win-tered at Île-à-la-Crosse in 1860–61 and then undertook a protracted pastoral visit to the Oblates' northern missions, a visit that would last three years (1861–64). While he was on this tour the territory of Atha-basca–Mackenzie was made into a distinct apostolic vicariate entrusted to Henri Faraud. Grandin then spent the years 1864–67 at his residence at Île-à-la-Crosse, visiting Oblate missions on the Churchill River. During his sojourn in Europe in 1867–68 to attend Oblate General Chapter meetings, he was informed that the Alberta portion of the diocese of St. Boniface, the one centred in St. Albert, was to become, in 1871, an autonomous diocese that would be entrusted to him. Therefore, upon his return to Canada in 1868, Grandin took up residence in St. Albert, near Edmonton, the town that would remain his episcopal seat until his death in 1902.

During his five years as missionary priest, and his subsequent forty-three years as bishop, Vital Grandin established a reputation as a saint. The man whom Louis Veuillot labelled the "lice-covered" bishop because of his poverty was not averse to describing to his friend and confidant Alexandre Taché some of his more mundane sufferings, and frequently with a touch of humour and self-deprecation. He occasionally referred to his problem with hemorrhoids, his "emeralds,"[5] that rendered him "a wandering Jew"—that is, always standing. By the time he was into his fifties he was complaining of growing problems with hearing, rheumatism, and asthma. He even described the difficulties that beset him when he needed to urinate while travelling on HBC barges. While the crew members simply stood on the side of the boat and relieved themselves, Grandin was too bashful to do so, even when he knew that nobody could see him. This resulted in his waiting all day to relieve himself, because even when docked the barges usually remained some twenty or thirty feet from shore. The result, according to Grandin, was that several missionaries, himself included, ended up suffering from bladder problems, an ailment that eventually would kill Archbishop Taché. He noted that the sisters were particularly vulnerable in this regard.[6]

Vital Grandin managed his church as well as could be expected in the circumstances, given the vast distances involved, the general poverty of the region, and the serious difficulties caused by some of his clergy. He always got along well with Archbishop Taché, for both men could be very frank and direct with each other, thereby settling a number of potential problems before they festered into animosity and resentment.

His relations with Henri Faraud were, however, another matter entirely. In 1869, upon Archbishop Taché's insistence, Grandin had temporarily ceded to the apostolic vicar of Athabasca–Mackenzie the use of the Lake La Biche mission, a station within the jurisdiction of St. Albert. If he did not do so, Faraud threatened to leave the country and return to France.[7] As we have seen, Faraud founded his demands on the transportation and supply requirements of the northern missions.

For the next twenty years, control of the Lake La Biche mission became a bone of contention between bishops Faraud and Grandin—an issue that would poison relations between the two men. Many felt that Faraud could not properly administer his vicariate of Athabasca–Mackenzie when he was so far removed from the scene. Archbishop Taché and bishops Grandin and Clut were of this view; they felt that he should have resided in Fort Chipewyan, or, preferably, Providence. As well, beginning in 1873 Bishop Grandin argued that changes in the HBC supply routes made it possible for Faraud to avail himself of them, that he no longer needed his own distinct supply system. Faraud disagreed. The argument continued, Grandin claiming that Faraud was neglecting the spiritual welfare of the Lake La Biche mission while bleeding it dry materially, and Faraud claiming the post was indispensable for the supply of his northern missions. In fact, one suspects that both bishops were primarily interested in the comfortable living and revenues provided by Lake La Biche, a post which at that time could boast of two stone houses, a large stable, three wooden sheds, thirty-two cattle, a water-driven mill, and more than twenty acres under cultivation.

Archbishop Taché found himself caught in the middle of the controversy between the two men, Faraud writing that Grandin had indulged in less than honourable behaviour in this regard, Grandin noting that there was no reasoning with Faraud. A few months before his death, in spite of—or possibly because of—the fact that the controversy had finally been resolved in Grandin's favour, Bishop Faraud was more adamant than ever. He wrote to his coadjutor, Bishop Clut:

> Bishop Grandin has behaved as he always has towards me, unjustly, foolishly, insanely, falsely, ridiculously, and a few other things... We must break with these people and treat them like strangers, without hatred, but granting them only the respect that basic courtesy requires. We can expect no help from that quarter, only pettiness and stinginess.[8]

Given Faraud's cantankerous nature, one must question the fairness of his judgement of Grandin.

Bishop Grandin was to enjoy much more harmonious relations with another of his Oblate colleagues. The Canadian priest Albert Lacombe (1827–1916) is perhaps, along with Alexandre Taché, the best known of the Oblate missionaries in the Northwest. We know that Lacombe spent the first two years after his ordination to the priesthood (1849–51) working under the supervision of Father Bellecourt in Pembina, North Dakota. In the wake of serious disagreements with Bellecourt, he returned to Montreal in the fall of 1851 and served in the parish ministry for some six months before returning to the Northwest in the company of newly consecrated Coadjutor Bishop Alexandre Taché. He immediately proceeded to Edmonton (1852–53), then to Lake St. Anne, where he made his final vows as an Oblate in 1856. After ten years in Lake St. Anne (1853–63), he moved to the new mission of St. Albert for two years before undertaking a roving missionary commission in the prairies during the next seven years (1865–72); he ministered primarily to the Blackfoot and Cree Indians for whom he founded the mission of Saint-Paul-des-Cris (1865), as well as to Métis people for whom he founded the mission of Saint-Paul-des-Métis (1896).

Beginning in 1872, Albert Lacombe spent a decade away from his beloved Indians of Alberta, working successively as an episcopal immigration agent endeavouring to recruit French-speaking settlers for the West, as pastor of St. Mary's parish in Winnipeg (1874–80), and as missionary to railway construction gangs in the Kenora area (1880–82). Solicited by Bishop Grandin, who was reeling from the loss of fathers Petitot and Scollen,[9] he then returned to Alberta, where he continued his diversified ministry—which included one hour as president of the Canadian Pacific Railway (CPR) in August 1883 on the occasion of celebrations marking the completion of the railway from the East as far as Calgary. After being entrusted with other sensitive missions by his superiors, Father Lacombe eventually retired to a home he had designed himself, his hermitage at Pincher Creek in southern Alberta.

Albert Lacombe was always held in the highest esteem and enjoyed the trust of his episcopal superiors, Archbishop Taché and Bishop Grandin in particular. The man had his weaknesses, but he always showed uncompromising zeal for his mission of evangelization. While Bishop Grandin observed that the priest liked to travel too much, he also acknowledged that he was beloved by all, whether Catholic, Protestant, infidel, Blackfoot, or Cree, because of his perennial qualities of Christian charity and kindness—in addition to the patience of Job. As early as 1868, Grandin declared to Oblate Superior General Fabre that the antipathy that some priests displayed towards Lacombe could be attributed to their jealousy at his widespread popularity and success. "In all the territory, for Protestants as for Catholics, Father Lacombe is the model missionary. I would add that I consider him as good an Oblate as he is a missionary."[10] Bishop Grandin would never waver in the high esteem in which he held Father Lacombe.

Effective in 1871, the Catholic missions of the western prairies were part of the diocese of St. Albert. Then, on 20 January 1891, the apostolic vicariate of Saskatchewan was formed, covering a northerly portion of today's Saskatchewan and Manitoba, along the Churchill and North Saskatchewan rivers, and extending northward along the western shore of Hudson Bay.[11] Oblate Father Albert Pascal was the first bishop, with residence at Prince Albert. North of the height of land separating the watersheds of Hudson Bay and the Arctic Ocean, and encompassing the vast Mackenzie River basin in addition to the Yukon Territory, lay the apostolic vicariate of Athabasca–Mackenzie, an ecclesiastical division that would in 1901 be divided into two distinct vicariates, Athabasca and Mackenzie.

First chapel in St. Albert, built by Father Albert Lacombe in 1861. This temple served for a decade.

When he became bishop of the new diocese of St. Albert in 1871, Vital Grandin supervised the work of fifteen priests, fourteen of them French, the other French Canadian. They were assisted by five catechists and thirteen Sisters of Charity of Montreal (Grey Nuns), who staffed convent schools, orphanages, and infirmaries. The sisters' initial establishment at Lake St. Anne (1859) was moved to St. Albert in 1863. Île-à-la-Crosse (1860) and Lake La Biche

The interior of the first chapel in St. Albert.

St. Albert's first cathedral, built in 1871 upon the appointment of Vital Grandin as first bishop of the diocese of St. Albert. This temple replaced the former chapel as the primary centre of worship.

(1862) boasted two other houses of the Grey Nuns in the diocese of St. Albert. In St. Albert, a town of some 700 souls and fifty houses, Bishop Grandin had a house and a new cathedral, in addition to a flour mill and a large farm that included sixty head of cattle, sixty horses, and some sixteen hectares of cleared land; there were six other churches or chapels at St. Anne, Edmonton, Lake La Biche, Saint-Paul-des-Cris, Île-à-la-Crosse, and Reindeer Lake. The Saint-Paul-des-Cris mission was founded by Albert Lacombe in 1865 for the benefit of the Cree, and was located northeast of Edmonton. The station was abandoned in 1873. From these resident missions Oblates toured various other seasonal mission posts such as Jasper House, Rocky Mountain House, Lesser Slave Lake, and Fort Pitt. As noted, the more northerly posts of the diocese, Lake La Biche and Lesser Slave Lake, for example, were entrusted to priests from Bishop Faraud's vicariate of Athabasca–Mackenzie.

While the key and historic mission of Île-à-la-Crosse served surrounding stations such as Green Lake, Cold Lake, and Portage la Loche, new missions were gradually established over the last third of the nineteenth century. This was the case for Fort Saskatchewan near Edmonton, as well as Fort Carlton and Battleford. Cumberland District on the lower Saskatchewan River, stretching as far as York Factory and Fort Nelson on the western shore of Hudson Bay, was largely Protestant. The Catholic penetration of the area was slow and gradual during the 1870s, 1880s, and 1890s. Catholic chapels rose in Fort Cumberland, Pelican Narrows, The Rapids, and Fort Nelson.

When this northeastern part of the diocese of St. Albert was detached to form the vicariate of Saskatchewan in 1891, Apostolic

Vicar Pascal supervised seventeen Oblate priests and six brothers in the evangelization of the area's 20,000 people. The bishop took up residence in Prince Albert, a town of 1,800 inhabitants, including 350 Catholics.

Southern Alberta was another area that developed after formation of the diocese of St. Albert. Albert Lacombe had ranged far and wide in this area between 1865 and 1872 and again after 1882. The invasion of the area by American whiskey traders had brought about the creation of the North West Mounted Police in 1873, which built Fort MacLeod in 1874. In October 1873 Oblate fathers Constantine Scollen and Victor Bourgine returned to St. Albert from a missionary journey among the Blackfoot near the junction of the Bow and Elbow rivers. They reported that they had established an excellent mission station on the Bow River but that within a week of their arrival a Wesleyan minister (George McDougall) had founded his own mission only a few kilometres downriver from them.

Fathers Scollen and Vital Fourmond were immediately despatched back to the area; the race was on once again. It was from this mission of Our Lady of Peace on the Bow River that Catholic evangelization of all of southern Alberta would flow, the missionaries visiting Fort MacLeod, Pincher Creek, and Fort Calgary. The latter was primarily a Mounted Police post until the CPR drove its transcontinental tracks through there in 1883, the year of the first Oblate visit to the village of MacLeod on the international border at the foot of the Rockies. Thereafter, Calgary boomed. By 1884, tracks stretched 160 kilometres west of Calgary; by 1891, another line had joined Calgary and Edmonton. Meanwhile, in 1885, six Faithful Companions of Jesus arrived in Calgary to staff a Catholic girls' school; they soon had more than fifty children in their care. For their part, the Oblates continued to develop the area's Church, solemnly inaugurating a new stone church on 8 December 1889.

In addition to Lacombe, one of the region's foremost missionaries was the Oblate Émile Legal, who had arrived from France in 1881. Legal devoted the next sixteen years to the evangelization of the Blackfoot, until his appointment in 1897 as coadjutor bishop of St. Albert. He succeeded Grandin upon Grandin's death in 1902.

The British Columbia Campaign

At the turn of the nineteenth century, the Pacific Northwest was inhabited by more than 100,000 aboriginal people, divided into several nations that had little relation to the Amerindians of the Canadian prairies. They were divided into numerous linguistic families, including the Athapaskan, the Tlingit, the Haida, the Tsimshian, the Wakashan, the Chimakuan, the Salishan, the Kootenayan, the Sahaptian, and the Chinookan. The Athapaskan and Salishan linguistic families became the foremost objects of Catholic missions.

It will be remembered that one result of the fanciful ecclesiastical structures created on the west coast in 1846 at the urging of F.-N. Blanchet of Oregon City was that Modeste Demers became a bishop in a land that was still largely wilderness; he was ordained on 30 November 1847. After taking up residence in Victoria, Demers spent his first four episcopal years (1847–51) travelling abroad in a largely fruitless attempt to recruit clergy.

A more positive event in Demers's years in office was the arrival within his diocese of the Oblates of Mary Immaculate and the Sisters of St. Anne. It was in 1847, the year of Demers's episcopal consecration, that one brother, one priest, and three soon-to-be-ordained Oblates first set foot in the Pacific missions, specifically in Oregon. They had come directly from Europe. After eleven years of difficult and often frustrating ministry to the Amerindians around Puget Sound, they moved their Pacific headquarters to Esquimalt, near Victoria, in 1858.

Victoria was made Pacific headquarters of the HBC in 1847, and capital of the colony of Vancouver Island in 1849, as well as the permanent residence of Governor James Douglas, a good friend of the Catholic missionaries. When the gold rush on the Fraser River brought hordes of prospectors and camp-followers into the HBC territory of New Caledonia in 1858, Great Britain immediately created a colony on the mainland, called it British Columbia, appointed Governor James Douglas of the colony of Vancouver Island as governor of British Columbia, and sent troops and lawmakers into the new colony. As early as 1859, the town of New Westminster on the north bank of the Fraser Delta was proclaimed capital of the colony, a status that would stand until 1868, two years after the two British colonies were united, when the joint capital was acknowledged as Victoria. During the first two years after the fusion of the colonies, it was New Westminster that served as capital.

Bishop Demers had been soliciting the services of the Oblates for several years, for the man was desperate for clergy, his entire clerical establishment amounting to only two priests in 1858 in spite of extensive and expensive recruiting journeys in earlier years. Indeed, all he had to show upon returning from his four-year recruiting journey of 1847–51 were three priests, all of whom would abandon the country within a few years; another year-long recruiting journey (1857–58) netted the bishop another two priests. One of the two, the Canadian Pierre Rondeau, would devote himself to the region's Indian missions until his death in 1900. However, such exceptional perseverance did not change the fact that the Catholic Church in the Pacific Northwest was in danger of having more bishops than priests.

From his headquarters in Esquimalt, the Oblate superior Louis-Joseph D'Herbomez managed the Oblate missions in the Pacific Northwest. On the mainland, the first resident missionary stations were at Lake Okanagan (1859), New Westminster (1860), and St. Mary's, or Mission City (1863), sixty-six kilometres above New Westminster on the Fraser River. During the 1860s it was from these stations that Oblates travelled, always concerned lest Anglican and other Protestant missionaries pre-empt them.

Louis-Joseph D'Herbomez
(1822–90)

Bishop Demers died in 1871. During his quarter century as bishop, he was an unhappy man, always short of clergy, indecisive, and poor. He wanted to resign, but Rome refused to accept his October 1859 resignation, instead attempting to assign him a coadjutor bishop. As more Oblate personnel arrived during the early 1860s, the missionary establishment grew apace. Problems arose between Bishop Demers and Father D'Herbomez, leading to an 1862 request by Oblate Superior General Joseph Fabre that Demers be given either an Oblate successor or an Oblate coadjutor bishop. When the Pope had refused to accept Demers's resignation of 1859 and decided to give him a coadjutor bishop, the intended victim had been the Canadian Oblate Alexandre Trudeau. However, Trudeau, with the consent of Bishop de Mazenod, refused the appointment for reasons of conscience.

Fabre, with the endorsement of the bishops of Canada, thereupon proposed the appointment of D'Herbomez; otherwise, it was reasoned, the mainland should be separated from the diocese of Vancouver Island and given its own bishop. When the Holy See was at the point of appointing D'Herbomez in March 1863, Bishop Demers intervened and opposed his rival's appointment. Rome then (December 1863) appointed a Canadian secular priest, Father Morrison, and issued his bulls, only to discover that the man had resigned the office before occupying it, claiming that he was not qualified for the job; in truth, he could not bring himself to accept episcopal rank in order to run a diocese that was in fact nothing more than a large parish. In the end Rome abandoned its planned appointment of a coadjutor bishop to Demers; in December 1863, mainland British Columbia was made into an apostolic vicariate, and Father D'Herbomez was appointed first apostolic vicar. The troubled marriage between Bishop Demers and Father D'Herbomez was to end in a legal separation.

Apostolic Vicar D'Herbomez was ordained bishop in Victoria on 9 October 1864 and installed in his see of New Westminster on 16 October. By the end of 1866, the last Oblates had left Esquimalt, and Vancouver Island, transferring their parish and college work to Bishop Demers. Thereafter, Oblate work on Canada's Pacific coast would be limited to mainland British Columbia; the Oblates would not return to Vancouver Island until the twentieth century.

In addition to recruiting two priests, when Bishop Demers visited Canada in 1857–58 he also recruited four Sisters of St. Anne to operate a school in Victoria. The band of women was the creation of Montreal's Esther Sureau who had founded a new congregation of women devoted exclusively to teaching schoolchildren. With the approval of Bishop Bourget, Sureau and four companions made their first religious vows in 1850. Her group came to be known as the Sisters of St. Anne, with headquarters in Lachine (1864) in the former residence of the late HBC Governor George Simpson. The congregation numbered forty-five women when it sent four of its members to Victoria in 1858.

They journeyed by train from Montreal to New York, by ship to Panama, by train across the eighty-three-kilometre isthmus, and by steamer up the west coast to Victoria, where they arrived on 5 June 1858. Within weeks of arriving, sisters Salomé Valois (age 28), Angèle Gauthier (30), Mary Lane (32), and Marie-Louise Brasseur (25) had opened a girls' school, which by November 1858 could boast of being entrusted with the education of Governor James Douglas's three daughters. Another two sisters arrived the following year, and the procession continued for decades; in fact, forty Sisters of St. Anne were sent to the Pacific missions over the following twenty years, eight new sisters arriving in 1863 alone.

The Sisters of St. Anne were not alone. In 1856, the Sisters of Providence, another Montreal congregation, founded in 1843 by the widow Émilie Tavernier-Gamelin, had sent the first five of its members to work in Oregon, marking the beginning of another major chapter in the history of Pacific Catholic missions. Moreover, in 1859, no fewer than twelve Sisters of the Holy Names of Jesus and Mary, another new Montreal congregation of the 1840s, had responded to Archbishop Blanchet's call to Oregon. The many wild and unruly settlers, prospectors, and miners of the Pacific coast must have been taken aback at this invasion of holy women.

Indeed, by the 1860s, the Catholic Church in British Columbia was solidly rooted. The number of bishops, missionaries, and sisters was relatively high, although all religious superiors constantly pleaded for more. During the last third of the nineteenth century, the challenge for these men and women would be the extent and speed of expansion.

In 1890 Bishop D'Herbomez of British Columbia died. His successor as apostolic vicar was Paul Durieu, who had worked as his coadjutor since 1875. Within three months of his accession to office, Durieu's church was raised to the rank of diocese of New Westminster (2 September 1890). Durieu's successor in 1899 would be Augustin Dontenwill. All these bishops were Oblates.

When the colony of British Columbia became part of Canada in 1871, two Catholic bishops were in place—Modeste Demers, overseeing his Church's work in the diocese of Vancouver Island, and

Paul Durieu (1830–99)

Louis D'Herbomez on the mainland, where every missionary and priest was Oblate.

During the last third of the nineteenth century, Oblates cast their missionary net throughout British Columbia. Based at New Westminster (1865) at the mouth of the Fraser River, they had key stations at St. Mary's (Mission City), inland at Lake Okanagan (the mission of the Immaculate Conception, founded in 1859), and at Williams Lake (1867). That is where Father James McGuckin purchased a farm in February 1867, only three months before receiving reinforcements in the persons of Father François Jayol and Brother Philippe Surel. In May of the following year, Bishop D'Herbomez visited St. Joseph's mission and appointed Father Jean-Marie Le Jacq superior of the new mission, which included all of the interior of British Columbia from the 52nd to the 56th parallels. McGuckin became superior in 1872.

In 1873 this vast mission was divided in order to create a new northerly missionary district between the 53rd and 57th parallels and the 122nd and 128th meridians—in other words, all the land located above the 53rd parallel and enclosed by the Rocky Mountains in the east and the Coastal Range in the west. This was the mission of Our Lady of Good Hope, centred at Stuart Lake. Meanwhile, in 1864 the Oblates had founded St. Michael's mission on an island off the northern tip of Vancouver Island; their failure to make any headway among the area's aboriginal people led to the closing of the station in 1874, the year in which the last Oblates working in U.S. territory, in the diocese of Nesqually, were repatriated to British Columbia. The handful of additional missionaries who became available as a result of the two station closures of 1874 allowed Bishop D'Herbomez to open the new station of St. Eugene (1874) among the Kootenays at the province's southern extremity. In 1878, he would establish another Oblate residence, St. Louis, at Kamloops.

In 1875, seventeen years after founding their first residence in Victoria, the Oblates had left the island, but they had an unchallenged monopoly of Catholic missions on the mainland. Excluding the two missionary districts that would be closed in 1874, from his residence in New Westminster Bishop D'Herbomez supervised Oblate work in St. Charles of New Westminster and its satellite St. Mary's, St. Joseph's of

The mission station at Fort St. James on Stuart Lake, British Columbia, built during the 1870s.

Williams Lake, Our Lady of Good Hope at Stuart Lake, the Mission of the Immaculate Conception at Lake Okanagan, and St. Eugene of the Kootenays. Each of these resident missionary stations served vast surrounding areas.

Aside from the bishop's headquarters in New Westminster and its associated college, the most important station was at Williams Lake, where McGuckin's 400-hectare farm boasted 150 head of cattle and seventeen horses. In addition to providing revenues and supplies for many of the vicariate's missions, the St. Joseph mission served some 2,500 Indian people in its own district, a number similar to the aboriginal population in the Okanagan and Stuart Lake districts. By 1898, Bishop Paul Durieu, D'Herbomez's successor, could report that he had two bishops, twenty-five Oblate priests, two seminarians (scholastics), and eleven Oblate brothers in his diocese of New Westminster. However, given that fully ten of the twenty-five priests were employed as superiors, bursars, or teachers, and that two were elderly, only thirteen Oblate priests were actually engaged in the ministry. They were entrusted with the evangelization of the province's estimated 80,000 people—23,000 Indians, 6,000 Chinese, and 50,000 whites. The bishop estimated that 50,000 were Protestant—that is, most of the white population in addition to a handful of Indians. The number of Catholics was set at 24,000, mostly Indian, while another 6,000 inhabitants were not Christian. At the time, Vancouver was rapidly becoming the province's major centre.

So it was that by 1900 most of the Canadian land mass was spotted with Oblates or Oblate-related clergy. Every single one of the Catholic bishops in the Northwest, except for Vancouver Island, was an Oblate, while most of the priests and brothers were as well. The Oblate monopoly was so pervasive that many of the other priests who came to work in the area soon chose the Oblate way for themselves. This was the case for fathers Lacombe, Gascon, and Grouard, for example. Among the sisters active in the area, the largest group, the Sisters of Charity of Montreal, were well known as the preferred companions of the Oblates throughout the country; the Sisters of the Holy Names of Jesus and Mary had been founded in Montreal in 1844, largely at the instigation of an Oblate, and the Sisters of St. Anne would prove just as amenable to their influence.

In sum, while the pathfinding was initially due to secular clergy, the occupation of the country for the Catholic Church was almost exclusively an Oblate achievement, strongly seconded by the sisters.

The Missionary Oblates of Mary Immaculate were not to go unchallenged, however. The Church of England, more specifically its

Harvesting potatoes at St. Joseph mission at Fort Resolution. Potatoes were an important part of the diet in the missions where it was possible to cultivate a garden.

Dog team pulling plough at Fort Resolution. Dog teams were used for ploughing fields, until oxen and horses became available.

evangelical Church Missionary Society (CMS), resented this new invasion of British territory by the papist French; they fought them every step of the way.

Notes

1. The apostolic vicariate of Athabasca–Mackenzie (1863), the diocese of St. Albert (1871), and the apostolic vicariate of Saskatchewan (1891).

2. See Martha McCarthy, *To Evangelize the Nations: Roman Catholic Missions in Manitoba, 1818–1870.*

3. See Ritchot biography by Philippe R. Mailhot in *DBC* 13, pp. 952–3. Also L.A. Prud'homme, *Monseigneur Joseph-Noël Ritchot.*

4. An administrative restructuring of the Catholic Church in western Canada occurred in 1871, when the Diocese of St. Boniface was raised to the status of archdiocese, or ecclesiastical province, including within its boundaries the new diocese of St. Albert and the apostolic vicariate of Athabasca–Mackenzie.

5. In French the word *émeraudes* is closer to the word *hémorroïdes,* than are the similar words in English.

6. Vital Grandin, *Souvenirs* (St. Albert: n.p., n.d.), 84.400, 1006, APA. Grandin to Taché, Cauterets, 5 August 1878. Copy AASB, 84.400, 911, APA. Grandin to Taché, Île-à-la-Crosse, 1 April 1861. Copy AASB, 84.400, 911, APA.

7. V. Grandin to A. Taché, Île-à-la-Crosse, 19 June 1869. Copy from AASB, 84.400, 911, APA.

8. H. Faraud to I. Clut, St. Boniface, 12 December 1889. Faraud papers, AG.

9. Father Constantine Scollen (1841–1902) worked in Alberta during the last third of the century. In the 1880s, he became an alcoholic and, after many years of difficulties, abandoned the ministry in 1885.

10. V. Grandin to A. Taché, St. Albert, 20 December 1868. Grandin papers, AG.

11. Maps showing the evolving ecclesiastical territorial divisions are found in Claude Champagne, *Les débuts de la mission dans le Nord-Ouest canadien,* pp. 52, 57, 58.

CHAPTER V

THE PROTESTANT ENEMY

THE Protestant Christianity that confronted the Oblate missionary campaigns is not easy to define. While Protestantism began as an historical entity at the time of the Reformations of the sixteenth century, it represents more than a movement of opposition to Roman Catholicism, just as Orthodox Christianity cannot be reduced to a movement of opposition to Roman Catholicism. Nor can Protestantism be fairly presented as the sum of its various denominational and theological parts, because most Protestants believe that they are bound together in a common unity. Yet it is not easy to define this commonality. Two leading Protestant authors have written:

> Efforts to develop independent statements of Protestant "principles" of "beliefs" tend to be so general and filled with all manner of qualifications as to be often meaningless, or they are sufficiently partisan as to exclude important motifs.[1]

Given the difficulty of sketching the nature of the Protestant opposition to the Oblates, we will try to steer a middle course between endless meaningless qualifications on the one hand and a partisan discourse on the other, always keeping in mind that in spite of their constant wrangling both Catholic and Protestant clergymen declared themselves to be Christians.

From the beginning, Catholic missionaries in the Northwest and British Columbia had to contend with Protestant rivals—that is, missionaries sent by various Protestant churches, the Methodists and the Church of England in particular. The latter, through its lay evangelical Church Missionary Society (CMS), was far and away the primary challenge to Catholic and Oblate hegemony over the people of north-western Canada. While the typical Catholic priest of the nineteenth century perceived any Protestant as a heretic who had yet to see the error of his ways, the typical Protestant minister, particularly the one of evangelical persuasion, perceived the Roman Catholic Church as the "Whore of Babylon," an institution of oppression and repression of freedom-loving people everywhere; Catholics were not Christians. The God-fearing Protestant was duty-bound to counter Catholic influence wherever it was found.

British Protestantism

The Reverend John West,[2] who set foot in Red River in 1820, was the first of a long series of ambassadors of the Church of England to come to the Northwest in the nineteenth century. In that it was Protestant, the Church of England represented the vast majority of Englishmen, Roman Catholics barely surpassing one percent of the population of England at the time.

English Protestants were not, however, unanimous in their ecclesiastical allegiances, the diverse theologies of the sixteenth-century Protestant reformers coupled with two centuries of internal political and theological debates having left a legacy of a plurality of Protestant churches. In the United Kingdom,[3] therefore, the Church of England competed with dissenting churches, a group that included the diverse brands of dissidents that separated from the established Church—Baptists and Methodists, among others. Moreover, the Church of England itself was divided, in that a growing number of its faithful lent an ear to the evangelical movement, a movement of theology and spirituality that was growing during the first half of the nineteenth century and that came to influence most Protestant denominations.

Like all churches established by law, from its outset in the sixteenth century the Church of England was challenged by sundry faithful who felt that the State Church was selling its soul by negotiating various compromises with the Crown, be it in regard to taxation, church subsidies, military service by clergy, or the swearing of oaths. The Church of England was accused of failing to abide by the pure Word of God. This led to the emergence of the Puritan movement in the sixteenth and seventeenth centuries, followed by the rise of John Wesley's Methodism in the eighteenth century.

These powerful Puritan and Methodist movements were fuelled by a great concern with abiding by the Word of God, the Bible, experiencing conversion through a personal and intimate encounter with God, and living a life of holiness and obedience to God. Such intense holiness meant that society and Church had to be reformed whenever and wherever it proved necessary. Puritans and Methodists also considered individual experience very important. This sometimes required not only a personal conversion experience, but also personal expressions of possession by God. A minority of these dissident Christians, driven by eighteenth-century German Pietism and the growing romanticism in Europe at the turn of the nineteenth century, went so far as to give importance to blatant expressions of possession by God—such as tears, fainting, speaking in tongues, or the instantaneous healing of the sick. Although these sensational manifestations would become the badge of distinction of later Protestant movements like Holiness, Adventism, and twentieth-century Pentecostalism, it is true to say that emotion and feelings were much more important for evangelical Christians than they were for traditional Christians, Protestant or Catholic.

Those Protestants primarily concerned with preaching the Gospel—the Good News, the evangel—came to be called evangelicals. Their numbers were growing by the late eighteenth century, in reaction to the established Church whose theology and mindset seemed all too rationalistic, as Enlightenment people were wont to be. Evangelicals were and are suspicious of intellectual activity, of too much reasoning in matters spiritual. Theirs was a religion of the heart, the Holy Spirit speaking directly to each Christian through Scripture and prayer. God did not rely primarily on the mediation of sacrament, priest, church, or government; all his children were equally and directly accessible to him.

What came to be called evangelicalism in the nineteenth century thus had begun long before, in seventeenth-century Puritanism and in eighteenth-century Pietism and Methodism. Evangelicalism runs like a thickening thread through British Protestantism. It was not a new body of doctrine, but a new zeal, a new earnest abiding by the Word of God as understood by the Protestant reformers. In the nineteenth century, it spread throughout the various Protestant churches, the Church of England included.[4]

Beginning in the 1830s, when a group of Church of England divines and churchmen showed too much inclination to interpret their Christian heritage in the way that the Roman Catholics did,[5] the evangelicals rose to the challenge. So it was that the Oxford movement of John Henry Newman and his friends served to spark an upsurge in evangelical interest within the Church of England. Evangelicals would fight the Romanists within (Puseyites[6] guilty of Newmania) just as vigorously as they did those without who obeyed the Pope.

In addition, John West's Church of England had, since the seventeenth century, "become inseparable from [English] national consciousness."[7] Since the "Glorious Revolution" of 1688 when a Catholic king was deposed and exiled, the monarch and his or her spouse were required by law to be members of the established church; since 1673 legislation required that all important State officials assent to the Church of England. A series of penal laws relating to property rights, inheritances, and travel discouraged dissenters, but especially Roman Catholics, from full participation in English society. The universities of Oxford and Cambridge were considered not only English, but Church of England institutions; Oxford required all its students to subscribe to the Thirty-nine Articles, the basic doctrinal charter of the Church of England. English law required that all recipients of a university degree take the oath of supremacy, which recognized the monarch as head of the Church of England. Owen Chadwick writes:

> The Victorians changed the face of the world because they were assured. Untroubled by doubt... they... identified progress with the spread of English intelligence and English industry... Part of their confidence was money... And part was of the soul. God is; and we are his servants, and under his care, and will do our duty. The Victorian age continued till the war of 1914.[8]

One aspect of British Protestantism that became manifest in Canada's Northwest, as elsewhere, was a virulent anti-Catholicism or No-Popery. This import from Great Britain was part of the surging evangelicalism of the nineteenth century. It was only later in the century that it became a home-grown Canadian product, in the wake of the migration of large numbers of Ontario settlers to the West.

In Britain, the centuries-old undercurrent of No-Popery had been on the wane during the "enlightened" eighteenth century, at least among the upper classes. In spite of this, Catholics may well have remained legal pariahs for a very long time were it not for the threat of civil war in Ireland. This pushed the British government to act to ensure the loyalty of its Irish citizens, the majority of whom were Catholic. The result was legislation, adopted in April 1829 by the British Parliament, ensuring the emancipation of the Roman Catholics.

Meanwhile, the intense Protestantism of the evangelicals had been gradually eroding feelings of religious tolerance in Britain when the eruption of the Oxford movement controversy in 1835 made compromise more difficult, if not impossible, in matters of religion. Catholics were soon being abused more openly, associations for the defence of Protestantism were formed, doctrinal issues were debated in public, and John Henry Newman became a Catholic in 1845. Five years later the so-called "papal aggression" controversy occurred, resulting from the surprise announcement, in October 1850, that Rome had created thirteen English dioceses within the new archdiocese of Westminster, appointing Patrick Wiseman as the new archbishop and making him a Roman Cardinal. Englishmen reacted as one in denouncing this invasion of their beloved England by the satraps of the papacy. Newspapers vociferated, politicians threatened and legislated, and Protestant evangelicals smugly noted that they had predicted this very thing would result from the pestilence that was Newmania in the Church of England. Rome was the Antichrist.

The Church of England in Canada's Northwest, being an outpost of the church in the old country, would necessarily reflect the moods and feelings of the mother church.

The Church Missionary Society (CMS)

The evangelical movement gave rise to distinct institutions within the Church of England, the Church Missionary Society being one of the most important and prominent. The vast majority of Church of England missionaries in Canada's North and West, clerical and lay, were recruited, trained, appointed, remunerated, and supervised by the CMS, the primary Protestant regiment in the field. In Canada's Northwest, the CMS was the Protestant equivalent of the Oblate congregation.

At the turn of the eighteenth century, the Church of England had given birth to two societies devoted to the evangelization of other countries, the Society for the Promotion of Christian Knowledge (SPCK) and the Society for the Propagation of the Gospel (SPG). England's oldest missionary society, the SPG had relatively little involvement in the Canadian Northwest. It had been founded in 1701 to support Church of England missions in English colonies. By the end of the nineteenth century, it was withdrawing from its few commitments in the Northwest; for example, it had curtailed all grants to British Columbia in 1882. The SPG gave £9,000 per year to Canadian dioceses but discontinued all subsidies as of the year 1900. Its work was continued, at least in part, by the Missionary Society for the Church in Canada (MSCC), established by the Church of England in Canada's General Synod of 1902.

There was even less involvement on the part of another English missionary society, the Colonial and Continental Church Society (CCCS), a group founded in 1838 to support Church of England ministry in English colonies.[9]

The main agent of Protestant missions in the Northwest, the CMS, was founded in 1799 by the evangelical wing of the Church of England and dedicated to the evangelization of heathens. Originally established to provide missionaries to Africa and the Far East, the new society usually handled missions to aboriginal people, while its sister missionary societies tended to focus on white settlements.

In the early nineteenth century, the Church of England was just as badly in need of reform as the Catholic Church of France, described earlier. Not only was the clergy the largest and richest profession in the realm, but the Church of England was a tradition-bound, patronage-ridden institution, characterized by arbitrary and very unequal distribution of endowment income. Every benefice in the country had a patron, who could be any of a wide variety of people or corporations, including churchmen, colleges, companies, guilds, private citizens, or public institutions. A clergyman could be appointed to a benefice by a patron moved by the most laudable or the basest motives. What was important for the clergyman eager to make a living was to catch the attention of a patron. Social standing was thus central to obtaining a benefice in the Church of England.[10] The number of clergymen grew rapidly in England after 1830.

Intent upon evangelizing the heathen, the CMS founders organized themselves in order to collect funds, and to recruit missionaries, train them, and send them into the field. They would have preferred to recruit members of the English clergy, the majority of whom were graduates of the ancient universities of England,[11] but the clergy proved reluctant to respond to the appeals of the missionary societies. Most of the foreign missionaries therefore came from the lower-middle and artisan classes.

There is no fathoming the religious motivation of a missionary recruit, and such motivation no doubt was a key factor in drawing numbers of young men, and a few women, to the missionary life. But the CMS had other ways to entice them.

There were real economic advantages. A missionary was paid more than £200 per annum, the exact salary depending on the location of the mission and the size of the man's family. This was better pay than that of many English benefices. In addition, a wide range of fringe benefits came with the job, including a disability allowance, a widow's allowance, death benefits for surviving children, and free education in

England for missionaries' children. The CMS recruit had all of his financial concerns taken care of by the society.[12]

Moreover, one's social status was enhanced by joining the CMS. In return for joining its ranks, the society provided a prized education and ordination, both important guarantees of status in Victorian Britain. In fact, uneducated candidates were the most numerous applicants; the CMS educated them free of charge—at least after 1825, the year of the founding of Islington College.

Given the large number of missionary recruits bereft of university education, in 1825 the society opened its own training college. At Islington, academic pursuits were subordinate to spiritual ones, the moulding of Christian character taking precedence over scholarly achievements. Students entered with varying degrees of preparation, making it necessary for the college to serve simultaneously as elementary school, secondary or grammar school, and theological college. By mid-century, the CMS acknowledged even more the importance of training for their missionaries. By then, candidates without a university education were required to complete a four-year programme of study; other missionary societies did likewise. Theirs was not a specialist's training, however, but simply identical to that of English clergymen. No attempt was made to initiate the prospective missionaries in native languages or customs, or in other religions.[13]

First Protestant Missions to the Northwest

In the first quarter of the nineteenth century, the northern half of the North American continent had been uniformly British for half a century. Nevertheless, no English clergyman had penetrated the distant North and West since the chaplain Robert Wolfall had stepped off Arctic explorer Martin Frobisher's ship in 1578 and presided over a liturgical service of the Church of England on the desolate shores of Baffin Island. During the next quarter of a millennium, the only clergymen to visit the vast Hudson's Bay Company (HBC) hunting ground were the Catholic priests, usually Jesuits, who led or accompanied the explorers of New France.[14] This all changed with the establishment of the colony of Red River in 1811.

Requests by the Earl of Selkirk for Catholic priests were noted earlier. He obtained them in 1818 and late the following year the HBC committee in London, in consultation with the CMS directors, appointed the Reverend John West, a member of the society, as chaplain to Red River.

Arriving in 1820, West soon founded a CMS church and school in Red River, ensuring continuation of the Anglican work after he himself was called back to England in 1823. For the rest of the century, a succession of CMS missionaries, clerical and lay, came to Red River; they were frequently assisted by graduates of the Anglican school founded by West in Red River. One of the ministers was David T. Jones, who took up where John West had left off in 1823, assisted by the lay teacher George Harbidge. Another was William Cockran, who arrived in 1825 to begin a forty-year clerical career in the region.

Table 4
Church of England Ministers and Catechists before 1845

NAME	ORDAINED	ARRIVED	DEPARTED	DIED
John West	–	1820	1823	–
David T. Jones	–	1825	1838	–
William Cockran	–	1825	–	1865
Henry Budd	1850	native	–	1875
Abraham Cowley	1844	1841	–	–
James Hunter	–	1844	–	–
John Smithurst	–	1839	1851	–
Charles Pratt	–	–	–	–
James Settee	catech.	native	–	–
John Roberts	catech.	1842	1845	–
John Macallum	1844	1833	–	–
Joseph Cook	–	–	–	–

Sources: Thomas C.B. Boon, *The Anglican Church from the Bay to the Rockies*; Frits Pannekoek, *A Snug Little Flock*; CMS papers in the NAC; Frank A. Peake, "From the Red River to the Arctic."

In pre-1845 Red River, the Church of England had four parishes strung out along the Red River. The oldest was John West's St. John's, which stood three kilometres below the forks of the Red and Assiniboine rivers. David Jones founded St. Paul's in 1824, located ten kilometres downstream from St. John's. Then, in 1832, William Cockran established St. Andrew's, twenty-two kilometres further downriver. The fourth parish was St. Peter's, yet another twenty-two kilometres downriver. Like their Catholic colleagues, the Church of England's ordained clergymen were, in 1840, few in the Northwest (Jones, Cockran, and John Smithurst), and their sphere of action was limited to Red River. Then there occurred a surprise raid by a Methodist platoon of missionaries.

Methodist Reinforcements

Having coexisted for a score of years in the Northwest, in 1840 the Anglican and Catholic clergy had adjusted to the presence of one another. Their mutual forbearance was facilitated by the fact that each served distinct ethnic, linguistic, and cultural communities, those of the Métis on the one hand, the English governing class on the other. Each of the two denominations fielded a similar number of ministers, who confined their ministry to the Red River settlement and its immediate surroundings. They existed side by side rather than together.

The small white and Métis settlement on the Red River continued to be dominated by the HBC, as was all of the Northwest. HBC Governor George Simpson ruled the churches as he did the rest of his wilderness empire, for he controlled the means of communication and transportation, as well as any form of commerce and government. The company's monopoly had real advantages for the churches, not only in free transportation and lodging for missionaries, but also because under Simpson's stewardship liquor was gradually diminishing in importance in the fur trade. Indeed, the unbridled licentiousness of the era preceding 1821, when the HBC and the North West Company fought each other armed with brandy, gin, and rum, had been replaced in 1840 by a policy of partial elimination of alcohol. In 1840, the trade in liquor was largely banned from the northern districts of English River (Churchill River), the Athabasca River, and the Mackenzie River, although it continued elsewhere, fuelled by the competition of independent traders from the United States.

By the late 1830s, however, the tame Catholic and Anglican clergy of the Northwest were showing signs of restiveness at being confined to Red River. Catholic Bishop Joseph Provencher badgered Governor Simpson until he relented and supported the sending of Catholic missionaries François-Norbert Blanchet and Modeste Demers to the Pacific coast in 1838. During the 1830s also, while Catholic Father George Bellecourt established his agricultural mission of St. Paul's fifty kilometres up the Assiniboine River, the Anglican clergy simultaneously opened its own agricultural–Indian village on the lower Red River; in both cases, the clergy was reaching out to the aboriginal people and assuming that it was best to "civilize" them in order to evangelize them. The change of lifestyle among Amerindians threatened to have deleterious effects on the Indian traplines that supplied the HBC with its furs. To the extent that the new missionary policy of the churches succeeded, the aboriginal people of the Northwest would be less inclined to earn their living as trappers. They would be drawn to settle in the central colony of Red River where Anglican and Catholic boarding schools were already in operation, and they would become unavailable as boatmen in the HBC's vast transportation network, the lifeline of the Northwest.

So it was that Governor Simpson and Chief Factor Ross of the company's Northern Department decided to invite Methodist missionaries into Rupert's Land. Not only were the Methodists rivals of the Church of England clergy, but as Protestants they could serve as foils for the Catholics whose British loyalty and HBC allegiance could be suspect. In addition, the British Wesleyan Methodist Missionary Society promised to evangelize, rather than civilize, the aboriginal people: its men would itinerate and evangelize the Indians without trying to settle them, a policy the HBC officers considered far less threatening to their interests. The HBC therefore agreed, at the request of the all-powerful secretary of the Methodist society's Committee of Missions, Dr. Robert Alder, to send missionaries to pre-selected posts in Rupert's Land at HBC expense. Four stations were to be occupied: Moose Factory at the foot of James Bay, Rainy Lake in northwestern Ontario, Norway House north of Lake Winnipeg, and Fort Edmonton on the upper Saskatchewan River. Governor Simpson had chosen the sites because of their key role in the fur trade.

The three British Wesleyan Methodist ministers sent to Canada in 1840 were George Barnley, William Mason, and Robert T. Rundle. For their work in Rupert's Land, they were joined by three missionaries of the Canadian Methodist Church—James Evans, Henry Steinhauer, and Peter Jacobs; all three were experienced Indian missionaries, Jacobs and Steinhauer being of Indian origin. Evans, the appointed supervisor of the new Methodist mission in the Northwest, settled at Norway House, assisted by Indian preacher Peter Jacobs. While Rundle headed for Edmonton assisted by the Métis Benjamin Sinclair, whom he had recruited en route, Mason took up station at Rainy Lake in the company of the Indian teacher Henry Steinhauer. George Barnley went overland from Montreal to Moose Factory. All four ministers in charge of the missions (Evans, Mason, Barnley, and Rundle) answered directly to the Missionary Committee of the British Wesleyan Methodist Missionary Society in London.

James Evans (1801–46) came to Upper Canada from England in 1822, converted to Methodism while at a camp meeting, and became a teacher at an Indian school at Rice Lake, Upper Canada. Having mastered the Ojibwa language, he was ordained and continued his ministry in Upper Canada during the 1830s. When Evans and his wife and daughter arrived in Norway House in August 1840, they took up residence in the HBC trading post alongside Chief Factor Donald Ross and his family. Within three years, tensions led the Evans family to move to nearby Playgreen Island, the site of the Indian mission; the latter was renamed Rossville. It became the headquarters of Methodist missions in the Northwest.

In addition to developing Cree syllabics along the same lines as the Ojibwa syllabics he had previously developed in Upper Canada, the Reverend Evans had become critical of the HBC's policy of Sunday travel; he invited his Christian Indians to abstain from working on the Lord's Day. Moreover, Evans advised his faithful that they were within their rights to trade furs with independent traders and were not restricted to trading with the HBC. Governor Simpson and Chief Factor Ross retaliated by inviting Evans to leave Norway House. Indeed, the Wesleyan Methodists were not proving as tractable as Simpson had anticipated.

In the summer of 1844, having heard of the missionary travels of Father Jean-Baptiste Thibault into the upper Saskatchewan and Athabasca country, Evans set out once more for the distant country he had first visited in the latter months of 1841, today's northern Alberta and Saskatchewan. He travelled by canoe in the company of his Ojibwa interpreter and assistant, Thomas Hassall. En route, having accidentally shot and killed Hassall near Île-à-la-Crosse (September 1844), Evans returned to Rossville only to face a growing series of accusations. Some accused him of having deliberately shot Hassall, others of engaging in sexual relations with the numerous Indian girls who boarded at his home. Meanwhile, Governor Simpson formally asked that Evans be recalled (June 1845), alleging that the missionary was emotionally disturbed and that he worked against the interests of the HBC. Dr. Robert Alder complied, and in June 1846 James Evans was ordered to return to England to discuss the matter. He died there in November 1846, shortly after his arrival.[15]

Since 1843, the Reverend William Mason had assisted Evans at Norway House. Mason's first three years in the Northwest had been spent at Rainy Lake (1840–43). When Mason left Rainy Lake for Norway House in 1843, he was replaced by the newly ordained Peter Jacobs, who remained there until 1854 when he moved to Upper Canada before falling into disgrace and being expelled from the ministry in 1857. In fact, the Methodist mission at Rainy Lake proved to be a dismal failure. Writing in the 1850s, long-time resident of Red River Alexander Ross quoted the Reverend Jacobs to the effect that the Methodist mission had not made a single convert nor established a school during the first eleven years of its existence.

After seven years of work at Moose Factory (1840–47), George Barnley left in a huff. He and his wife had got into a dispute with the post's chief factor over the use of post facilities. Governor Simpson felt that Barnley's wife was to blame, and reiterated his frequent admonitions against allowing white European women into the HBC trading posts, for trouble usually followed. In time, this would become grounds for preferring Catholic missionaries in the Northwest, for their celibacy eliminated the constant threat of social turmoil caused by white women in the tiny, closed society of a fur-trading post.

The fourth key region occupied by the Methodists was north-central Alberta. When Robert Rundle arrived there in October 1840, Fort Edmonton was a key station in the fur trade, for that was where supply convoys changed from the boats of the upper Saskatchewan River to packhorses to cross the 150-kilometre portage to Fort Assiniboine on the Athabasca River. From there, the convoys continued up the Athabasca to cross the Rocky Mountains through Yellowhead Pass, or down the Athabasca to the Mackenzie. For eight years, Rundle led the life of a dedicated missionary, before leaving the country in 1848.[16]

By 1848, the Wesleyan Methodist mission in Rupert's Land had all but disappeared. James Evans had left Norway House for England in disgrace in 1846, only to die in England; George Barnley had departed in 1847, in the wake of his dispute with Chief Factor Miles over the social conditions that were his lot in Moose Factory; suffering from a broken arm, Robert Rundle left the country in 1848, never to return; William Mason remained in Norway House but, having abandoned all hope of Methodist reinforcements, defected to the CMS in 1854. Although a handful of aboriginal ministers and catechists remained in the Northwest (e.g., Peter Jacobs, Henry Steinhauer),[17] the Wesleyan Methodist mission had in effect ended: in 1847 the British Wesleyans had transferred their Upper Canada missions to the Canadian Methodist Conference; they would do likewise with their Rupert's Land missions in 1854.

Ironically, when most Methodist missionaries left the country in 1848 they were held in high esteem by Governor Simpson who was commending Mason's "amiability and friendly demeanour" and his "highly satisfactory" performance at Norway House, and Jacobs's "indefatigable" work at Rainy Lake.[18]

Consolidating Methodist Forces

In 1854, upon assuming responsibility for Methodist Northwest missions, the Canadian Conference of the Methodist Church took over a mission field that needed attention. This mission was but a skeleton of its former self. In fact, not only had many of the first missionaries left the field, but William Mason transferred to the Church of England (1854), Peter Jacobs left for Upper Canada (1854), and Henry Steinhauer visited England (1854–55).

In the wake of the visit of Methodist superintendent the Reverend John Ryerson in 1854, the Canadian Conference of the Methodist Church injected new resources into the Northwest. In 1855, a newly ordained Henry Steinhauer returned from his visit to England in the company of the Reverend Thomas Woolsey. While Steinhauer, with his assistant Ben Sinclair, founded a mission at Lake La Biche, in direct competition with the two-year-old Oblate mission, Woolsey went to Fort Edmonton to take over Robert Rundle's old mission, which had been vacant since 1848. Within two years, in order to remove himself from Oblate competition, Steinhauer had moved his mission from Lake La Biche to Whitefish Lake, where he would spend the next quarter century of his life, until his death in 1884.

Meanwhile, Charles Stringfellow, Thomas Hurlburt, and Robert Brooking took over the Methodist missions of Norway House and Oxford House. By 1857, this handful of Methodist missionaries were the only resident clergymen at Norway House (Rossville) and Oxford House, and the only Protestant clergymen in today's Alberta.

While the Reverend Steinhauer ran his mission at Whitefish Lake, the Reverend Thomas Woolsey did likewise at Edmonton (1855). Two years before Woolsey left the country in 1864, both men were visited by the Methodist district chairman, the Reverend George Millward McDougall (1821–76). The Upper Canadian McDougall had attended Victoria College in Cobourg, assisted the Reverend William Case in Indian work near Orillia (1850–54), and been ordained to the Methodist ministry in 1854, six years before his appointment to the Rossville station.

One year after his exploratory visit of the upper Saskatchewan River, McDougall migrated West with his family in 1863, founding the mission of Victoria, on the north side of the Saskatchewan River some 133 kilometres east of Edmonton. He intended to show the area's Indians how to live in a settled agricultural community, while conducting extensive missionary forays into the wilderness of the western plains.

In 1865, McDougall extended his work by having his son, John, re-establish the mission of Pigeon Lake, located on an overland route between Fort Edmonton and Rocky Mountain House—a mission initially founded by Rundle but abandoned by the catechist Ben Sinclair in 1854, in favour of Lake La Biche. After renaming Pigeon Lake "Woodville," George McDougall opened a permanent mission at Fort Edmonton in 1871, intent on foiling Catholic efforts in the area. From

1873 until his tragic death from exposure to the elements in 1876, George McDougall and his son, John, also evangelized the Blackfoot of the Bow River, near today's Calgary, opening the mission of Morleyville (1873). By this time the two first Methodist stations of Victoria and Woodville were no longer active missions.[19]

The Methodists were the second Protestant denomination to field missionaries in the Northwest and the first to have a man resident on James Bay (1840). But their first minister among the Northwest's white population was George Young, at Winnipeg in 1868.

Five distinct Methodist denominations came to the Northwest in the nineteenth century, although they had all merged by 1884. First in the field, in 1840, the British Wesleyans transferred their territory to the Canadian Wesleyan Methodists in 1854. When the latter established their first distinct conference in the Northwest in 1872, it was divided into two districts, Red River and Saskatchewan. The Reverend George Young's Red River district contained three circuits: Red River, run by George Young; Norway House, by Egerton Ryerson Young; and Oxford House, by native convert John Sinclair. The Reverend George McDougall's Saskatchewan district encompassed his own circuit, centred at Victoria on the North Saskatchewan River; the Edmonton circuit, led by Peter Campbell; the Elk River circuit, run by George McDougall's son, John; and the Whitefish Lake circuit, by Steinhauer. Administrative expansion was very rapid, for by 1887 the Methodist Church in Canada counted no fewer than eight districts in the Northwest.

By 1884, the Methodist Church in Canada represented the four other Methodist factions that had come to the Northwest in earlier years: the British Wesleyans, and three splinter groups called the Methodist Episcopal Church, the Bible Christian Church, and the Primitive Methodists. The consolidated Methodist Church in Canada was able to continue its rapid expansion, in step with the increasing pace of migration from Ontario at the turn of the century. Indeed, in 1906 Alberta and Saskatchewan were made into separate conferences alongside Manitoba, all under the direction of superindendent James Woodsworth, who resided in Winnipeg.

Nineteenth-century Methodism in the Canadian Northwest reflects the denomination's gradual fall from grace into mediocrity. John Wesley's Methodism had been the cutting edge of the eighteenth century's "great awakening" and subsequent evangelical revival in British Protestantism. Early nineteenth-century Methodists distinguished themselves by their zeal, passion, commitment, and determination to bear witness to their conversion experience and resulting piety. As the nineteenth century wore on, this reforming zeal slowly transformed itself into a very conservative mindset, Anglo-Protestant racism and Ontario-centredness becoming more prominent than evangelical zeal. By the end of the nineteenth century, Methodists were more concerned with maintaining their institutional church system than with converting the world. One scholar has written:

> As the Methodists became less emotional and enthusiastic in the practice of their faith their institutionalism became more exclusively territorial. They were also forced to turn to such obvious concerns as Sabbatarianism and Temperance and anti-Catholicism in order to find a meaningful social role. In Canada, in the absence of anything else, they could always emulate national trends... The prevailing attitudes [in their newspapers]... were simply those of the English-speaking majority.[20]

The band of enthusiasts had become a flock of followers of current fads, carried on the bandwagon of public opinion. The Word of God had been replaced by that of the white Anglo-Protestant elite, as expressed in newspaper editorials or political speeches. In all the important social and political issues that bedevilled the Northwest during the last third of the nineteenth century, Methodist clergymen could be found in the forefront of crusades to repress minorities and impose the white Anglo-Protestant system of values. So it was with the first Riel insurrection, the amnesty debate before 1875, the repression of French as an official language, and the abolition of confessional (i.e., Catholic) schools in Manitoba and the Northwest Territories. These Methodist clergymen believed that the Northwest's aboriginal people were a weak and backward race that had to be brought, willy-nilly, to acknowledge the superiority of white Anglo-Protestant civilization. Progress and civilization demanded that any and all kneel and pay homage to their god—namely, the dominant group itself. Such were the teachings of the reverends George McDougall, John McDougall, Egerton Ryerson Young, and James Woodsworth. To quote again historian William Howard Brooks: "By 1912... there was nothing heroic or evangelical, or perhaps even religious, in the official attitudes of the bulk of the Methodist Church."[21]

Consolidating Church of England Forces

Clergymen of the Church of England were more numerous in the field than were the Methodists. John Ryerson counted thirteen in the Northwest in 1854, most of whom were located in Red River. There were none west of the Rocky Mountains. There was one at York Factory

(William Mason), one at Lake La Ronge (Robert Hunt), two at Moose Factory (John Horden and E.A. Watkins), and one minister (James Hunter) and a catechist (James Settee) at The Pas. The balance were located in the broader Red River area, including William Cockran, Abraham Cowley, and the teacher William Kirkby. They were paid and supervised by London's CMS, although the missionaries in the more northerly posts still received £50 in annual salary from the HBC. In 1856, this was the case for William Mason in York Factory and John Horden and E.A. Watkins on James Bay.

Bishop David Anderson had been in office in Red River since 1849, nominally in charge of the diocese of Rupert's Land, which had been created when a retired HBC officer left a grant for that purpose. In fact, Anderson was considered overly zealous by his clergy, while the country-born (English-speaking Métis) did not like him. The disenchanted prelate left the country in 1864, to be replaced the following year by Robert Machray.[22] A generous bequest also allowed for the establishment of the diocese of [British] Columbia in 1859, with Bishop Hills at the helm.

At the time of Confederation, the Church of England had two dioceses in the Northwest, Rupert's Land headed by Bishop Robert Machray (1865–1904) and Columbia headed by Bishop George Hills (1860–92). The onrush of white settlers accompanying the incorporation of the Northwest into Canada led to the rapid subdivision of these two sees. At Machray's request, in 1872 the CMS subdivided the diocese of Rupert's Land to create the diocese of Hudson Bay (Moosonee) and the diocese of Athabasca, which included all of the Northwest Territories and the Yukon north of Portage la Loche (Methye Portage). The veteran Hudson Bay missionary John Horden was consecrated Bishop of Hudson Bay (15 December 1872), while William Carpenter Bompas was appointed to Athabasca. Simultaneously, Archdeacon John McLean was made bishop of the new diocese of Saskatchewan, which included all the lands drained by the Saskatchewan River. At the time of the first synod of the ecclesiastical province of Rupert's Land, held in August 1875, four Church of England bishops were at work between Hudson Bay and the Rocky Mountains.

In the early 1880s, it was time to subdivide anew. In 1883, the synod of the province of Rupert's Land decided to make Athabasca's northern portion into the diocese of Mackenzie River, only eight years before the latter was in turn divided to create the diocese of Selkirk (later Yukon). In the southern prairies, the same synod of 1883 made the civil district of Assiniboia into the new diocese of Assiniboia, soon thereafter renamed Qu'Appelle; on 24 June 1884, Robert Anson was consecrated as its first bishop. Having moved his headquarters from Regina to Qu'Appelle, he resided there until resigning his see in 1892. His successors were W.J. Burn (1893–96) and John Grisdale (1896–1911).

In the northwestern prairies, William Cyprian Pinkham was chosen, in 1886, to succeed John McLean as second bishop of Saskatchewan. However, only five days after Pinkham's consecration on 7 August 1887 the provincial synod of the province of Rupert's Land formed the diocese of Calgary to encompass the entire civil territory of Alberta. Pinkham was designated joint bishop of Saskatchewan and Calgary, until such time that a sufficient endowment would allow a second bishop to be appointed to one of the two dioceses. This occurred in 1903, whereupon Bishop Pinkham resigned from the see of Saskatchewan in Prince Albert, continuing exclusively as bishop of Calgary. In 1902, the diocese of Keewatin was carved out of the western portion of the diocese of Moosonee.

On the Pacific coast, at the request of the synod of the diocese of Columbia (1878) Bishop Hills's diocese was divided in 1879 to form three dioceses: Vancouver Island, New Westminster, and Caledonia. While Hills continued as bishop of the reduced diocese of Vancouver Island centred in Victoria, Caledonia in northern British Columbia, centred in Port Simpson, was entrusted to William Ridley; New Westminster in the southern mainland went to Bishop Acton Windeyer Sillitoe, who was on the scene by 1880. The administrative organization of the Church of England was completed in September 1893 when its first general synod met in Toronto. Robert Machray was elected first primate of the Church of England in Canada. By the end of the century, no fewer than eleven Church of England bishops were active in the ecclesiastical province of Rupert's Land, nearly double the number of Catholic bishops.

Bishop Ridley presided over the dissolution and exile of the Metlakatla mission run by lay CMS missionary William Duncan, who had founded it in 1857.[23] Near Port Simpson, Duncan had managed to establish a closed community of Tsimshian Indians; management was shared by the Indian people, but all worked under the paternal supervision of William Duncan himself. The results obtained in Metlakatla were pleasantly surprising to most, as the Metlakatla residents gave up the all-too-frequent dependencies on alcohol and prostitution, plagues that bedevilled many Indian communities in close proximity to those of the white man. Duncan had found the means for the aboriginal people to police themselves, supported by the magisterial powers that Duncan himself managed to secure from the government of British

Columbia. Moreover, the community had founded several prosperous commercial enterprises that generated revenue for Metlakatla.

However, Bishop Hills of Columbia soon discovered that Duncan was not very amenable to supervision, direction, or even the companionship of other Church of England missionaries. There may have been a clash of personalities, because Duncan, much like his Catholic peer Adrien-Gabriel Morice (who arrived in British Columbia in 1880), had to be his own sovereign boss. Power had to be his alone.

The clash was compounded by the differing theological horizons of Duncan and Hills. Although not ordained, Duncan belonged to the evangelical wing of the Church of England, as did the CMS, a wing that viewed with suspicion any and all concessions to the Anglo-Catholic wing of the Church of England; the latter valued much more highly the Christian tradition, including the episcopacy, the sacraments, and the liturgy. Although Bishop Hills was not a Romanist by any stretch of the imagination, he did belong to the Anglo-Catholic wing.

When the diocese of Columbia was divided in 1879, Metlakatla became part of the new diocese of Caledonia, under the direction of Bishop William Ridley; Bishop Ridley enjoyed the support of the CMS, Duncan's employer. When the controversial missionary refused to allow the introduction of the rite of Holy Communion into his idyllic Metlakatla, he was dismissed from the CMS. Duncan thereupon pulled up stakes, leaving not only his Church, but also the country. In 1887, he led six hundred like-minded Tsimshian faithful to Annette Island in Alaska, where a new Metlakatla was founded.

While the tug-of-war between Hills and Duncan continued throughout the 1870s, another clerical squabble broke out in Victoria. In this case the antagonists were the Anglo-Catholic Bishop Hills on the one hand, and another evangelical missionary, the Reverend Edward Cridge, on the other. The two controversies were not unrelated, because Duncan and Cridge were friends, and not only saw eye to eye on theological matters, but also were united in their opposition to their cold, aloof, and patronizing bishop.

Conflict erupted in 1872 following several years of bickering between the two men, Cridge objecting to the ritualism, or Catholic leanings, of his bishop. The occasion for the outbreak of hostilities was a sermon delivered on 5 December 1872 at the ceremonies marking the consecration of Victoria's new Anglican cathedral. Archdeacon William Sheldon Reece preached a sermon commending the new "Catholic revival" in the Church of England. Cridge protested, and the battle was on.

As Victoria's Anglicans divided into two factions, in January 1874 Cridge published an open letter to his bishop in Victoria newspapers, writing "...that every local congregation, with its accepted pastor, is a complete church..., that a diocese is no necessary part of a church..., [and] that the bishop has no authority over a particular congregation."[24] Bishop Hills had Cridge convicted by a diocesan court on a charge of denying the bishop's authority. Hills withdrew the pastor's licence to preach and suspended him from his parish of Christ Church (1874). When Cridge refused to concede gracefully, Hills obtained an injunction from the Supreme Court of British Columbia (24 October 1874), ordering Cridge not to preach or officiate as a clergyman of the Church of England. The outcast minister reacted (1875) by leading a large number of his parishioners out of the Church of England and into the Reformed Episcopal Church of the United States, a denomination that consecrated Cridge to the episcopate that very year.

Just as the Catholic missions were largely funded by the French Society for the Propagation of the Faith, most of the human and financial resources for Church of England missions came from the CMS. In 1895, the CMS spent £18,000 on its Canadian missions, funding the work of forty-nine white clergymen, eleven ordained Indians, and five laymen. In the eyes of the CMS leaders, Canada's Northwest never attained the importance of the Indies or Africa; it was therefore all too frequently the least promising of the missionary recruits who were sent to the Northwest, those who did not earn high praise from the directors of the CMS seminary in Islington. Nevertheless, it was the CMS that proved to be the leading rival of the Oblates in Canada's Northwest.

Since 1822, when it had enrolled HBC chaplain John West as its first missionary to the Northwest, the CMS had supported most Church of England missionaries in the region. For example, when David Anderson arrived in Red River as first bishop of Rupert's Land in 1849, four of the six clergymen in his diocese were CMS appointees. It has been noted, by 1895 the CMS was supporting an impressive sixty-five missionaries in the Northwest.

In addition to providing financial support, the CMS published several magazines that served to bolster the morale of missionaries in the field and inform them about events outside their isolated outposts, and to motivate Englishmen to continue supporting the CMS. The missionary received *The Church Missionary Intelligencer*, a monthly magazine founded in 1849, containing excerpts from the letters of missionaries, histories of various mission stations, biblical and theological commentaries, and book reviews. The magazine reflected the evangelical point of view of the CMS and provided a forum for friends and supporters of the society. It may have given the Oblates the idea to do likewise, for the Oblate *Missions* that began appearing in 1862 served much the same purpose.

It is clear from the above that it was the Church of England that carried the banner of Protestant missionary work to the Indians of northern and western Canada. By the early twentieth century, the Church of England in Canada had a dozen bishops working in the Canadian North and West, residing in Moose Factory, Winnipeg, York Factory, Qu'Appelle, Prince Albert, Calgary, Dunvegan, Athabasca, Carcross, Victoria, New Westminster, and Port Simpson.

With the exception of the missions by the Moravian Brethren on the coast of Labrador after 1770, the same Church of England led in Protestant missions to the Inuit, a ministry that only began in the late nineteenth century with men like the Reverend E.J. Peck on Cumberland Sound (1892) and Isaac Stringer at the mouth of the Mackenzie River (1893). Although the Methodists had made an earlier (1840) important contribution to Indian mission work in the southern portion of the Northwest Territories, and along the coast of British Columbia with Thomas Crosby (1840–1914), they were effectively out of the running in the last quarter of the nineteenth century.

Notes

1. John Dillenberger and Claude Welch, *Protestant Christianity* (New York: Charles Scribner's Sons, 1954), p. ix.

2. See Richard A. Willie, "West, John," *DCB* 7, pp. 976–9; Arthur N. Thompson, "The Expansion of the Church of England."

3. After the turn of the nineteenth century, Ireland fell under the sway of Parliament, as did Scotland, England, and Wales.

4. On the diffuse yet important movement called evangelicalism see F.L. Cross (ed.), *The Oxford Dictionary of the Christian Church*, revised edition (Oxford: Oxford University Press, 1983); Owen Chadwick, *The Victorian Church*. For the North American situation, see Leonard I. Sweet, "Nineteenth-Century Evangelicalism," in Charles H. Lippy et al. (eds.), *Encyclopedia of the American Religious Experience* (New York: Charles Scribner's Sons, 1988), vol. 2, pp. 875–99. For the Canadian situation, see Phyllis D. Airhart; Michael Gauvreau, *The Evangelical Century*; John Webster Grant, *A Profusion of Spires*; George A. Rawlyk (ed.), *The Canadian Protestant Experience*; William Westfall, *Two Worlds*.

5. These tractarians (authors of tracts) led by John Henry Newman spoke and wrote of sacrament, holiness, obedience, fasting, the fathers of the Church, etc.

6. Edward Pusey was an associate of Newman.

7. Owen Chadwick, *The Victorian Church*, p. 3.

8. Ibid., p. 1.

9. Several other missionary societies existed in England at the time, including the London Missionary Society (LMS), the Wesleyan Methodist Missionary Society (WMMS), and the China Inland Mission (CIM).

10. Alan Haig, *The Victorian Clergy*, preface.

11. Ibid., p. 27.

12. C.P. Williams, "'Not Quite Gentlemen.'"

13. Ibid. See also Eugene Stock.

14. For a review of this history see Robert Choquette, "French Catholicism Comes to the Americas," in Lippy, Choquette, and Poole, *Christianity Comes to the Americas*, pp. 131–242.

15. On Evans see Gerald Hutchinson, "Evans, James," *DCB* 7, pp. 298–300.

16. See Hugh A. Dempsey (ed.), *The Rundle Journals 1840–1848*. For an overview of Rundle's life see Frits Pannekoek, "Rundle, Robert Terrill," *DCB* 12, pp. 1015–16.

17. See Isaac K. Makindisa.

18. George Simpson to Dr. Alder, Lachine, 4 December 1848. 3M25, D4/70. HBC Archives (microfilm copy), NAC.

19. On McDougall see James Ernest Nix, *Mission among the Buffalo*; "McDougall, George Millward," *DCB* 10, pp. 471–2.

20. William Howard Brooks, "Methodism in the Canadian West," p. 307.

21. Ibid., p. 210.

22. For a brief biography of Anderson see Frits Pannekoek, "Anderson, David," *DCB* 11, pp. 20–22. On Robert Machray see Christopher Hackett, "Machray, Robert," *DCB* 13, pp. 698–702.

23. The following lines on William Duncan are largely based on Jean Usher, *William Duncan of Metlakatla* and Morris Zaslow, "The Missionary as Social Reformer."

24. Cited in Frank A. Peake, *The Anglican Church in British Columbia*, p. 79.

CHAPTER VI

ENGAGING THE ENEMY
FROM RED RIVER TO ALBERTA

CATHOLICS and Protestants had been fighting each other since the Reformations of the sixteenth century. During the three centuries that followed, the battle waxed and waned depending on place and circumstance. Although the eighteenth century witnessed the diminishing of the worst excesses of confessional intolerance, the roots of anti-Protestantism and anti-Catholicism struck deep in both Europe and America. The nineteenth century's ultramontane (Catholic) and evangelical (Protestant) movements had only to tweak the nose of the somnolent monster of religious intolerance in order to have it roaring anew.

The history of Catholic–Protestant relations in the colonies of post-Conquest Canada had most frequently been one of Protestant majorities who, in the wake of the English conquests of the eighteenth century, treated their Catholic minorities differently from one colony to another. While Nova Scotia outlawed Catholicism in 1758, Quebec's new English government came to terms with it in the Quebec Act of 1774: it was important to ensure the loyalty of Canadians to the British Crown, which was threatened by the revolt that was brewing in the southern colonies. In Upper Canada (Ontario), British constitutional law (1791) favoured the Church of England; however, the new multidenominational population of the early nineteenth century compelled the government to forego its plans for an established Church in that colony. By the 1850s much of this legal discrimination had ended throughout Canada. This Canadian heritage had an impact on the Northwest after Confederation (1867).

As the Oblate regiment occupied the field of Canada's Northwest after 1845, they soon encountered their primary adversary, the Church Missionary Society (CMS) regiment. Their clash would be a continuous, long-standing, indeed permanent, one, and was played out in every arena of joint activity from Red River to the Pacific and Arctic oceans. Neither could abandon the field of battle. Each was under orders from God to gird its loins and engage the Protestant, or Catholic, enemy. Separated brethren indeed.

There were many similarities between the Oblate and CMS gladiators. Each band was controlled and funded from Europe—that is, from London or Marseilles/Paris/Rome—and consequently each was an instrument of the policy of either English Protestantism or French Catholicism. Each was the agent of the propagation of European civilization, truly believing that its way was best for any and all. Moreover, each was driven by its own brand of nationalism, be it English, French, or French-Canadian. Each was evangelical in theological and spiritual persuasion, if the word "evangelical" is taken in its broadest meaning as describing Christians driven by earnestness, zeal, and passion for the conversion of all humankind resulting from the Christian's personal conversion upon hearing the Word of God, and the resulting holy living. The obverse was a marked tendency to denigrate their rivals, blackening their reputations while claiming in apparent good conscience that it was their Christian duty to do so. Also, both CMS and Oblate regiments tended to attract their share of missionary recruits intent on fleeing civilization for the wilds and barren wastes of the most distant corners of the globe.

Coexisting in Red River before 1845[1]

Travelling at the expense of their hosts, in the summer of 1818 fathers Joseph-Norbert Provencher and Sévère Dumoulin and the seminarian Guillaume Edge journeyed to Red River. These first resident clergymen to set foot in the colony enjoyed the support not only of Governor General Lord Sherbrooke of Canada, but also of the wife of Lord Selkirk. In fact, Lord Selkirk had given the Catholic mission a piece of land of some twenty square miles on the right bank of the Red River, across from the mouth of the Assiniboine. The land would become the nucleus of the town of St. Boniface, therefore a Catholic colony founded with the support of the Protestant gentlemen Selkirk and Sherbrooke.

In fact there was hardly a shadow of misunderstanding between the Catholic priests and the administrators of Canada and the Northwest during this period. Not only did Governor General Sherbrooke chair the fundraising drive for the Red River mission, but Bishop Plessis instructed his missionaries to show complete loyalty to the British governors. Indeed, on 20 April 1818, the bishop asked fathers Provencher and Dumoulin to make known to the Indian people the advantages of living under the government of His Majesty; the priests were to teach, by word and deed, the respect and loyalty that were owed to the Sovereign.[2]

Appointed bishop in 1820 and consecrated in 1822, Provencher continued to benefit from the good offices of the Hudson's Bay Company (HBC). In the same vein, Governor George Simpson of the HBC wrote in 1824 that the behaviour of the Catholic missionaries was above reproach; they not only abstained from meddling in the colony's political and commercial affairs, but they avoided any controversy with the Protestants.[3] The following year, Simpson congratulated Provencher for his exemplary conduct, his indefatigable zeal, and the unexceptionable perseverance of his missionaries.[4] By a resolution of 22 August of that same year, 1825, the Council of the company's Northern Department endorsed the view of its governor and, as a gesture of gratitude, announced an annual grant of £50 to the Catholic mission. Bishop Provencher had equal respect for Simpson and the HBC officers, and frequently spoke of their generosity and good will.[5]

The arrival of the first Anglican missionary in the autumn of 1820 signalled the beginning of denominational rivalries in the Northwest. On 30 December 1819 Lord Selkirk informed Bishop Plessis of John West's appointment by the directors of the HBC in London, in consultation with the CMS. Lord Selkirk's letter to Bishop Plessis is revealing:

> Your Lordship well understands the importance of preventing discord in a new colony...; and you will appreciate how the maintenance of the union between inhabitants must depend on harmony and frank cooperation for the common good between the pastors of different communions. You will also appreciate that in the present situation of the colony of Red River, composed of people of different languages, between whom there have always been national prejudices..., it would be most dangerous to allow feelings of jealousy and hatred based on religious differences to arise. The appearance or extinction of such feelings will depend almost entirely on the conduct of these pastors: and I have the greatest confidence in the wisdom of the missionaries that your Lordship has chosen..., and that they will have no difficulty in maintaining among Catholics a sincere attachment to the faith they profess, without presenting their Protestant neighbours as the enemies of God, for whom there is no salvation. The unfortunate consequences of a different conduct became all too manifest in a different part of the British Kingdom [Ireland], where there are many priests more infused with a partisan

spirit than with a religious spirit, priests who are only capable of sustaining the zeal of their parishioners by making them hate all people of other communions.[6]

Selkirk continued by noting that although he did not know John West personally he had discussed his mission at length with a mutual friend. The earl strongly recommended to West "moderation in speech in regard to Catholicism, and to never meddle in matters of exclusive Catholic concern." Selkirk declared himself convinced that Catholic priests would be too busy to meddle in the business of others. He therefore hoped that the joint presence of priests and ministers would not hinder the development of Christian charity in Red River.

Bishop Plessis responded to Selkirk on 25 January 1820, stating that he was surprised at the news of the appointment of a Protestant minister in Red River, an appointment that seemed to contradict the spirit of the initial agreement that had led to the founding of the Red River mission.

Thus, the news of the appointment of a Church of England minister in 1820 sparked some feelings of resentment in Bishop Plessis, while Lord Selkirk was driven to write a homily inviting the clergy to practise Christian charity.

Before 1840, the only Protestant clergymen in the Northwest were the handful of Anglican ministers who existed alongside an equivalent number of Catholic secular priests. As a rule, the relationship of the Anglicans with the HBC officers proved more strained than that of the Catholic priests. Thus when John West definitively returned to England in 1823 it was to the great satisfaction of Governor George Simpson. The Reverend David Thomas Jones, who succeeded West at Red River, was better appreciated by certain local HBC administrators, even though he managed to alienate his parishioners of Scottish origin. So it was that the Presbyterian Alexander Ross wrote that "these English missionaries are furious against every other creed but their own."[7] This same Presbyterian, who spent his life in the Northwest, continued by describing the Reverend William Cockran, another Anglican minister of the period, as "wedded to the dogma of exclusiveness, and strongly prejudiced against everything that he regarded as sectarian."

The Reverend Herbert Beaver and his wife, Jane, stationed at Fort Vancouver between 1836 and 1838, also made themselves most unpopular. In addition to trying to convert to Protestantism the Catholic children of Fort Vancouver, the English couple unabashedly damned the local marriages *à la façon du pays*, the form of wedlock most common among the couples living in HBC trading posts. The Church of England clergymen were especially vitriolic in condemning this "immoral" and "sinful" custom, describing the spouses of fur traders as mere concubines engaged in satisfying the base passions of fornicators, as opposed to husbands. John West had indulged in such condemnations at Red River between 1820 and 1823, while the Reverend Beaver's successor, Robert John Staines, did likewise at Fort Victoria from 1849 to 1854.

The attitude of these Protestant clergymen stood in stark contrast to that of fathers Blanchet and Demers, for example, who were conciliatory and more appreciative of "natural marriage." The priests were content to ask the interested parties to normalize their union by renewing their marriage vows before the priest, a service that did not condemn the existing bond but supposedly enhanced it.

So it was that many Church of England ministers working in Canada's Northwest abandoned their posts after only a few years, to the considerable relief of their own faithful. The situation was similar in the case of schoolteacher George Harbidge, entrusted with the Anglican school at Red River from 1822 until his dismissal in 1825. Governor George Simpson described him as ignorant, vain, undisciplined, and dominated by his wife, Elizabeth, who was said to hold an excessively high opinion of herself. It is this shabby and sorry band of personnel that is judged so harshly by historian Frits Pannekoek, who writes that these clergymen were primarily responsible for the disintegration of the Red River community before 1870.[8] This clergy had alienated not only the colony's leaders, but also a good number of the Church of England's Red River faithful.

Before the arrival of the Oblates in Red River in 1845, relations between Catholic and Protestant clergymen were minimal. Provencher, Dumoulin, and most of the other Catholic priests who worked at Red River spoke little English; they busied themselves serving their francophone faithful, white or Métis, and had little to do with the colony's white Protestant community. The Reverend David Thomas Jones reported in 1824 that he enjoyed the best possible relations with the Catholics, for he rarely met any of them, and then only at the governor's table; on such occasions, only harmless and meaningless conversation took place, because Jones spoke no French. Nevertheless, time and again, he managed to denounce "Popish bigotry" and the Catholic Church's "spirit of domination" and intolerance, all the while praying for the purification of the Catholic Church.

Of all the Church of England clergymen active in Red River before 1845, undoubtedly the most prejudiced against Catholics was William

Cockran, who arrived from England with his family in 1825. His correspondence includes a continual litany of accusations against Catholics. Cockran began by describing his forty-two-day voyage from York Factory to Red River in 1825. The crews of the boats carrying his party to Red River were without exception Catholic Métis, who, according to Cockran, always behaved according to the dictates of their Church. In other words, they showed constant hatred of the heretical Cockran. Their hostility, according to Cockran, extended to frequently dropping his baggage into the river, all the while ignoring the instructions proffered by the minister. He accused the men of blaspheming with equal skill in French and English, and of swearing in the names of God, the devil, the saints, the Church, and the various parts of the body of the Virgin Mary.[9]

Anti-Catholic tirades occurred again and again under Cockran's pen. After eight years of ministry in Red River, he commented on the region's Indians:

> These savages make good Roman Catholics; the priests sprinkle them with holy water and tell them they are safe; they hang a cross about their necks and tell them they are invulnerable. This symbolical deception suits their carnal minds, they go away satisfied with the lie which the mystery of iniquity had put into their right hand.[10]

On the eve of the arrival of the Oblates in Red River, the four or five Catholic priests in the country were leery of the Protestant clergymen, but rarely discussed them. However, the equivalent handful of Anglican ministers were so prejudiced against the Catholics that they regularly wrote about them. It is noteworthy that the 1830s, 1840s, and 1850s were decades of an intensive anti-Catholic crusade in the English-speaking countries of the Western world. Nevertheless, in the Canadian Northwest, HBC administrators not only held no quarrel with the Catholic missionaries, they showered praise and money upon them, while experiencing strained relations with at least half of the Anglican missionaries. The arrival of six Wesleyan Methodist missionaries in the Northwest in 1840 brought no noticeable change to the quality of relations between Catholics and Protestants.

It is apparent that a spirit of harmony and friendship characterized relations between Catholic priests and HBC officers in the early nineteenth-century Northwest. The HBC took up where the North West Company and Lord Selkirk had left off, treating the Catholic missionaries with every courtesy, providing transport, lodging, and food, usually free of charge. The HBC even went so far as to build several Catholic chapels and cabins in the mission stations, pay a modest annual salary to the Catholic bishop at Red River, and make itself useful to the missionaries in several ways. The declarations of Governor George Simpson and others demonstrate that the HBC officers in Rupert's Land appreciated the presence of the Catholics and sought to make life as easy as possible for them. The Catholic missionaries earned this support by showing loyalty to the British Crown, by refraining from meddling in commercial and political matters, and by leading a frugal and austere life.

HBC officers in Rupert's Land had a very different attitude to the ministers of the Church of England, in spite of the fact that it was the HBC's board of directors, motivated by evangelical concerns, that had invited the Church of England clergymen into the country in the first place. Once on the scene in Red River, these British clergymen soon proved to be troublemakers. We know that John West returned home after three years, but only after having quarrelled with Governor Simpson and others. West's successor, David Jones, was better appreciated by Simpson, but in 1829 he antagonized his Presbyterian parishioners by publishing unflattering commentaries about them in a London journal. The Scots did not forget their pastor's back-stabbing. As for the Reverend William Cockran—he accused the Catholics of every sin under the sun, thereby stirring up controversy. On the Pacific coast, the reverends Beaver and Staines also proved most able at fomenting discord. Other Church of England ministers of this period—John Smithurst, for example—did likewise.

The different attitudes of the HBC officers in Rupert's Land in dealing with Catholic clergymen on the one hand and Church of England clergymen on the other cannot be explained on theological grounds: the company should have favoured its Anglican coreligionists and shunned their Catholic rivals. Nor can this behaviour be explained by the linguistic, cultural, or national identities of the clergymen: once again the company should have preferred the English Protestants to the French Catholics.

The HBC's hostility to the Church of England clergymen, and their converse amiability towards the Catholic priests, can best be explained by the personal qualities of the individual missionaries. The Catholic priests were not above reproach; nevertheless, they managed to win the respect and friendship of the HBC officers in Rupert's Land, while the Church of England ministers usually managed to earn their scorn and ridicule. The Catholic priests displayed greater flexibility in adjusting to the customs of the region, whether the marriage customs *à la façon du pays* or Sunday work, two issues that frequently proved explosive when Protestant ministers were around.

The Protestant ministers, who, with few exceptions, had been chosen and sent by the CMS, were not the cream of the Church of England missionary crop of the period. The CMS was primarily concerned with staffing its missions in the Far East, in India particularly; only the society's leftovers were sent to the Northwest—those candidates who were not considered of sufficient quality to be sent to the Indies. The CMS missionaries sent to Rupert's Land viewed anything and everything through the very peculiar and bigoted lenses of an uneducated, credulous, and evangelical Englishman. They tried to reproduce a little England in the Northwest; they proved to be incapable of constructive compromise and incapable of understanding that Rupert's Land was a land very different from their country of origin.

This same poor education and these same national characteristics became apparent in the attitude of the Church of England clergymen towards the Catholics. Protestant laymen like Lord Selkirk, George Simpson, and Alexander Ross could evaluate Catholic priests on their merits; on the basis of their daily experience, these men set aside the scurrilous accusations and calumnies that were current fare in the anti-Catholic literature of the times. The Protestant ministers were unable to do so.

While these factors may explain the often difficult relations between Church of England clerics and HBC officers, it is their evangelical theology that accounts for the ministers' consummate bigotry and prejudice against Catholic clergymen. Petty clerics like William Cockran revelled in repeating the calumnies trumpeted by the anti-Catholic tradition: for these evangelical Protestants a Catholic did not even qualify as a Christian and therefore could not attain salvation. Ironically, the medieval *extra ecclesiam nulla salus* (outside the Church there is no salvation) had come back to haunt the Catholics.

In the eyes of an evangelical Protestant, the Catholic was a tool of Satan, the slave of a system of superstition and oppression. These evangelical Protestants proved to be apostles of hatred and division, rather than of peace and reconciliation. Although the Catholic priests were not without fault, theirs was a milder and more innocuous form of bigotry. For example, the Reverend David Jones was furious in 1825 on learning that a Catholic carpenter in Red River had refused to work on the doors of an Anglican church under construction. According to Jones, the tradesman must have been forbidden by a priest to work on the construction of a heretical temple.

During the first twenty years of the Red River colony, Catholic and Anglican clergymen seldom crossed swords, for each worked in homogeneous and distinct linguistic and cultural communities. They rarely ventured outside the colony of Red River and met only occasionally, usually at the governor's table. Moreover, neither spoke the language of the other. Each served his own francophone-Catholic or anglophone-Protestant community, with little interest or concern with that of the other. Even as late as 1854, the Canadian Methodist visitor John Ryerson described the Red River colony as follows:

> The Roman Catholics and the Protestants are very nearly equal to each other in point of numbers. The former almost universally speak French, and the latter almost universally speak English. They are separated, too, by locality as well as by language, very few of the Roman Catholics being found among the Protestants, and still fewer Protestants among the Roman Catholics. Hence the two denominations live, as far as religion is concerned, in perfect harmony, without collision, and without proselytism.[11]

In fact, in the period preceding 1840 Catholic priests in Rupert's Land usually behaved as if the Protestant clergymen did not exist. They did not take them seriously, confident that they alone had the true religion, the Catholic one. The correspondence of the priests contains very few comments about the Protestant ministers, whereas the correspondence of the Protestant clergymen is shot through with sweeping and scurrilous attacks against the Catholics.

The first twenty years of Catholic–Protestant coexistence in Rupert's Land reflected tensions that were current elsewhere. Anti-Catholicism reared its ugly head, fuelled by the bigotry of petty English clergymen. Conversely, the anglophone Protestants who governed the country got along very well with the francophone Catholic clergymen. This early ecumenism was therefore the work of Protestant laymen and Catholic priests.

Skirmishes in Manitoba

Everything would change with the arrival of the Methodists in 1840, when Anglicans and Catholics challenged the monopoly that had been granted to Wesley's followers by the HBC. In fact, the battle pitted the Anglicans and the Methodists against the big, bad Catholics—for Methodists and Anglicans more often than not cooperated with one another.

It all started in 1840 when the Methodists established a mission at Rossville near Norway House and, with the support of the HBC, placed missionaries at Rainy Lake, Moose Factory, and Edmonton. In defiance of the HBC, which wanted to prevent Catholic priests from gaining access to these regions, in 1842 Bishop Provencher charged

Father Jean-Baptiste Thibault with founding a mission on the upper Saskatchewan River.

Also in 1842, Father Jean-Édouard Darveau undertook the first of his three annual missionary voyages to Duck Bay on Lake Manitoba, some 190 kilometres northwest of St. Boniface, a station first visited by Father Bellecourt in 1839 and 1840, then by Father Thibault in 1841. In 1843, Father Darveau went as far as The Pas on the lower Saskatchewan River. It is surely mere coincidence that 1842 was also the year in which the Church of England's Abraham Cowley, who had arrived from England the previous year, established a rival Anglican mission on the same Duck Bay (Partridge Crop).

Meanwhile, in 1840 the Métis schoolteacher and Anglican catechist Henry Budd[12] founded an Anglican mission post at The Pas, preparing the way for Reverend James Hunter,[13] who settled there in 1844. Simultaneously, the Catholic bishops of Canada were trying to obtain HBC authorization to found a Catholic mission on James Bay to compete with that of Methodist minister George Barnley. However, they were unsuccessful, Governor George Simpson arguing that every means had to be taken to avoid denominational rivalry in any part of Rupert's Land.

During the early 1840s, therefore, the situation of Catholic and Protestant missions was changing in Rupert's Land. In 1840, the six Methodist missionaries and the two Anglican clergymen (reverends Cockran and Smithurst) made up the contingent of eight Protestant ministers in the territory. They coexisted alongside Catholic Bishop Provencher and three priests[14] at Red River. The multiplication of mission stations that began in these early 1840s meant that the two groups of clergymen would cross swords more and more frequently. So it was that on 22 August 1842 when Abraham Cowley glimpsed a Catholic priest near his mission on Lake Manitoba he confided to his diary that the man (Father Darveau) seemed pleasant enough but that Cowley suspected him of opposing him (Cowley) by every means at his disposal.[15] Six months later, Cowley's colleague, William Cockran, warned him from Red River:

> The Romanists I assure you are the most dangerous enemies which you have to contend with. They will never stick to truth as far as you are concerned, they will think every means just that will defeat your purposes and oblige you to abandon your design.[16]

After having stayed overnight at Father Bellecourt's house in the village of St. Paul on the Assiniboine River, Cowley wrote in 1844 that "the miserable appearance" of the village formed "a wretched comment upon the system to which the villagers belong."[17] His colleague continued to warn both Cowley and his superiors in London that the Catholics threatened to surround them and to continue to pervert the Indians with their lies.

Thus daggers were drawn in the early 1840s. However, the Catholic priests, although less numerous, enjoyed distinct advantages. The fact that they were poorer worked in their favour in the eyes of the colony's leaders, who were Protestant for the most part. Eden Colville, associate governor of Rupert's Land, wrote to Sir George Simpson in 1851:

> I am sorry to hear that there is so much prejudice against Catholic missionaries, as I feel bound to say that in my opinion, they are much better fitted for missionaries in this country, than members of the English Church—from their self-denial, and the way they accommodate themselves to the circumstances of the country.[18]

The fact that Catholic missionaries accorded more importance to the learning of Indian languages also worked in their favour. Before 1840, Catholic priests did not distinguish themselves in this regard, since only fathers Thibault and Bellecourt had mastered Indian languages. However, after 1840, facility in the Indian languages was considered a necessity by most Catholic missionaries, the Oblates especially. Inhabitants of the Northwest came to acknowledge that the Catholic priest usually spoke the language of the people he sought to evangelize, while the Anglican or Methodist missionary usually had to rely on the services of an interpreter. This gave considerable comfort to the Catholics. In 1842, Bishop Provencher purred with satisfaction on noting that only Methodist missionary James Evans in Rossville could speak the Indian languages.[19] Anglican Reverend James Hunter, who arrived in the country in 1844, also learned the languages. However, Presbyterian Alexander Ross rubbed salt in the Anglican wound by writing that during the twenty years between John West's departure in 1823 and Abraham Cowley's arrival at Partridge Crop in 1842 no Protestant minister even attempted to move out of the white settlement at Red River in order to evangelize the Indians.[20]

Thus when Oblate Father Pierre Aubert and his subdeacon, Alexandre Taché, arrived in Red River in 1845, Catholic–Protestant rivalry was well entrenched in the Northwest. While the two groups coexisted peacefully, albeit separately, in Red River, they were on a war footing on Lake Manitoba and all along the North Saskatchewan River, at The Pas and Edmonton in particular; both parties led dogged contests at Rainy Lake and along the Winnipeg River—without, however, scoring any points under the heading of "conversions."

Skirmishes on the Saskatchewan River

Travelling up the Saskatchewan River from the Manitoba lakes, the first mission station one encountered was that of the Church of England at The Pas, staffed as of 1840 by Indian catechist Henry Budd. That is where CMS minister James Hunter was sent on his first appointment upon arriving from England in 1844. William Cockran[21] may have proved to be the leading Anglican apostle of intolerance before 1845, but in subsequent years he was matched in anti-Catholicism by the Reverend James Hunter. Fearing the visit of a Catholic priest (Louis-François Laflèche) in the summer of 1845, Hunter was hardly settled in at The Pas on 5 November 1844 when he chose to preach to his Indian and Métis people from the classic anti-Catholic text drawn from the Book of Revelation, dealing with the Whore of Babylon:

> I saw a woman sitting on a scarlet beast which was full of blasphemous names, and it had seven heads and ten horns. The woman was arrayed in purple and scarlet, and bedecked with gold and jewels and pearls, holding in her hand a golden cup full of abominations and the impurities of her fornication; and on her forehead was written a name of mystery: "Babylon the great, mother of harlots and of earth's abominations." And I saw the woman, drunk with the blood of the saints and the blood of the martyrs of Jesus. (17: 3–6)

After having sketched the history of popery and of the Protestant Reformation, Hunter pointed out to his parishioners that the Church of Rome fulfilled the biblical description of the Whore of Babylon in every respect. He stressed that flagrant contradictions existed between the Word of God and the doctrines, idolatry, and abominations of the Church of Rome.

The Reverend Hunter continued to write in this vein during subsequent years, the 1845 missionary journeys of Father Laflèche to The Pas and Father Thibault to Lake Athabasca only serving to provoke his ire. When Hunter and Budd heard that their erstwhile rival and others were headed for Île-à-la-Crosse in the summer of 1846, they sought to checkmate the priests by founding a rival Anglican mission at Lake La Ronge (Stanley Mission) on the Churchill River below Île-à-la-Crosse. However, the only personnel the CMS could afford to send there in 1846, to keep the "papists" in check, was the Indian catechist James Settee, a man without theological training. Settee was compelled to hold the fort for four years—that is, until 1850 when the Reverend Robert Hunt, newly arrived from England in 1849, was stationed at Stanley Mission as its first ordained resident missionary. The Catholic missionaries were nevertheless gaining ground over their Anglican rivals in these northern regions. As noted, from their base at Île-à-la-Crosse the Catholics had already founded the mission of the La Nativité on Lake Athabasca (1849) near Fort Chipewyan; this became another resident mission station, which, in addition to those of Lake St. Anne and Île-à-la-Crosse, allowed Catholic missionaries to range far and wide in the surrounding countryside.

This Catholic expansion into the Northwest was a prime concern of the Reverend James Hunter at The Pas and of Métis catechist James Settee at Lake La Ronge. Both knew that the Indian people tended to remain loyal to the church of the first missionary who worked among them. That is why the regions of The Pas and Lake La Ronge were largely Protestant, in striking contrast to Île-à-la-Crosse and Lake Athabasca, which had become, or were becoming, largely Catholic. Hunter went so far as to write that the Indians of these regions would gladly receive any religious teacher, that they were unaware of the differences between the Catholic Church and the Church of England,[22] the religion of the French and the religion of the English.

Hunter was doubly concerned because the new CMS mission near the trading post at Lake La Ronge was a commercial satellite of the HBC trading post at Île-à-la-Crosse, and was located halfway between The Pas and Île-à-la-Crosse. The priests had therefore managed to seize a pivotal station in northern Saskatchewan. In his instructions to Settee in July 1846, Hunter advised his catechist to warn the Indians of some of the essential differences between the churches of Rome and of England in order to prevent the propagation of "popery" and of its doctrines that were so destructive of souls. Time and again, Hunter begged his superiors in London to send more ministers in order to oppose "popish" propaganda; he was disappointed at their lack of constructive response. He was even more disappointed in 1848 when he learned that a third Catholic priest, Father Henri Faraud, was on his way to Île-à-la-Crosse, with a probable view to proceeding as far as Lake Athabasca. Until his departure from the mission at The Pas in 1854, Hunter continued to preach the necessity of appointing more ministers to Rupert's Land; he acknowledged in the same breath the zeal and manifest activity of the Church of Rome, which nevertheless preached error and idolatry.[23]

Again and again, Hunter denounced the ignorance, idolatry, and obscurantism of the Church of Rome, a corrupt and dangerous church that all too often seduced the poor Indians. Hunter's dictums served to reinforce the prejudice of the CMS directors in London, particularly in the wake of the 1850 controversy surrounding the restoration of the

Catholic hierarchy in England, the "papal aggression controversy." These Anglican evangelicals feared the aggressivity of the Catholics, all the while respecting their devotion and self-denial.[24]

The Anglican contingent was reinforced by the arrival of the Methodists after 1840, but the only one of the six Methodist ministers in the field to have to contend with a rival Catholic missionary resident in his territory was Robert Rundle in Fort Edmonton. Although Rundle remained unchallenged during the first two years of his ministry, in the summer of 1842 Father Thibault arrived and remained active in the area for many years thereafter.

Robert Rundle, like his Wesleyan Methodist colleagues, displayed all the hatred and rancour of a nineteenth-century evangelical Protestant against the "Romanists." In the spring of 1841, when he was still the only Christian missionary in Alberta, he wrote prophetically:

> The Roman Catholics are... casting a jealous eye over the plains of the Saskatchewan; I not only want to rescue...[the Indians] from the strongholds of heathenism but also to save them from the fascinations and abominations of the Church of Rome.[25]

Two years later, Rundle commented on Thibault's 1842 visit:

> The priest left last autumn for Red River... after having succeeded in beguiling away very many from the simplicity of the gospel. The greater part, however consisted of half castes of French descent, many of whom are [as] deeply rooted in popish superstition as the Canadiens themselves.[26]

On 6 January 1844, while Thibault was wintering at Frog Lake, Rundle remarked to James Evans that Fort Edmonton was "a hotbed of Popery."

Throughout his eight years in the western plains, Rundle railed against the vices and abominations of popery. He wondered when the Catholic system of "lying vanities" would end. He found that most of the HBC employees, especially the Métis, were of Catholic origin and naturally gravitated to Thibault. This rendered posts like Fort Edmonton, Fort Pitt, and Fort Carlton hotbeds of Romanism. The HBC post at Lesser Slave Lake, which had given him such encouragement since 1841, had mostly reverted to the Catholic fold as soon as Father Thibault began visiting in 1842. In sum, the Methodist mission was being decimated by the rallying of the Métis to the faith of their fathers.

Although Robert Rundle never changed his views on Catholicism, views that were fed by the centuries-old anti-Catholicism of

England, we shall see that, strange as it may seem, he did develop some friendships among the few Catholic priests who crossed his path in Alberta.

By the middle of the nineteenth century, when the Oblates were just getting their missionary campaigns off the ground, Catholic and Protestant clergymen had locked horns whenever and wherever they shared a common territory. In the case of Red River, the conflict was minimal, given that both groups served distinct constituencies. On the Saskatchewan River, where they competed for the hearts and minds of the Métis and Indian people, they began crossing swords. In the Mackenzie basin, an area penetrated simultaneously by CMS and Oblate pathfinders, they clashed openly and vigorously.

Notes

1. This section closely resembles my "Les rapports entre catholiques et protestants dans le Nord-Ouest du Canada avant 1840," in Raymond Huel (ed.), *Western Oblate Studies 1/Études oblates de l'Ouest 1*, which constituted an initial study of this portion of my book.

2. J.-O. Plessis, Instructions to Provencher and Dumoulin, Québec, 20 April 1818, in Grace Lee Nute, p. 59.

3. 5 June 1824. 3M4, D4/7. HBC papers, NAC.

4. 22 August 1825. 3M4, D4/7. HBC papers, NAC.

5. J.-N. Provencher to A. Dionne, St. Boniface, 17 July 1826 and 1 July 1829, *Les Cloches de Saint-Boniface* 31, 4 (April 1932): 88–92, 93–94.

6. Selkirk to J.-O. Plessis, 30 December 1819. Cited in Nute, pp. 257–8.

7. Alexander Ross, p. 181.

8. "The Anglican Church and the Disintegration of Red River Society, 1818–1870," in Francis and Palmer, *The Prairie West*, p. 101. See also by the same author: "The Churches and the Social Structure of the Pre-1870 Canadian West," unpublished Ph.D. dissertation, Queen's University, 1973; "The Historiography of the Red River Settlement, 1830–1868," *Prairie Forum* 6, 1 (Spring 1981): 75–85; "Protestant Agricultural Missions in the Canadian West to 1870," unpublished M.A. dissertation, University of Alberta, 1970, 140 pp. The substance of Pannekoek's argument is found in his recent *A Snug Little Flock*.

9. W. Cockran to the secretary of the CMS, Red River, 29 July 1826. CMS Mission books, reel A-77, NAC.

10. William Cockran, *Journal*, 30 September 1833. MG 17, Class C, C.1/M.2, reel A-77, p. 14. NAC.

11. John Ryerson, p. 71.

12. See T.C.B. Boon, "Budd, Henry," *DCB* 10, pp. 108–9; Katherine Pettipas (ed.).

13. See Bruce Peel, "Hunter, James," *DCB* 11, pp. 480–2.

14. Fathers G.-A. Bellecourt, J.-B. Thibault, and J.-A. Mayrand.

15. MG 17, Class C, C.1/M.3, p. 211. NAC.

16. Cited in A. Cowley, *Journal*. MG 17, Class C, C.1/M.3, p. 226. NAC.

17. 18 March 1844, in A. Cowley, *Journal*. MG 17, Class C, C.1/M.3, p. 226. NAC.

18. 14 July 1851. Cited in James C. Macgregor, p. 57.

19. J.-N. Provencher to J. Signay, St. Boniface, 30 June 1842. *Bulletin de la Société historique de Saint-Boniface* 3 (1913): 204.

20. A. Ross, p. 303.

21. See J.E. Foster, "Cockran, William," *DCB* 9, pp. 134–7.

22. James Hunter, *Journal*, 16 June 1846. MG 17, Class C, C.1/M.4. NAC.

23. J. Hunter to H. Venn, Cumberland Station, 6 December 1852. MG 17, Class C, C.1/M.5. NAC.

24. See Eugene Stock, pp. 9, 320.

25. Cited in William Howard Brooks, "Methodism," p. 38.

26. 24 May 1843, cited ibid., p. 40.

CHAPTER VII

THE BATTLE OF THE MACKENZIE

IN 1858, while Father D'Herbomez was moving his headquarters to Victoria, his Oblate colleagues in the northern prairies had just reinforced their central supply station at Lake La Biche with more personnel (1855). They had also opened the resident mission of St. Joseph (1858) near Fort Resolution on Great Slave Lake, the inland sea located 1,000 kilometres north of Île-à-la-Crosse and 400 kilometres north of Lake Athabasca. The Oblates would spend the next half century engaging the Anglican adversary in the vast and desolate land of the Northwest and Yukon territories.

Grollier versus Hunter and Kirkby

Oblate Father Henri Grollier was stationed at the most distant Oblate outpost of St. Joseph that same year. There he learned that Archdeacon James Hunter, pastor since 1855 of the Church of England parish of St. Andrews at Grand Rapids on the Red River, was aboard a Hudson's Bay Company (HBC) barge and headed for Fort Simpson, intent on founding a permanent mission there. Fort Simpson was the HBC headquarters in the Mackenzie basin, a vast territory of more than 2,600,000 square kilometres, fully one quarter the size of today's Canada. The race was on, Hunter having been impelled on his journey by the threat of rapidly advancing Catholic mission stations, while Grollier was determined that the Protestants not be given an opportunity to "corrupt" the Indians with their false doctrines.

Sisters of Charity and girls of orphanage and boarding school at
St. Joseph mission at Fort Resolution clean and prepare fish for storage
during winter.

In November 1857, Hunter had asked Bishop Anderson for authorization to visit Fort Simpson the following year, with a view to establishing a permanent Church of England mission there, thereby "opening up" the area for Anglican missionary operations. While informing Church Missionary Society (CMS) secretary Henry Venn of his plans, Hunter wrote:

> At Cumberland [The Pas] we drove out the priests. They are now gone beyond us into the Isle à la Crosse and Athabasca districts, and six priests have arrived here [Red River] this autumn, some of whom will no doubt enter the Mackenzie River district next summer. We must endeavour to outflank them, and take possession of Fort Simpson... Thus if the priests attempt to go beyond us again, we shall drive them into the Arctic sea. I propose... to go alone... I shall leave... in June next, and be absent for about a year and a half.[1]

Having obtained Governor Simpson's authorization for the trip, at HBC expense, Hunter set out on company boats in early June 1858. He travelled from Red River via Portage la Loche, Lake Athabasca, and Great Slave Lake, arriving at Fort Simpson on 16 August. On the boats, he was not overly surprised to find himself in the company of two Oblate priests (Isidore Clut and Germain Eynard) and two Oblate brothers (Joseph Patrick Kearney and Jean Pérréard); Clut and Kearney were going to the Lake Athabasca mission to join Father Faraud, while Eynard and Pérréard were en route to Great Slave Lake to join Father

Grollier at that most distant Catholic mission. As he crossed the twenty-kilometre Portage la Loche, Hunter pleaded with CMS secretary Henry Venn to send at least two missionaries to the area, all the while brandishing the spectre of the Church of Rome. He commented:

> I deeply regret that we have delayed so long and allowed Isle à la Crosse, Athabasca and Fort Resolution... to be occupied by the Church of Rome. The latter has only been occupied this year, and at each of these places the Church of Rome had doubled her staff by sending in a priest to each this year. There are now or will be in a few weeks two priests at each of these three stations; and if I had not made the effort and entered the district this year, Mackenzie River would also have been occupied by them... We have taken the priests, I think, rather by surprise.[2]

Surprised at this expedition by the portly Archdeacon Hunter, Fort Resolution's short and rotund Father Henri Grollier reacted instantaneously. He joined the same boat brigade, determined to prevent his Protestant rival from claiming the Mackenzie unchallenged. So it was that on 16 August 1858 a Church of England archdeacon and a Catholic priest set foot in Fort Simpson at the same time.

Hunter enjoyed a decided advantage, however, for not only were the HBC officers of the Mackenzie district Protestant almost to a man, but the newly appointed officer for the district was Bernard Rogan Ross, Hunter's brother-in-law, who also happened to strongly favour Protestant missions.

Having pre-empted the Catholics, Hunter hoped to be left in peace to develop his missions. But the scrappy Grollier would not hear of it. The Oblate was given a cool reception and so only stayed a few days at Fort Simpson, but he nevertheless served notice to Hunter that he had a fight on his hands. Moreover, Eden Colville and the HBC Committee in London, at the request of Bishop Taché, had already authorized the founding of a Catholic mission at Fort Good Hope on the lower Mackenzie, as well as a Catholic presence in the territory. Hunter was incensed. He wrote to Ross, accusing the Oblates not only of disloyalty for competing with the Protestant missions, but of harbouring anti-British sentiments as well.

> There are not only religious but also national differences, propagated amongst the servants and Indians... Here in British possessions, the English name is held up to ridicule and contempt.[3]

Ross reacted immediately to the alleged ungentlemanly and un-Christian conduct on the part of Grollier, as well as his anti-English behaviour. "I feel deeply hurt at our common country being held up as a mark for reproach and scorn by alien priests of a hostile superstition."[4]

Chief Trader Ross immediately organized a petition by the HBC officers of the Mackenzie district, asking the HBC to withdraw permission for the Catholics to establish missions at forts Simpson and Good Hope. The reasons advanced for their opposition were that since the traders in the area were all Protestant, only Protestant missions should be favoured, and that the "alien French priests" were responsible for imposing on the Indians "a system... of anti-English feeling and Protestant damnation."[5]

Hunter was pleased. Within a week of arriving in Fort Simpson, he had witnessed the departure of Father Grollier and the signing of a petition by HBC officers against the Catholics. Jovial and self-satisfied, he headed up the Liard River to spend three weeks at Fort Liard, only to discover, upon his return to Fort Simpson, that the priests had already been at work at forts Dunvegan and Vermilion on the Peace River,[6] and they had made "little scruple of the means they employed for the attainment of their purposes."[7]

While Hunter wintered at Fort Simpson (1858–59), his nemesis was at his St. Joseph mission near Fort Resolution, sharpening his anti-Protestant spear. Grollier first crossed the vast inland sea to establish a Catholic station in the wilds of Fort Rae (March 1859), just as he had done at Fond du Lac on Lake Athabasca in 1853. Then, once the Mackenzie was free of ice, the crusading little priest headed downriver, past forts Simpson and Norman, to establish the Catholic mission of Our Lady of Good Hope (31 August 1859) above the Arctic Circle, a station that would thereafter be his base of operations until his premature death from asthma in 1864. It was from his base at Fort Good Hope that, in 1860, Grollier first went down the Mackenzie River and up the Peel River to Fort McPherson, where he began to evangelize the Loucheux Indians.

Upon his return to Red River in the summer of 1859, Archdeacon Hunter discovered that HBC Governor Simpson had dismissed his anti-Catholic petition. All was not lost, however, for Hunter oversaw the ordination and appointment of his St. Andrews schoolteacher and deacon, William Kirkby, as resident missionary at Fort Simpson. Bishop Taché described Kirkby as neither a giant nor a gentleman, but a man with an iron will and great daring. He was the sole Church of England missionary in the Mackenzie district between 1859 and 1862, with the arrival of Robert McDonald. However, McDonald took up station at the distant Fort Yukon (1862–71) and Fort McPherson (1871–1904). In effect, Kirkby remained alone to carry the Church of England standard in the Mackenzie basin until William Carpenter Bompas arrived in 1865.

We have seen that Henri Grollier was at best a difficult person, a man who appears to have lived with a perpetual scowl on both his face and his personality. The Protestants were high on his list of targets.

A lengthy letter by Grollier to Bishop Taché, dated 20 July 1860, gives the measure of the man. From his base at Fort Good Hope, Father Grollier journeyed up the Mackenzie River to arrive in Fort Norman on 5 June 1860. He picked up his pen to defend himself against the calumnies of the "Orangeman" B.R. Ross, who had apparently accused Grollier of arrogance, "Satan's emissary" having been the Reverend Kirkby, who was responsible for the accusations. Grollier proceeded to write a diatribe of more than ten pages against Kirkby, his schoolmaster at Fort Norman, John Hope, and Protestants in general. He declared that the Indian people of Fort Norman were impossible to convert, while Protestant ministers and their followers were capable of anything. "What is lacking in our missions is the blood of martyrs... I believe that an Englishman and a savage are perfectly identical."[8] Protestantism made no demands, wrote Grollier, except that of naming "God"; it was a school of hypocrisy. And Indians were a hopeless, faithless people.

Responding to Bishop Taché's judgement that Grollier's letters showed fanaticism, the missionary declared that his kind of fanaticism was necessary in dealing with Protestant ministers; otherwise Catholics would pay a severe penalty—for Protestant ministers, traders, and merchants were perpetrating a system of open persecution against Catholics.

> In persecuting us as Catholics, it is a question of nationality that they are primarily concerned with... I truly believe that in all justice, God must have England broken by France. Otherwise, the whole world is doomed; England with its corrupting gold will bury everything in Protestantism... I hope that if such a war takes place the Anglican missions will receive a death blow.[9]

Clearly, Henri Grollier was not a man for compromise or accommodation. The Reverend Kirkby discovered this on 5 June 1860, when he proposed to Grollier a *modus vivendi* in the missions, whereby each would recognize the other's sphere of influence and agree not to encroach on the other's territory. Grollier refused. Kirkby then suggested that they offer each other room and board, Kirkby making his house and table available to Grollier when he visited Fort Simpson if the priest would reciprocate at Good Hope. Grollier refused anew. He was engaged in a war to the finish against English Protestantism in the Mackenzie district.

Until his death at Good Hope in 1864, Henri Grollier continued to spend amazing amounts of energy expounding against the Protestants and against his own colleagues. He uttered the usual strictures upon Protestants, the Reverend Kirkby in particular, suggesting that what he needed was a few good kicks in the rear end.

By 1860, in spite of regional HBC opposition, the Catholic priests seemed to have gained the advantage over their Church of England rivals in the Mackenzie district. As had been the case at Red River and on the plains, this advantage resulted from a variety of factors: the Métis employees' predilection for French-speaking and Catholic ministers, the priority given by Oblate missionaries to learning aboriginal languages, and, not least, the greater abnegation of the Oblate missionary. Indeed, upon James Hunter's return to Red River in 1859, no less a personage than Bishop David Anderson commented: "Romanism gains, her priests penetrate, because they carry nothing. Send us the one [minister] who will be content to travel with a single box or at most a couple."[10] It would seem that the Oblate vow of poverty was paying dividends. During the 1860s, the Reverend Kirkby regularly reported on the progressive Catholic occupation of the best sites for mission stations. Hunter himself added: "The priests have the language, and this gives them a great hold upon the Indians... [In Mackenzie River] we are losing the golden opportunity."[11]

One explanation for Catholic ascendancy in the Mackenzie valley after 1860 is the simple law of numbers. They were sending more missionaries into the area than were the Protestants. Moreover, the Catholic missionaries had a resident bishop in their midst as of 1860, when Vital Grandin returned following his consecration in Europe.

Thus beginning in 1858 the Oblates founded mission stations down the more than 1,300 kilometres of the Mackenzie River below Great Slave Lake. Although Fort Simpson became a primarily Anglican mission, with resident minister, the Oblates visited annually, while establishing their own permanent stations at Fort Good Hope on the lower Mackenzie (1859) and Providence on the upper river (1862). It was from Good Hope and Providence that, during the 1860s, a long series of new mission outposts was established at places like forts Dunvegan and Vermilion on the Peace River, Fort Rae on Great Slave Lake, forts Liard and Halkett on the Liard River, Fort Norman on the Mackenzie, Fort Franklin on Great Bear Lake, Fort McPherson on the northerly Peel River, La Pierre House, and Fort Yukon on the Yukon and Porcupine rivers. Over the years some of these outposts would become permanent mission stations.

The Battle of the Mackenzie

In 1860, Bishop Anderson of Red River had one Church of England missionary (Kirkby) in the Mackenzie basin; a second (McDonald) arrived in 1862 and headed for Fort Yukon. By 1860, the Catholics had one resident bishop (Grandin) in the territory, while a second (Faraud) was in place in 1865 and another (Clut) in 1866. Oblate headquarters in Marseilles and Paris conducted their race for the northern sea using bases at Fort Chipewyan on Lake Athabasca (La Nativité mission), Fort Resolution (St. Joseph mission) on the south shore of Great Slave Lake, Providence on the upper Mackenzie, and Fort Good Hope, more than 1,100 kilometres down the Mackenzie River. There was at least one priest, usually two or more, stationed at each of these posts, sometimes assisted by one or more religious brothers who served as the post's handymen, hunters, and fishermen. During the 1860s, additional resident Catholic missions were established at Fort Liard on the Liard River (1863) and Fort Dunvegan on the Peace River (1867). A chain of other stations was also visited by the missionaries on a seasonal or occasional basis.

From his base at Fort Simpson, the Reverend Kirkby earnestly endeavoured to best his Catholic rivals, but he was outnumbered from the outset. From his new mission at Fort Good Hope, Father Henri Grollier visited Fort Norman midway between forts Simpson and Good Hope, spending two months there in the summer of 1860; Kirkby had preceded him, however. Grollier then travelled to Fort Simpson and joined forces with Father Zéphirin Gascon,[12] who had come from Fort Resolution after earlier evangelizing the Indians of Fort Rae. On the orders of Bishop Grandin, who had learned that Kirkby planned to visit Fort Liard, the two priests went up the Liard River to Fort Liard, arriving in September 1860, only days before Fort Simpson's Protestant minister arrived to resume Hunter's mission of 1858. After two weeks of mission work, Grollier, Gascon, and Kirkby travelled back to Fort Simpson together, Gascon going on to Fort Resolution. However, in March 1861 Bishop Grandin sent Gascon back up to Fort Liard, having again gotten wind of Kirkby's plans to do likewise. The Catholic priest and Protestant minister made the twelve-day voyage by snowshoe and dog team together; it was effected without their speaking a word to each other, both having taken the gloves off in their competition for the allegiance of Fort Liard's aboriginal people.

During the forty-five days that Kirkby and Gascon worked at Fort Liard (7 April to 22 May 1861), Kirkby was assisted by the postmaster—whose Métis wife helped Gascon—who reported that he was gaining ground on his nemesis. They returned to Fort Simpson together, and

Oblate brother with trout
caught in Great Slave Lake near
Fort Resolution.

Missionary on Great Slave Lake
removing his catch from net
with his teeth.

Indian woman ice-fishing on Great Slave Lake.

Oblate brother hauling his wood out of the bush, using a dog team.

Missionaries cutting wood in the bush. Wood was cut during the winter months to allow for drying during the following spring and summer, before being used as fuel.

Firewood accumulated at Fort Resolution before being stored.

after only four days of rest Kirkby boarded HBC barges once more, to descend the Mackenzie River. He was heading out on his longest voyage yet, visiting forts Norman, Good Hope, McPherson, Yukon, and Lapierre House, the latter four trading posts having never been visited by a Protestant minister. While Father Grollier had visited Fort McPherson in 1860 from his base at Good Hope, no Catholic priest had yet set foot at the more distant Lapierre House and Fort Yukon.

While the Reverend Kirkby sailed down the Mackenzie, Bishop Grandin undertook his own protracted missionary journey in the region. In the company of a thirteen-year-old boy who served as his cook and servant, Grandin left Fort Chipewyan by canoe on 1 July 1861, spending eighteen days at Fort Resolution and another eight days at the missionary outpost of Big Island on Great Slave Lake, another HBC trading post. Always acknowleging the hospitality and friendliness of the vast majority of HBC officers, Grandin regretted that he was now compelled to speak to the Indians against Protestantism, thereby occasionally provoking some unpleasantness. Descending the Mackenzie River, Grandin chose the site for the mission of Providence, which he intended to develop into the Oblate central mission station on the Mackenzie. While there, he received a letter from the Church of England minister at Lake La Ronge, Robert Hunt, applauding the fall of the Antichrist and foretelling the triumph of Protestantism and the ruin of Catholicism. Grandin thought these feelings had been provoked by the fires that had destroyed the Catholics' St. Boniface establishment in December 1860 and spring 1861.

Ice floes at breakup at Fort Providence on the Mackenzie.

After spending a week at Fort Simpson (14 to 21 August 1861), Grandin and Gascon went up to Fort Liard (mission of St. Raphael), whence Gascon proceeded further upriver to Fort Halkett before returning to Fort Liard and wintering there. Father Gascon wrote of the hospitality provided by Postmaster William Lucas Hardisty, who remained nonetheless a staunch Protestant. Meanwhile, Bishop Grandin returned to Fort Simpson, where the chief trader, also a Protestant and a supporter of Kirkby, nevertheless proved to be very hospitable. On 30 September, the bishop re-embarked on his journey down the Mackenzie, stopping at Fort Norman (mission of St. Theresa). On 9 October 1861, he arrived at Fort Good Hope, where the sickly Grollier had been joined, since the preceding August, by Father Jean Séguin and Brother Patrick Kearney. There the bishop stayed for three months (9 October 1861 to 9 January 1862), experiencing first-hand regular daily temperatures of minus forty and minus forty-five degrees Fahrenheit. He then ascended the ice-bound Mackenzie to Fort Norman, where he worked from 20 January to 6 March 1862 before returning to Fort Resolution via Fort Simpson. While at Good Hope, always conscious of his Protestant rival, Kirkby, who was scheduled to go north again after the ice broke up, Grandin had ordered Séguin to attend to

Beach landing at Fort Providence.

the more northerly posts of Fort McPherson, Lapierre House, and Fort Yukon. On Holy Saturday 1862, the priest obediently hitched up his dog team and, leaving Grollier and Kearney at Good Hope, undertook the 500-kilometre trip to Peel River.

At Fort McPherson, Séguin initially reported very positive results in his mission to the Loucheux[13] Indians. Kirkby arrived there on 22 June but, in Séguin's opinion, was welcomed by the Indians only to the extent that they could obtain tobacco from him. When the Reverend Kirkby continued onwards to Lapierre House the next day, Séguin accompanied him. After four days of very difficult overland travel, the clergymen arrived to find that the postmaster at Lapierre House favoured Kirkby, who had visited the post the preceding year. Séguin attributed Kirkby's success with the local Loucheux Indians not only to his generosity with tobacco, but also to his spreading rumours to the effect that Séguin, and other Catholic missionaries as well, secretly kept several wives. When Kirkby proceeded onwards to Fort Yukon, Séguin returned to Peel River and Good Hope, arriving on 3 August 1862 after an absence of more than three months.

There Father Séguin received a letter from Bishop Grandin ordering him to travel to Fort Yukon in the company of a new Protestant minister, Robert McDonald, who had just arrived from Red River. Therefore, on 3 September 1862, while Kirkby had just returned to Fort Simpson, Séguin again descended the Mackenzie River, ascended the Peel, and then crossed the mountains to finally reach Fort Yukon on 23 September.

According to Séguin, both Kirkby's and McDonald's success with the Loucheux at the three posts along the way was a result of their generosity with tobacco, a substance that the Indians could not easily do without. At Fort Yukon, McDonald's success was even more manifest, Father Séguin complaining that he did not manage to gain a single Indian to his cause. He invoked the usual explanation of gifts of tobacco, plus the fact that this was the third visit by a Protestant minister to Lapierre House and Fort Yukon, whereas no Catholic priest had ever been there. Also, it seems that a Canadian Métis, who served as interpreter at Fort Yukon, sided with the Protestant minister and arranged to have all the local Indians flock to his banner. Given Séguin's ignorance of the language of these Tukudh Indians, he was hamstrung. He wintered at Fort Yukon in loneliness, his desolation exacerbated by the arrival, in the fall of 1862, of the Reverend Robert McDonald, a man who would make of Fort Yukon his residence for the next nine years. Indeed, the Amerindians of the Yukon and Peel areas, the Tukudh and the Loucheux, would prove the Church Missionary

Society's most promising field of missionary endeavour in the Northwest.

While the Séguin–McDonald saga unfolded in the remote Northwest, Kirkby had returned "south" to Fort Simpson, only to find that Father Gascon had decided to raid Kirkby's own mission station. In the latter part of 1862, Gascon visited various Indian homes at the post, singing Catholic hymns, much to Kirkby's horror. Kirkby began to watch the priest and to follow him, trying to "outsing" him while accusing him of breaking the rules of civilized religious warfare by attempting to convert Protestant Indians.

Protestant and Catholic missionaries clashed wherever they met. Each watched his adversary closely, reminding himself of the other's limitations and weaknesses, real or imagined. Thus Bishop Grandin and fathers Séguin, Grollier, and Petitot reminded their correspondents that the Reverend Kirkby had been a mere stableboy before transforming himself into a schoolteacher, and then a minister. As for Robert McDonald, he had been a Red River brewer before coming to the Northwest and being ordained.

In fact, as had been the case at Red River since 1820, individual clergymen sent by the CMS experienced a significant increase in status and income when they came to Rupert's Land. Nevertheless, after five years in the Mackenzie basin, Kirkby still did not speak the aboriginal languages and still worked through an interpreter, which did not help his cause. According to Grandin, the fact that Kirkby was married further handicapped him, because the aboriginal people considered him as a "man of a woman," like themselves, rather than a "man of God." Séguin argued similarly that Kirkby's wife and children were a considerable bonus for the Catholic cause. This was no doubt the reason for Kirkby's allegations that the Catholic missionaries had several wives.

Every missionary spoke of his encounters with either the "man of sin" or the "minister of error." One example of the clash between priest and minister was the encounter between William Kirkby and Émile Petitot at Fort Resolution in July 1863. Since his arrival in the Mackenzie basin in 1862, the Oblate Petitot had been stationed at St. Joseph Mission near Fort Resolution, where he studied the Athapascan languages with a view to evangelizing the Indians in the summer of 1863. Upon the arrival of the Indians at the post in June 1863, Petitot undertook his mission. Between morning and evening sermons in the native language, he taught reading and catechism to the children, heard confessions, taught hymns and prayers, and instructed his people in Catholic doctrines. After a few weeks of this routine, on 2 July 1863 the

Running rapids in a river barge on the Mackenzie.

Reverend Kirkby arrived on the HBC barges that went from Fort Simpson to Portage la Loche. The minister immediately called the Indian people together and began reading the Bible to them. When Petitot learned that a "wolf had stuck its nose into his sheepfold,"[14] he was consumed by a fever and could no longer eat nor sleep. The Oblate moved from his neighbouring mission to Fort Resolution, called the Indian people together, and proceeded to refute point by point the teachings of the Protestant minister, including Kirkby's attack on the Catholic belief in the Virgin. While thus engaged, Petitot broke down in tears before his Amerindian audience; the sobbing priest so impressed his flock that they allegedly gave no more credence to Kirkby, in spite of his promises of generous gifts of tobacco. According to Petitot, the Athapascans then lit their pipes with the prayerbooks distributed by Kirkby, while retaining their beads and Catholic hymns— much to Petitot's satisfaction. After Kirkby's departure, Petitot continued his missions around Great Slave Lake until he was ordered to replace the deceased Grollier at Good Hope in 1864.

William Carpenter Bompas versus the Oblates

While the CMS's Robert McDonald served his Loucheux and Tukudh people for fully forty-two years from his stations at Fort Yukon and Fort McPherson, and while the Oblates' own Émile Petitot served several outposts from his base at Fort Good Hope, there arrived in the region the most celebrated of the Church of England's Arctic missionaries. From his newly established mission station on Great Bear Lake, Petitot noted the arrival of William Carpenter Bompas on 15 April 1866:

> a tall, dry, and cartilagenous minister of the pure Gospel, the third of his species currently travelling in these Arctic wastes. He is gifted with an angelic mien, a celestial look, a honeyed and cooing voice, and is infused with science. He reads the Bible in Greek, and burns with an ardent zeal, over-excited with the idea that he has received a special divine mission to extricate the poor Indians from the fangs of the priests.[15]

The Church of England was launching its best effort at evening the score with the Catholics.

The work of Bompas during his early missionary years has already been noted.[16] Although raised a Baptist, he was confirmed in the Church of England in 1858, made a deacon in 1859, and ordained a priest by Bishop Machray in 1865. The CMS recruited him that same year and sent him to Rupert's Land to replace Robert McDonald at Fort Yukon. It took him four years to get there.

Upon his arrival at Fort Simpson on 25 December 1865, Bompas met William Kirkby, the only CMS missionary in the territory other than Robert McDonald. Fort Simpson's was the only chapel, as it still was in 1874. However, by 1885 eleven men were at work, manning ten missionary stations, six of which had churches. This upsurge in personnel and churches followed Bompas's consecration in 1874 as first bishop of the new diocese of Athabasca–Mackenzie.

From the outset, in 1865, Bompas had decided not to replace Robert McDonald at Fort Yukon, choosing instead to become an itinerant missionary in the Mackenzie area. During the next few years—in fact until the end of 1873, when he left for England to be made a bishop—Bompas travelled from one remote post to another (forts Norman, Franklin [Great Bear Lake], Rae, Resolution, Chipewyan, Simpson, Liard, Vermilion, Dunvegan, McPherson, and Yukon). He spent most of the year 1867–68 at Fort Chipewyan, and the year 1868–69 at Fort Simpson replacing Kirkby, who had left for England on furlough.

When the new missionary, the Reverend Reeve, arrived in Fort Simpson in 1869, Bompas began the first of his journeys to the distant Yukon. After spending one year at Fort Yukon (1869–70), he returned to the Mackenzie, via Peel River, and wintered at Fort Vermilion on the Peace River (1871–72). At the request of the CMS, he again journeyed to Fort Yukon in the fall of 1872 to replace Robert McDonald, who had moved to Peel River the previous year. During his stay (1872–73) at that remote trading post on the Porcupine River, near its junction with the Yukon,[17] Bompas learned that he was to be made bishop of the new diocese of Athabasca–Mackenzie. He thereupon left for England in the early months of 1874, was consecrated and married in May 1874, and was back in Fort Simpson in August.

Upon taking over his new diocese of Athabasca–Mackenzie, Bompas became responsible for the evangelization of an immense territory inhabited by some 10,000 people, half of whom were Catholic, another 3,000 Anglican, and the remainder not Christian. Shortly before calling his first diocesan synod at Fort Simpson in September 1876, the bishop had three catechists and one schoolmaster under his supervision, in addition to the reverends McDonald, Reeve, and Shaw. These clergymen were respectively entrusted with the missions at forts McPherson, Simpson, and Chipewyan; Bishop Bompas himself resided at Fort Simpson when not travelling. In addition, three other mission stations (Fort Norman, Hay River on Great Slave Lake, and Rampart House) were placed in the hands of resident catechists William Norn, Hardisty, and

Kenneth McDonald, while the schoolteacher, Alfred Garrioch, worked at Fort Chipewyan.[18] After 1875, Bompas succeeded in increasing the number of his mission stations, founding posts at Fort Rae on Great Slave Lake, Fort Dunvegan, and Fort Vermilion on the Peace River. At Fort Dunvegan, where the Oblates had had a resident missionary since 1867, Bishop Bompas managed to establish a resident missionary and begin a large farming operation in 1879.

The Church of England's farm at Fort Dunvegan was described by Catholic Bishop Émile Grouard in 1893. It was a model farm whose purpose was to teach the Indian people agricultural skills, and consequently generously funded by the government of Canada. Vast fields had been cleared, ploughed, sown, and harvested with the use of state-of-the-art machinery. A flour mill operated at full capacity alongside a prosperous herd of cattle and other farm animals. The mission's school was so successful that many Catholics enrolled their children there, in spite of the existence of a neighbouring Catholic mission that sought to compete.[19] Bishop Grouard reported that 500 kilometres down the Peace River at Fort Vermilion the Church of England had a similarly prosperous establishment. Indeed, by 1893 Vermilion had become the see of the Church of England's diocese of Athabasca.

Bompas constantly sought new clergy for his growing number of mission stations, and he was never satisfied with the number of men the CMS sent him. By the late 1880s, in his reduced diocese of Mackenzie River, north of the 60th parallel, Bompas had eight clergymen and four teachers and catechists running ten mission stations. He was disappointed by the defections of some of his men, the Reverend Shaw and the catechist Kenneth McDonald, for example,[20] but others were soon obtained to replace them.

During his eight years as an itinerant missionary in the Athabasca–Mackenzie region, and his subsequent thirty-two years as bishop, William Carpenter Bompas regularly reported on the conditions of his mission field. In the late 1860s, Fort Simpson, the HBC district headquarters and central Church of England mission, was inhabited by a dozen Protestant servants, most of whom were Presbyterians, and a handful of episcopalian HBC officers and servants. This latter group was the main object of Kirkby's and Bompas's ministrations. The resident clergyman's lot was a humble one indeed. Bompas noted in 1869 that "opposition to Romanism appears to be the main part of mission work in that district."[21]

During his stay at Fort Chipewyan in 1867–68, Bompas again worked primarily among the residents of the trading post, who numbered 100 altogether; another 200 to 300 Indians inhabited the forests in the surrounding area and visited Fort Chipewyan from time to time. Bompas wrote:

> The Indians in the woods are mostly Romanists in name and this makes it difficult for me to visit them... At the Fort, the Romanists and Protestants are nearly equally divided... There is only one European here besides myself, and I know of only two or three in the whole district. The other Protestants are all country born, some of English descent and some pure Indians.[22]

There was a great diversity of languages (Cree, French, Chipewyan, and English) at Fort Chipewyan, Bompas confessing that he did not know which of them predominated. Indeed, Bompas was always handicapped by the language barriers he encountered, so much so that when he tendered his resignation in 1871 it was partly because of his linguistic difficulties:

> The syllabics employed in this country are, as you are aware, a great stumbling block to me and form an additional reason why I would gladly withdraw from the work if my place here can be supplied by another. I take the alphabet to be a divine gift to man and to be the foundation of all true knowledge.[23]

As was the case elsewhere, throughout his long career in the North Bompas was engaged in a running battle with the Oblates. In 1866, while Petitot built a log house for his seasonal visits to Great Bear Lake, the Reverend Bompas supervised the construction of a much larger house, informing Petitot that he and Kirkby[24] had decided to build a mission and an orphanage there, apparently in reaction to the Catholic orphanage that the Oblates were establishing at Providence.

To manage their new station and teach in its school, the CMS missionaries hired a Métis named MacLeod, a former cook at Fort McPherson described by Petitot as a libertine and an ignoramus. In order to meet the Protestant challenge, Petitot, while at his permanent station of Good Hope in 1866–67, painted various colourful religious scenes on canvas, paintings that were bound to impress the Indians of Great Bear Lake. However, upon returning to the outpost in March 1867, he discovered that Bompas had already left the place, abandoning his house and projected orphanage. One year later, MacLeod was charged with sexually abusing two of his female students, thereby putting an end to his school.

In February 1867, Bompas headed overland to Fort Rae, on the northern shore of Great Slave Lake. Noting that his Indians of Great Bear Lake had not succumbed to Protestant seduction, Petitot immediately warned his colleagues at Fort Chipewyan of Bompas's visits;

Father Henri Audémard (kneeling), with four Oblate brothers and
forty-one children from the Fort Providence orphanage on an outing in
1890.

Father Faraud thereupon ordered Father Gascon to set out on the four-
day journey by snowshoe and dog team from Fort Resolution to Fort
Rae, a mission opened by Father Grollier in 1859 but visited only occasionally and for short periods afterwards. The Bompas threat galva-
nized the Oblates.

Upon Gascon's arrival at Fort Rae on 12 March 1867, he was
relieved to discover that Bompas had already left, headed for the HBC
trading post at Big Island at the source of the Mackenzie on Great Slave
Lake. Gascon settled down for a three-month mission, baptizing forty
adults and thirty-one children, hearing 600 confessions, and teaching
catechism to eighty children every day, all the while praising the Lord
because he had bettered the Protestant minister once more.

The story was similar for Father Faraud, who, from his base at
Providence, sent Father Émile Grouard to evangelize forts Liard and
Halkett on the Liard River, in addition to Fort Simpson, the Reverend
Kirkby's base. Further north, fathers Petitot and Séguin worked the
lower Mackenzie from Good Hope; they were disappointed with the
meagre results obtained among the Inuit (Eskimos), first contacted in
1867, and among the Loucheux of Fort McPherson, a station that
tended to favour the CMS missionaries.

Unidentified missionary from Fort Chipewyan shoes dogs to protect their paws.

Upon leaving Fort Rae and the Great Slave Lake region in the summer of 1867, the Reverend Bompas settled at Lake Athabasca, once more crossing swords with the Oblates at their mission of La Nativité near Fort Chipewyan. The Protestant Bompas and the Catholic Bishop Isidore Clut competed up and down the Peace River, at Fort Vermilion in particular, and among the local Beaver Indians. As a rule Bompas made little headway. Finally, in 1869, he left Fort Simpson and headed in the direction of Peel River and Fort Yukon, whose Loucheux and Tukudh Indians had from the outset proven much more receptive to the CMS missionaries. It was in those most distant reaches of the Canadian Northwest that he was destined to make his most important contribution to Church of England missions.

The Reverend Bompas endorsed his Church's policy of endeavouring to staff Indian churches with Indian pastors, leaving the European missionaries free to work among the "heathen." Upon becoming a bishop, he offered his suggestions for the selection of future CMS missionaries to the North. English candidates should be chosen from among the country's agricultural population, men used to outdoor life and farming. They should be humble, frugal, and contented with rough fare and exposure to the elements. He considered that most of the men who graduated from the CMS's Islington College were townspeople, and consequently ill-prepared for Canada's North. The young men trained at St. John's College in Red River tended to be too young and uncommitted to persevere in the North.[25]

When the diocese of Mackenzie was carved out of that of Athabasca–Mackenzie in 1883, but particularly when the diocese of Yukon was formed in 1891, Church of England missions were much more prosperous than they had been in the 1860s, at least in the southern part of the territory, the diocese of Athabasca. Upon each of these territorial divisions, William Carpenter Bompas chose to become bishop of the more remote and poorer diocese,[26] although his rank and seniority would have entitled him to stay in the more prosperous south. Like Petitot, Morice, and George McDougall, Bompas was happiest when roughing it in remote and isolated places. He spent the last fifteen years of his episcopate in the distant Yukon.

Upon being appointed first bishop of the new diocese of Selkirk (Yukon), separated from the diocese of Mackenzie in 1891, Bompas set out down the Mackenzie River and up the Peel River, crossed the mountains, descended the Porcupine River to the Yukon River, and went upstream to Forty-Mile where he established his headquarters. Ever since the visit of William Kirkby in 1861, and the arrival of resident missionary Robert McDonald at Fort Yukon in 1862, the Yukon was Church of England territory, the Catholic priests having proven unable to unseat the Anglicans. Bompas knew the area well, having wintered there in 1869–70 and again in 1872–73.

When he arrived in Forty-Mile (near the Alaska border) in 1891, Bishop Bompas brought with him the Reverend Canham, who would shortly thereafter be appointed to Fort Selkirk, the old (1848) HBC trading post at the junction of the Yukon and Pelly rivers. The schoolteacher Totty was also a member of the group, stationed at Moosehide. The bishop's wife had been in England since 1887 but joined him at Forty-Mile in 1892.

It was from Forty-Mile that Bompas ran his diocese until 1903, when he moved to Carcross (Car[ibou] Cross[ing]), located on the railway line at the southern perimeter of the Yukon Territory. The mission work was slow and uneventful, Bompas managing to obtain the services of a handful of clergymen to assist him, men like R.J. Bowen (1895), H.A. Naylor (1896), F.F. Flewelling (1896), and H.A. Cody (1904). When the gold rush began in 1896 and created the town of Dawson overnight, it was the Reverend Flewelling who was charged with ministering to the new community's spiritual needs. While celebrating these first Church of England services in Dawson in 1896–97, he observed Jesuit Father Judge celebrating Mass, also for the first time in Dawson. While Judge built the first Catholic church, the Reverend Bowen was transferred from Forty-Mile to Dawson to build the first Anglican church in the fall of 1897.

By 1898, the ecclesiastical landscape was becoming more familiar as the Oblates took over Catholic ministry in the Yukon Territory, competing as they did elsewhere with the Church of England. When Bompas died in Carcross in 1906, his successor, Isaac O. Stringer, was already in place. By this time, other Protestant denominations like the Presbyterians and the Salvation Army had also made an appearance in the Yukon Territory.

The half-century battle for the souls of the Mackenzie's aboriginal people had resulted in an Oblate victory throughout most of the Athabasca and Mackenzie regions, although the neighbouring Yukon was definitely CMS land.

Notes

1. Red River, 4 November 1857. MG 17, Class C, C.1/M.6, reel A-80. HBC Archives (microfilm copy), NAC.

2. 31 July 1858. MG 17, Class C, C.1/M.6, reel A-80. HBC Archives (microfilm copy), NAC.

3. Fort Simpson, 21 August 1858. MG 17, Class C, C.1/M.6, reel A-80. HBC Archives (microfilm copy), NAC.

4. B.R. Ross to J. Hunter, Fort Simpson, 23 August 1858. MG 17, Class C, C.1/M.6, reel A-80. HBC Archives (microfilm copy), NAC.

5. [B.R. Ross] and HBC officers, Fort Simpson, 23 August 1858. MG 17, Class C, C.1/M.6, reel A-80. HBC Archives (microfilm copy), NAC.

6. From his base on Lake Athabasca, Father Faraud had toured this area in the fall of 1858.

7. Hunter to the secretaries, Fort Simpson, 30 November 1858. MG 17, Class C, C.1/M.6, reel A-80. HBC Archives (microfilm copy), NAC.

8. Grollier to Taché, Fort Norman, 20 July 1860. HEB 6874 .L88L 3, AD.

9. Ibid.

10. To Henry Venn, Red River, 27 September 1859. MG 17, Class C, C.1/M.6, reel A-80, p. 411. HBC Archives (microfilm copy), NAC.

11. To J. Chapman, Red River, 1 April 1867. MG 17, Class C, C.1/M.6, reel A-80. HBC Archives (microfilm copy), NAC.

12. The secular priest Zéphirin Gascon was in the process of becoming an Oblate; he made his vows in 1861.

13. The French word *loucheux* means cross-eyed.

14. Émile Petitot to Joseph Fabre, Great Slave Lake, September 1863, in *Missions OMI* 6, 1867, p. 372.

15. Émile Petitot to Joseph Fabre, Great Bear Lake, 31 May 1866, in *Missions OMI* 7, 1868, p. 295.

16. For a general if dated biography of Bompas see H.A. Cody.

17. Fort Yukon had originally been located farther down the Yukon River. When the U.S. purchased Alaska from Russia in 1867, it was discovered that the trading post lay in American territory. When an American team effectively took over the post in 1869, in the presence of Bompas, the HBC planned to move its operations to the new Fort Yukon on the Porcupine River, a short distance above its confluence with the Yukon. Robert McDonald moved out with the company in 1870. He established his new mission at Fort McPherson on Peel River in 1871. When Bompas returned in 1872, it was to the new Fort Yukon, the old one being in the hands of an American fur-trading company.

18. The names of the missionaries and of their stations of residence are taken from W.C. Bompas, to the secretaries of the CMS, Fort Simpson, 30 March 1875. MG 17, Class C, C.1/M.10, reel A-80, p. 133. CMS papers, NAC.

19. Émile Grouard, "Rapport sur le vicariat d'Athabaska-Mackenzie," *Missions OMI* 31, 1893, p. 369ff.

20. W.C. Bompas to Lay Secretary, Fort Simpson, 18 May 1876. MG 17, Class C, C.1/M.10, p. 386. CMS papers, NAC.

21. Fort Simpson, 5 May 1869. MG 17, Class C, C.1/M.7, p. 164. CMS papers, NAC.

22. W.C. Bompas to secretaries of CMS, Fort Chipewyan, 9 December 1867. MG 17, Class C, C.1/M.7, reel A-80, p. 24. CMS papers, NAC.

23. W.C. Bompas to Secretaries, Fort Chipewyan, 6 July 1871. MG 17, Class C, C.1/M.8, reel A-80, p. 97. CMS papers, NAC.

24. Kirkby returned to England in 1868.

25. W.C. Bompas to secretaries, Fort Chipewyan, 17 August 1875. MG 17, Class C, C.1/M.10, reel A-81, pp. 216–7. CMS papers, NAC.

26. Bompas was successively bishop of the dioceses of Athabasca–Mackenzie (1874–84), Mackenzie (1884–91), and Selkirk (1891–1906).

CHAPTER VIII

CATHOLIC–PROTESTANT RELATIONS

W HEN Catholic ultramontane clergy collided with their Protestant evangelical counterparts, sparks usually flew, Protestant No-Popery clashing with Catholic anti-Protestantism. Each was a mindset that tolerated no dissent.

However, this was not always the case, the Protestant gentlemen who were officers of the Hudson's Bay Company (HBC) usually having a friendly rapport with Catholic priests. On the Protestant side, only the clergymen were infected with endemic anti-Catholicism, and then some more so than others. More surprisingly, some of the Protestant clergymen who uttered the most scurrilous attacks on Catholic priests seemed to reverse themselves instantaneously, and in almost the same breath become friends with their victims.

Catholics and the Hudson's Bay Company

We have seen that before the arrival of the Oblate missionaries in 1845, the Catholic clergy and the HBC officers in Red River got along superbly, each frequently showering praise upon the other; this in spite of the fact that the 1830s, 1840s, and 1850s were decades of an intensive anti-Catholic crusade in the English-speaking countries of the Western world.[1] Nevertheless, in the Canadian Northwest, HBC administrators not only held no quarrel with the Catholic missionaries, they heaped praise and resources upon them—while experiencing strained relations with many of the Anglican missionaries. The arrival of six Wesleyan Methodist missionaries in the Northwest in 1840 brought no noticeable change to the quality of relations between Catholics and Protestants.

The HBC as a business enterprise evaluated everything, clergymen included, in the light of its commercial value to the company. Although the HBC Committee in London would occasionally indulge in evangelical posturing, as a general rule HBC directors, and Governor George Simpson in particular, tried to treat Protestant and Catholic missionaries equitably. Because it wanted to avoid denominational conflicts in a given territory, the HBC sometimes refused to accede to Catholic requests to establish missions in a territory already occupied by a Protestant minister. This was the case on James Bay during the 1840s, at York Factory in 1851, on the upper Saskatchewan in 1838, and in Oregon in 1835. But those incidents were exceptions to the rule of courtesy, hospitality, and generosity on the part of HBC officers towards all missionaries.

Bishop Taché was but one of several Catholic missionaries who acknowledged the indispensable support of the HBC. In a series of letters to his mother, written between July 1845 and January 1851, the future bishop of St. Boniface praised the HBC for always showing great hospitality to travellers. This was the case when the young subdeacon Taché first journeyed to Red River in 1845; all along the route, at Mattawa, Sault-Sainte-Marie, and Fort William (Thunder Bay), the clergymen and their party were welcomed with open arms. When Father Taché travelled to Île-à-la-Crosse in 1846, he did so in the company of HBC trader McKenzie and his son, both of whom earned nothing but praise from the priest. When Taché and Laflèche wintered in the HBC trading post at Île-à-la-Crosse in 1846–47, the young Oblate wrote his mother that they "could only rejoice at the courtesy and attention [they] were given by the respectful Mr. McKenzie."[2]

Having gone to Fort Chipewyan on Lake Athabasca during the latter months of 1847, Taché reiterated his appreciation for the "gracious welcome" he received everywhere; at Fort Chipewyan he was treated with friendship that he would never forget.[3] Six months before being elected coadjutor bishop to Provencher, Father Taché evaluated the work of the HBC:

> I do not share the view of those who see nothing but evil in the [HBC]... I believe that one cannot reasonably ask more from a company of merchants who purchase with the harshest privations a mediocre fortune for their old days. One is greatly mistaken to judge this company as similar to the [defunct] North West Com-

pany... In all the land of the Montagnais [Athapascan]... I find that the trade of the honourable Hudson's Bay Company is always conducted within the boundaries of the strictest justice... Moreover..., without the company, and forced to rely on the meagre resources that we now possess, it would be morally impossible for us to continue missionary work here.[4]

Bishop Taché would reiterate these feelings in his "Vingt années de missions," published in 1866:

> As a rule, the members of the honourable Hudson's Bay Company have not only assisted us, but on several occasions have proven to be sincere and devoted friends... The officers... definitely deserve our gratitude and our esteem, and... we owe them part of the success of our missions.[5]

The esteem Taché felt for the HBC never faltered. While visiting Reindeer Lake in the spring of 1848, he boarded at the HBC trading post. Taché wrote:

> My host, Protestant by birth, persists in his belief, because he believes that Protestantism is the doctrine that St. Paul preached in England, while St. Peter taught another doctrine in Rome. However, he is far from fanatical. He respects our religion and treats its ministers much better than would many Catholics. Every Sunday he attends Mass and, after he offered his services, I appointed him my sole cantor.[6]

Oblate Father Nicolas Laverlochère, the first nineteenth-century Catholic missionary to James Bay, sang the same tune. On 15 August 1847, he wrote from Moose Factory:

> [During] the fifteen days that we spent at the home of [Mr. Miles, head of the HBC trading post], he never ceased extending to us every care and attention, and he did so with the kindness and consideration that distinguishes the English gentleman. Not only did he always invite us to his table, but he had us bless it even though neither he nor any other guest was Catholic. Moreover, he frequently ensured that we lacked for nothing, graciously inviting us to consider ourselves at home... In every trading post that we have visited, the agents of the honourable Company, and this one in particular, frequently make us believe, that we are among family.[7]

In sum, things could hardly have gone better in the relations between Oblates and the HBC. The company not only provided room and board to the missionaries during their voyages, but frequently transported them, at its own expense, in its canoes and barges.

With rare exception, the officers in charge of the trading posts, be they Catholic or Protestant, seemed to prefer the Catholic priest to the

Protestant minister. The reason was perhaps the simplicity of the Catholic missionary: he not only required little in terms of supplies or lodging, but was also grateful for anything that he was given. The Protestant minister frequently demanded that both he and his wife be lodged, fed, and provided with every amenity. Moreover, certain ministers meddled in political or commercial affairs, behaviour that was bound to alienate the HBC.

In addition to being expensive to maintain and a burr under the HBC's commercial saddle, the ministers of the 1840s and 1850s all too often spread hatred and condemnations, be it of popery, the Métis, the French, or marriages à la façon du pays. A contemporary historian cites HBC officers:

> We are rather getting tired of Wesleyans and quite sick of Episcopalians... The Catholic clergy here... are exemplary. The Indians see them living perfectly alone and caring for nothing but converting them and often they think more of such men than those who come with families and bully for every luxury and complain of every appearance of neglect getting literally furious on the slightest annoyance felt by them or their accomplished ladies.[8]

Not only did the Protestant ministers make unreasonable demands, but they believed in the superiority of everything British. The Métis, the French, and the Canadians—that is to say, all Catholics—were the object of their religious, racial, and linguistic spite. Recorder Adam Thom (1839–54) symbolized this white Anglo-Protestant racism in Red River.

In all respects, the Catholic priest demonstrated more flexibility. He showed greater appreciation for the Métis people, qualifying their customary form of marriage as "natural marriage" that only required a formal blessing to become fully licit. In other words, for the Catholic priest, such unions were good in themselves, albeit lacking a formality to conform to the law of the Church. He rarely uttered sweeping condemnations of Protestantism, and when he did so his words were moderate in tone. For example, the following words of veteran missionary Albert Lacombe addressed to his superior general compare favourably with the incendiary statements of the reverends Hunter and Cockran:

> We never hold public discussions about religion with the Protestant missionaries, and such discussions would do us more harm than good in the eyes of the Indians. But if, as frequently happens, we are questioned on the difference in religious beliefs between Protestants and ourselves, we simply explain Catholic doctrine, particularly with regard to the specific points in question...: celibacy of the clergy, and oral confession.[9]

In sum, while the reverends Hunter and Cockran denounced Catholic priests and their Church, that "Whore of Babylon," their Protestant lay coreligionists valued and praised the priests, who responded likewise.

Protestant No-Popery

The 1840s and 1850s are particularly important decades in the history of Catholic–Protestant relations in Canada. On the international and national scenes, these years included the Union of the Canadas, the advent of responsible government, the "papal aggression" controversy in England, the Protestant campaign of proselytism in Quebec by the French-Canadian Missionary Society, the Separate School crisis in Ontario, and the apogee of the "Know-Nothing" movement in the United States. In Rupert's Land, during the same two decades, the expansion of Catholic and Protestant missions and the arrival of the Oblates are particularly noteworthy. Denominational rivalry became a permanent feature of the "Great Lone Land." Also, many of Canada's people had never witnessed denominational rivalry. In sum, before the 1840s Protestant–Catholic conflict was not current fare for most Canadians.

Beginning in 1840, however, denominational rivalry put down roots that would endure for more than a century in Canada's Northwest. The rivalry first appeared in the race to occupy missionary stations at strategic locations along the endless fur-trade water routes leading to the Arctic and Pacific oceans. Soon it would also become apparent in the preaching, the financial management of the churches, and the behaviour of the clergy. Both Catholic and Protestant clergymen were conscious of this rivalry, which frequently motivated their actions.

It was usually the Protestant minister who attacked the Catholic priest. Other than regularly noting in their correspondence that Protestant clergymen were "ministers of error," the Catholic priests rarely spoke of them. The mood of Protestants *vis-à-vis* Catholics is reflected in the report of an Ontario Baptist delegation to Red River in 1869. Noting that nearly half the population of Red River was Catholic, the delegates reported that "priestcraft" was as old as the settlement itself, and had grown with it "first in its influence over the masses, and secondly in the acquisition of property." They then spoke of the political and ecclesiastical power of that "monster influence."[10]

William Carpenter Bompas, one of the most dedicated Protestant missionaries in the Northwest, can be taken as representative of the anti-Catholicism among ministers of the latter third of the nineteenth century. Bompas was not only better educated than most ministers sent to the Northwest, but also more devoted and committed to the difficult living and travel conditions of the missionaries in the North. Bompas even gained grudging respect from Oblate historian Adrien-Gabriel Morice—no mean achievement. Morice wrote that Bompas was not only more capable than his Protestant colleagues, but also an adversary "worthy of attention."[11] Bompas spent the last forty-one years of his life (1865–1906) working in the North, and he did so with as much devotion and commitment as the best of his Oblate rivals.

Yet it is this same Bompas who wrote that he found the power of Rome "greater than heathenism in opposition to the gospel."[12] The correspondence of this devoted Christian missionary regularly includes gratuitous attacks against the Catholic priests. From the time of his arrival in Fort Simpson on Christmas Day 1865 to his departure for his episcopal consecration in England in 1874, the Reverend Bompas never spared the Catholics. While resident at Fort Chipewyan in 1867–68, he expounded on the sad situation of the Indian people of the area, who had all joined the priests' party, in spite of the fact that "Romish errors are fatal to the soul, and... conversion to that faith does not... raise or improve the character or heart of the Indian above his natural state as a heathen."[13] Bompas declared that he understood this misguided behaviour of the Indians, because "while they are unregenerate... they will mostly prefer at first the Romish religion because of its external show."[14]

In the summer of 1871, while at Fort Chipewyan, Bompas tendered his resignation to the Church Missionary Society (CMS), noting that he was in the midst of "Romanists," whereas he had been sent to evangelize the heathen. He begged the CMS to send him a larger supply of Bibles, tracts, prayerbooks, and schoolbooks, and

> as our conflict here is chiefly against the man of Sin, a few illustrated copies of Foxe's *Martyrs* and other easy books against popery, would probably do more good than the missionaries own voice; but it is the fashion nowadays to deal tenderly with Romish error.[15]

Two months later, while at Rocky Portage in the Peace River district, Bompas noted that no Protestant missionary had penetrated the New Caledonia District, across the mountains in British Columbia, where fur-trade posts were now accompanied by new mines.

> The Indians in New Caledonia are under the teaching of Romish priests who also visit the forts and baptize the children of the Protestants. They occasionally preach in English to the men and... try

to entrap the English half-breeds into joining their Church especially by refusing to marry them unless they are rebaptized in the
Romish faith. The priests are said to have been successful in that
district in checking... among the Indians the sins of drunkenness
and gambling, having organized constables among them who flog
them for these offences.[16]

In the autumn of 1871, after six years of missionary work, the
Reverend Bompas had not mellowed in his appreciation of Catholicism:

> While learned men at home may discuss doctrinally how far Rom-
> ish error is truly designated anti-Christian, the question is
> answered practically in this country in this simple way, that just in
> so far as the Indians come under the influence of the priests, just so
> far do they become "anti-Christian," that is opposed to the Gospel,
> while without the priests' influence they seem always favourably
> disposed to its reception.[17]

While continuing to fear and decry "Romanism," Bompas and his
colleagues nevertheless acknowledged some of the advantages enjoyed
by the Catholic missionaries. So it was that Bompas regularly asked the
CMS for more teachers, catechists, ministers, and supplies. He wanted
to develop schools as foils for Catholicism, and was never satisfied that
the Protestants were doing enough. He wrote that "the administration
of the Romish missions appears carried on with so much more zeal and
vigour than our own, that in this respect, they deserve success."[18]

As was the case for his Catholic rivals, Bompas regularly indulged
in wishful thinking, predicting either major shifts in denominational
allegiances in Catholic areas or unflagging fidelity to the Church of
England in predominantly Protestant areas. In fact, it would seem that
many Indian people told any and every missionary what he wanted to
hear, in return for tobacco, clothing, and food.

Bompas and his Protestant colleagues continued to denounce
Catholicism and the "Man of Sin," not so much because of what they
witnessed in the Northwest, but because of their own theological and
ideological brainwashing and indoctrination before they ever set foot in
the Northwest. The warped education of the ministers could explain
much of the denominational hostility.

Catholic Anti-Protestantism

The writings of Catholic missionaries are shot through with denunci-
ations of alleged machinations and lies by the "ministers of error."

Publications by Catholic authors like Dom Benoît[19] and Adrien-Gabriel Morice[20] are replete with indignation and accusations against both the generalized anti-Catholicism and francophobia of the Anglo-Protestant majority and the specific dishonesty of various Protestant clergymen scattered throughout the Northwest. The general accusations, which became much more frequent in the later years of the century, were often provoked by the heated debates surrounding the Riel question and the school and language questions.

So it was that Dom Benoît, Archbishop Taché's biographer, wrote:

> In Alberta, Saskatchewan, and Assiniboia, the majority of government employees, English and Protestant, always showed great intolerance for the Catholic religion and the French language.[21]... There has always been in Canada, over the past century, a group of fanatics who never miss an opportunity to oppress French-speaking Catholics.[22]

Father Morice also described the Protestant ministers working in the Northwest; in fact he plagiarized the following statement from Bishop Vital Grandin:

> The apostles of error are recruited more easily than those of truth; less is required of them, and they undergo less training. They generally arrive in the country as schoolmasters; then we learn that they have become "reverends," and behave as such. We sometimes meet Métis or Indians who, although barely able to read the Bible in English and translate it incorrectly into native languages, are promoted overnight to the rank of minister. Their fellow Métis or natives look upon them as wise men..., although civilized people are humiliated by their "reverends," and make no bones about it.[23]

Morice frequently reiterated the familiar accusation by Catholics that the ministers purchased the conversions of Indian people.

Many of the Catholic missionaries in the Northwest contributed to the indictment of Protestant ministerial rivals. While on his annual summer visit to James Bay and the Catholic mission station at Fort Albany in 1883, Oblate Father Nédélec denounced the Protestant presence and threat to the only Catholic mission in that Anglican territory. Nédélec claimed that the Catholic Indians were under siege, their Protestant tormentors resorting to lies, insults, calumnies, and false promises. "Everything is against us, except God and truth."[24] Ten years later, Father François Fafard, founder of the Catholic resident mission at Fort Albany (1892), expressed identical sentiments, while jealously eyeing the plentiful supplies enjoyed by the Church of England mission.[25]

On the western side of Hudson Bay, in the province of Manitoba, and in southern Saskatchewan, the story was similar during the last quarter of the nineteenth century. Oblates wrote of the "terrible opposition" they faced and the "tenacious war" against them by a rapidly growing number of Protestant ministers of various sects. Newly installed Archbishop Langevin of St. Boniface (1895) wrote of the "perfidious doings of the ministers of error, true creatures of the devil,"[26] who had taken upon themselves the task of distancing people from truth. Clearly, Bishop Bompas had found his match in hyperbole; the more moderate Taché was no more.

Other than the Yukon Territory, the part of the Northwest where Protestant missionaries had been most successful was northern Manitoba and the easterly portion of northern Saskatchewan. In fact, these areas remained almost exclusively Protestant, the stations of York Factory, Fort Churchill, Norway House, Fort Stanley, and The Pas testifying to many decades of either Methodist or Church of England missions. The Catholics began competing in earnest in this area only during the last quarter of the century; previously, the only Catholic mission was at Reindeer Lake.

Étienne Bonnald (?–1928)

Spearheading the Oblate campaign to make inroads into that Protestant preserve was Father Étienne Bonnald, who in 1876 opened a permanent Catholic mission at Pelican Narrows, on Pelican Lake adjoining the Churchill River, the site of a new HBC trading post (1874) in the Cumberland District. Pelican Lake was 225 kilometres from Fort Cumberland on the Saskatchewan River, Cumberland in turn standing seventy-five kilometres from The Pas. On the Churchill River, Father Bonnald served the mission post of Paktawagan, 250 kilometres downriver from Pelican Narrows; Fort Nelson stood 250 kilometres further, at the mouth of the adjoining Nelson River.

For twenty-six years (1876–1902), Father Bonnald worked from his base at Pelican Narrows, ranging down the Churchill and Nelson rivers to Fort Nelson on Hudson Bay; he was soon assisted by Father Ovide Charlebois,[27] who served the more southerly part of the district, along the lower Saskatchewan River, visiting the stations at Fort Cumberland, The Pas, and Grand Rapids two or three times per year. The Oblate missionaries rarely stopped at the CMS mission of Fort Stanley (Lake La Ronge), where everyone was Protestant. In fact, the entire district was largely Protestant, the only exceptions being small groups of French-speaking Métis, the people who made up a good proportion of the Catholic congregations of the itinerant Oblates.

While The Pas and Fort Stanley were CMS missions, the more northerly Norway House and Fort Nelson were Methodist. Bonnald reported that the entire region of the lower Hayes, Nelson, and Churchill rivers was Methodist country. The arrival of Catholic priests after 1876 must have caused an intensification of Methodist activity, although Fort Nelson still boasted of only a resident Methodist catechist in the 1890s. It seems that both Catholic priests from Pelican Narrows and Methodist ministers from Rossville developed a greater interest in the Indian people of Fort Nelson once the two bands of clergymen began competing.

Father Bonnald was not overly kind in his assessment of his rivals. He spoke of "several... who lived in concubinage and even in adultery" and who had come to spread lies and unbelief.[28] He derided the Methodist practice of sighing and crying to God while in prayer,[29] and had nothing but contempt for the Methodist catechist at Fort Nelson, who allegedly fled the post in 1894 when an epidemic took forty lives among the post's Indian people.[30]

When the Oblates decided to further penetrate that Protestant country, it was again Bonnald to whom they turned, instructing the veteran missionary, in 1902, to found a Catholic mission at Cross Lake midway between York Factory and Norway House. Bonnald and his companion, Father Beys, built their establishment directly across the lake from an extant Methodist mission, and in the neighbourhood of an HBC post; the CMS had its own mission further downriver at Split Lake. At Cross Lake, Methodists and Catholics undertook another chapter in their ongoing competition, both opening schools and seeking to entice children into them. Within three years, Bonnald was claiming victory in his school and chuckling over the fact that the Methodist catechist at Cross Lake was caught "in the act" of committing adultery.[31]

Bonnald and two companions were then ordered to establish another Catholic mission at Norway House, the Methodist stronghold in northern Manitoba. Upon their arrival on 30 December 1905, the Methodists must have been shocked, given that no Catholics were then to be found near Norway House. Typically for a missionary of either denominational camp, Bonnald reported that many Indian people looked with favour upon the new messenger of the Gospel, and promised several conversions in the not too distant future. In fact, the Catholics erected their first house/chapel at Norway House in the summer of 1907.

In southern Saskatchewan's Qu'Appelle Valley, Oblates and Protestants also competed for the allegiance of the Indian people. If anything, Oblate Father Théophile Campeau was more intransigent than his brothers in religion when discussing Protestant ministers. Stationed at Montagne de Tondre, in the extreme western portion of the Oblate missionary vicariate, Campeau pulled no punches when fighting the Protestants. In 1890 he proudly told of visiting all the Indian reservations in the area, and dealing at length with various questions pertaining to Protestant–Catholic differences. Campeau reported to his Oblate superior the gist of his message to the Indian people:

> The Catholic religion is the only true religion instituted by Our Lord Jesus Christ for the salvation of souls. Protestant religions were invented by perverse men, and do not deserve any credit.

> I had to refute the lies and calumnies that the ministers never cease uttering against us, and against our industrial school at Qu'Appelle... The apostles of error... come to the native people loaded with gifts: clothing, money, food, everything is offered to them... The Indians... go to see the ministers... in order to eat. However, when they want to pray, they come to us.[32]

Campeau continued by denouncing a dishonest and adulterous interpreter in the employ of a Presbyterian minister. The unnamed villain allegedly purchased Indian converts, giving each fifteen dollars at the time of their baptism. Many had sold out. Father Campeau continued to denounce his Protestant rivals during the 1890s, repeating the accusation that they were liars for having falsified statistics on the denominational attachments of Indian people. Campeau claimed that Protestant Indians were only half as numerous as the statistics indicated.[33]

In Alberta, it was more of the same. Although the Church of England never had an ordained minister in place before 1875, the Methodists had been there since 1840. Oblate Father Hippolyte Leduc reported in 1870 that Protestant ministers suddenly became very scarce when an epidemic broke out among the Indian people, much to the credit of the priests and the shame of the ministers.[34] The Oblates reported regularly on the shameful rivalry of the ministers in education or in missions; occasionally they denounced the fanaticism of certain Protestant HBC officers,[35] although they were usually the objects of praise. Father Leduc reported to Oblate assistant general Aubert in 1872:

> The ministers of error... try to hinder us as much as possible... They want to topple, destroy Catholicism. They loudly proclaim that Catholicism is finished. They repeat to the poor Indians that the great chief of the Catholics is a prisoner, and condemned to wash the dishes of King Victor Emmanuel.[36] Although they may invent lies upon lies, the gates of Hell will never prevail against the Church of Jesus Christ. Although the ministers don't always treat us with charity in our absence, one must acknowledge that in person they are truly courteous and considerate. One of them even did me the honour of calling me his brother on a solemn occasion.[37]

During the 1880s and 1890s, the Oblates reported the presence of many more Protestant ministers in southern Alberta; these belonged to several denominations and continued to dispose of far greater wealth than did the Catholic missionaries. In addition, they had become very active, swamping the Catholics with "frenetic propaganda"[38] and using their greater wealth to build better schools and make generous handouts to the Indian people.

A novel phenomenon was that, according to the Oblates, some of these ministers pretended to teach the same religion as the Oblates, allegedly to entice the Indian people into accepting their Protestant message. Bishop Grandin noted in 1881 that not only were his Protestant rivals in southern Alberta antagonistic, but "they pretend to teach the same religion that we do."[39] Six years later, Oblate Father Leduc commented on Church of England bishops in the Northwest:

> In order to better succeed in their tactics against the Church, with few exceptions these bishops have adopted the principles of ritualism. They and their ministers claim to be truly ordained; they celebrate Mass, endeavour to re-establish the sacrament of Penance in their churches, do not oppose the invocation of saints, admit the existence of purgatory, etc.... They bring an extraordinary energy to the propagation of their form of worship, and spare no expense.[40]

In Alberta, Catholic missionaries also denounced the bigotry and partisanship of government employees, who were usually Protestant, in spite of the fact that most Indians were Catholic. Bishop Grandin wrote that it was this "unavowed, but always skilfully dissimulated, real, and active fanaticism"[41] that caused such uneasiness in the Northwest.

We have seen that the Catholic–Protestant rivalry frequently centred on schools, for the parties vied for the conquest of the younger generation. An example of this rivalry was the Catholic mission of St. Bernard on Lesser Slave Lake, northwest of Edmonton.

Father Alphonse Desmarais had taken over this mission in 1885. Upon witnessing the arrival of a Protestant minister at the HBC fort, and his opening a school, Desmarais immediately did likewise (1886). The battle was joined, and it was unrelenting in the succeeding years, each missionary trying to recruit as many of the Indian children as possible. Fearing that he would be outclassed by the more generous provisions found at the Protestant school, in 1888 Desmarais issued a challenge to his Protestant rivals: the Catholic schoolchildren would compete against the Protestants in a public exam, in order to demonstrate which school was superior. The minister declined the invitation,[42] much to Desmarais's frustration. He nevertheless claimed that his school was succeeding (forty-five children in 1888) in forcing the Protestant school out of business. The Oblate never let his guard down, however, setting out every autumn to recruit as many children as he could. In 1889, he also planned the construction of a Catholic chapel alongside the Protestant one, across the bay from the Catholic mission. Desmarais did so in the greatest secrecy, keeping his plans from the minister until the land was purchased and the building materials were delivered to the site.

In the more northerly parts of the Northwest, Catholic scorn and depreciation of Church of England ministers and catechists continued unabated during the 1870s, 1880s, and 1890s; the Oblates reported regularly that the Protestants were intensifying their efforts in the region. Father Émile Petitot, working on the Mackenzie River in the early 1870s, reported various inane or burlesque anecdotes about his CMS rivals: Bompas was baptizing any and all Indians, using water of any form—even tea. The Reverend Robert McDonald had been beaten up by a Loucheux Indian at Fort McPherson when the minister tried to stop the men from playing ball on the sabbath, threatening them with his revolver. In another incident, a group of Catholic Loucheux had undertaken a marathon of prayer in competition with a band of Protestant Loucheux; the Catholics emerged victorious because they were equipped with a larger collection of prayers, hymns, and invocations, enabling them to outlast their Protestant brothers. The tournament had lasted half a day.

When Bishop Isidore Clut, in the company of Father Auguste Lecorre, journeyed to the Yukon in the autumn of 1872, he not only discovered that the Reverend Bompas was hot on his heels, but that the region remained largely Protestant. Clut was incensed at discovering that his Protestant rivals, Bompas in particular, were telling the Indian people that the Catholics were God-killers. Lecorre claimed to have heard the charge repeatedly in several Indian villages. To prove the accusation, Bompas had allegedly simply pointed to the cross that hung around the necks of the Catholics, the Oblates in particular. At Fort Yukon in February 1873, Clut and Lecorre confronted Bompas with the accusation; Bompas denied it, but allegedly refused to say so in front of the assembled Indian people.[43]

In sum, the Catholic–Protestant fight continued in the Northwest Territories as it did elsewhere. Even when the rivals bore a grudging respect for each other, they continued to demean each other. When more substantial accusations could not be found, the Oblates derided Robert McDonald for being a former brewer, or chuckled at Bishop Bompas for travelling "with his breviary under his arm"—a French-Canadian saying signifying that the minister travelled in the company of his wife. Because most Protestant ministers were married, they had been rendered "men of a woman," as opposed to "men of God," in the eyes of the Indian people.

Friends Nevertheless

This pattern of controversy, animosity, mistrust, misunderstanding, and accusations dominated Catholic–Protestant clerical relations in the Northwest during the second half of the nineteenth century. However, Catholic and Protestant clergy and laity were not all of this persuasion. In spite of the theological, ideological, and political conditioning that favoured, indeed demanded, such hostility, some clergy and lay people, both Protestant and Catholic, managed to overcome their prejudices and develop constructive and charitable relationships with people of the other camp.

As was the case in the Northwest from the outset, HBC officers usually had positive and friendly relations with Catholic missionaries. Bishop Grandin was only one of many to acknowledge the generosity of the HBC officers, in spite of the fact that most were Protestant.[44]

The same was usually true of relations between Oblate missionaries and high-ranking government officials in the Northwest Territories. Suffice it to cite Oblate Father Joseph Lestanc, who wrote from Battleford to the Oblate assistant general in 1879:

> Governor Laird... has proven very polite and affable... Although Protestant himself, he is a fair and impartial man, motivated by the best intentions. In all our meetings, I have found him likeable, patient, and extraordinarily generous. All the priests who have had

dealings with him are unanimous in praising his qualities and his good intentions.[45]

Surprisingly enough, in spite of the tense and often bitter quarrels over the first Riel insurrection and the amnesty question, Father Lacombe could write from Winnipeg in 1877:

> In Winnipeg, although the majority of the population is Protestant, the Catholic priest is respected everywhere. We always wear our ecclesiastical garb on the streets, and we have never had to deal with the least discourtesy. Even among Protestants, people are eager to show us sympathy and goodwill.[46]

In fact, the Alberta territory, one of the earliest battlefields of Protestant and Catholic clergy, illustrated the apparent frequent contradictions in the behaviour of the Protestant missionaries. Robert Rundle's strong anti-Catholicism has been noted. Although the Methodist missionary never changed his views on Catholicism, views that were nurtured by the centuries-old anti-Catholicism of England, he did develop some lasting friendships among the few Catholic priests who crossed his path in Alberta. Although Rundle had little to do with Thibault, he did spend the last two weeks of April 1846 travelling in the company of Father Joseph Bourassa, from Lesser Slave Lake to the Lake St. Anne Road. Only two months later, in the summer of 1846, Rundle visited the Lake St. Anne mission on his own initiative. The previous autumn, Rundle's usual fall mission to Rocky Mountain House had proven a unique experience. There he met and spent a month with the itinerant Jesuit Pierre Jean de Smet. The two men became fast friends, discussing anything and everything, even proposing combined religious services and prayers. They parted on the best of terms, Rundle continuing to rail against the evils of popery but never uttering a personal accusation against the priests. He seemed to have been programmed to detest the Catholic religion, yet growing to appreciate the individual Catholics whom he encountered.

Catholic priests also told of cases of unusual cooperation and assistance from Protestant lay people. In 1881, Oblate Casimir Chirouse bore witness to the talents and goodwill of the Protestant administrator of New Westminster Hospital; he not only showed respect and affection for the priests, he allowed them every liberty for their ministry in the hospital; in addition, he sent his children to the Catholic schools, in spite of the fact that there were free Protestant schools in the neighbourhood.

Oblate Father Vital Fourmond told of a more unusual case at Duck Lake, Saskatchewan, where the Catholic mission of the Sacred

Heart had been established, first visited by Father Alexis André in 1868. Upon settling in the area in 1874, the wealthy Anglican merchant Mr. Stobard agreed with Father André, who resided at neighbouring St. Laurent, that a church should be built at Duck Lake. Stobard paid for it, employing a Presbyterian contractor to do the work. Another wealthy Protestant named Moore completed the job, graciously supplying the Catholic mission with construction materials from his sawmill in Prince Albert. Two other generous Protestants from the neighbourhood, particularly HBC officer Clark from Fort Carlton, then provided a bell for the church. In sum, a Catholic mission had been established at the sole expense of Protestant laymen.[47] Needless to say, Father Fourmond was more than grateful. Clearly, not all Catholic–Protestant relations were hostile and rancorous.

When Catholic social services were at issue, it seems that with few exceptions Protestants were supportive of Catholics. This was the case at St. Albert in 1874, when Father Leduc reported that the town's Catholic orphanage (twenty-seven children), run by the Grey Nuns, enjoyed the full moral and financial support of the area's Protestants. Five years later, Leduc reported that the largely Protestant population of Prince Albert, Saskatchewan, an Anglican see, asked the priests to establish a congregation of sisters to run a hospital and a boarding school.[48]

Several Catholic missionaries reported that they were always granted a sympathetic and hospitable reception by Protestant people. Father Charles Cahill, from his base at Rat Portage (Kenora), evangelized the lumber camps along the shores of the Lake of the Woods and Rainy Lake. Although most workers were English-speaking Protestants, Cahill reported in 1891 that he was always very well received and that several Protestants attended his evening prayers, which included a hymn, a prayer, and a sermon—all delivered in both French and English.[49]

Oblate Father Jules Decorby, working out of Fort Ellice in the southern prairies, reported that the white settlers of his territory, whether of Canadian, English, Irish, Polish, or German stock, all received him well. The majority were Protestant. Father Decorby declared in 1893 that in the twenty years the Catholic priests had been visiting the area, none had encountered incidents of bigotry, hostility, or disrespect. In fact, he told several anecdotes about special sympathy and support for the missionary. The Oblate reported that on several occasions during his itinerant ministry, rather than sleep outdoors, he had knocked on a settler's door, asking for shelter for the night. Not only was he never turned away, but he was usually given the most generous and cordial hospitality. His hosts always took care of him, and his horse, never accepting payment in return, and always making him promise to return whenever he was in the area.

In the missions of British Columbia, Father François Thomas told the same story. Based at Williams Lake, the Oblate always received the most cordial hospitality by Catholic and Protestant alike; he noted that the community of Quesnel Forks, some 100 kilometres away, was especially welcoming.

Although it was the relations between clergymen that usually left little room for Christian charity, there, too, one finds cases of unusual cooperation and fellowship, albeit not as frequently as some would expect from apostles of Christian charity.

In some ways, Catholic and Protestant clergymen were engaged in a love–hate relationship: the same ministers or priests who denounced the "monstrous and evil" influence of the "man of Sin" or of the "minister of error" could shower the same adversary with praise. This was the case with Father Jean-Baptiste Proulx, who, in his book about Bishop Lorrain's visit to James Bay in 1884, notes that there was no denying that the Anglican missionaries to James Bay had shown zeal and energy in their apostolate.[50] The Protestant author Malcolm McLeod was cited by Father Morice, when praising the "noble zeal of the Catholic clergy" in civilizing the North American Indians.[51] The same Morice, who could never be suspect of Protestant partisanship, cited Protestant author George M. Grant, who wrote very favourably about Catholics,[52] and then proceeded to describe the friendly and cooperative relations between St. Albert Catholics and Protestants in 1877. That year, six local Protestants, four of whom were clergymen, worked hand in hand with Bishop Grandin to alleviate the suffering of the settlers of St. Albert, who had experienced severe crop damage.[53]

The Baptist clergymen C.C. McLaurin, the historian of the Baptist denomination in the Northwest who wrote of the "monstrous influence" of Catholicism, also wrote the following:

> Much credit must be given to the priests of the Roman Catholic Church for the zeal displayed in their sacrificial effort to minister to the Indians of Western Canada. In this country, as in others, they are the pioneers in introducing Christianity to the aborigines. There seems to be a greater willingness on their part to enter new countries, to endure hardships and to face opposition than among ministers of other religious bodies...

> It is impossible to conceive what the early priests of the Roman Catholic Church have endured in Western Canada, living in wigwams..., terrible journeys..., scarcity of food... Very few Protestant

missionaries have undertaken the hard tasks which those priests willingly performed... We talk of sacrifice, but compared with what these early messengers of the Roman Catholic Church endured, we have made meagre sacrifices... What those men and women have suffered, no one can describe... Personally, I have visited the missions at Grouard, Peace River, Dunvegan, Lake McLeod, and have marvelled at their work. As Baptists, we have not done much for the Canadian Indians.[54]

Courtesy and mutual respect were the norm for other Protestant and Catholic clergymen. For example, in September 1883, on the occasion of the twenty-fifth anniversary celebrations of Bishop Grandin's episcopal consecration, the Anglican bishop visited his rival, tendering his congratulations and good wishes. In August 1884, Anglican Bishop Sullivan of Algoma preached in Trinity Church, Winnipeg, and in the words of a Catholic newspaper showed "odious scorn" towards Catholics, relegating them to the rank of pariahs. Within a week, Church of England Bishop T.R. McLean of Saskatchewan mounted the same pulpit to repair the damage, speaking of the Catholics in the Northwest with praise and respect.[55] The interdenominational bridge had been rebuilt.

The wide range of theological convictions among ministers also made it difficult to group all Protestant clergymen under the same banner. This was illustrated in 1886 when Father H. Leduc went to Pincher Creek in southern Alberta to bless a new Catholic church. After noting that the local Methodist minister quietly listened to his sermon, Oblate Father Leduc told an unusual anecdote. As he was about to embark upon his return journey to Fort MacLeod, the local Anglican minister asked if he could join him in his wagon; they discussed religion during the entire voyage. Leduc discovered that the minister was Anglo-Catholic in the full sense of the word—"an advanced Ritualist," to use Leduc's phrase. The minister uttered whole-hearted anathemas against Presbyterians, Methodists, and any and all other dissenters. He informed Leduc that whenever he was going to be away from Pincher Creek he instructed his flock to attend the Catholic Mass, and to avoid other Protestant services at all costs. He told Leduc that the Catholic Church was the mother Church, the Church of England being one of its finest branches. The minister, himself the son of a Church of England minister and a Catholic mother, was not only well versed in the Catholic faith, and a defender of it against Presbyterian and Methodist attacks, but he was also a friend of the Catholic missionary in Pincher Creek.[56] Decidedly, things were not always what they appeared to be in Protestant–Catholic relations.

In the remote mission station of Dunvegan, on the Peace River, the missionaries managed to cooperate on a day-to-day basis. Father

Émile Grouard, the future bishop, reported in 1883 that both Anglican and Catholic mission stations were short of hired help, and that the missionaries were reduced to doing their own chores in the fields. They began helping each other at harvest time. Getting to know each other led to much more favourable evaluations of the other, Father Grouard noting that the CMS missionary was a "good man."[57]

From his station at Pelican Narrows in the heart of Protestant territory, Father Étienne Bonnald told several anecdotes illustrating the sometimes harmonious and brotherly relations between Catholic and Protestant clergymen. Over the course of the years, Bonnald had developed a strong friendship with an Anglican archdeacon who worked in the territory. Bonnald recalled that he had initially met the man, sitting forlorn on the banks of a lake, his journey interrupted by persistent high winds. When Bonnald crossed his path, the archdeacon was running out of food. The Oblate gave him several pounds of moose meat that he was carrying, creating a lifelong friendship: "The good man overflowed with thanks, granting me all the blessings of the Patriarch Jacob."[58] On another occasion, Bonnald and the minister ended up sleeping in the same bed, when they stayed overnight in the same house.

On his annual or semi-annual return trek from Pelican Narrows to Prince Albert, a distance of 583 kilometres, Bonnald had many opportunities to encounter Protestants. He wrote in 1896:

> It is a Protestant country, and the priest is welcomed with much respect and treated with generosity. We arrived one night at the home of the wealthiest and most influential Protestant of the area, the Company's [HBC's] first pilot. [We were offered] good food, good beds, fish for our dogs, and all kinds of kindness and hospitality. Nothing was lacking, and all was free. After supper, our host asked me to say our Catholic prayer and to preach to the assembled people. This I proceeded to do.[59]

Father Bonnald continued that the Protestant gave him money and then accompanied him on the next sixty-six kilometres of his journey. During this trek of some seven days, Bonnald reported that other Protestants welcomed his party into their homes and offered to mend their torn shoes; this included a Protestant minister, who offered him dinner, shelter, and free provisions for his men and his dogs.

In sum, Oblate Father Bonnald, the same man who crossed swords with various Protestant ministers at Fort Nelson and Norway House, had very warm and friendly relations with several other Protestants, both lay and clerical. Indeed, Protestant–Catholic relations could be complex, not easily reduced to simplistic formulae. The same people who hurled ideological and theological missiles at each other one day could end up embracing each other on the next.

In addition to the constant deep respect and friendship that existed between lay Protestants and Catholic missionaries, a number of Protestant and Catholic *clergy* managed to cooperate, appreciate each other, and even become friends, in spite of the fact that their churches were on a war footing throughout the North and West until the end of the nineteenth century.

Nevertheless, it was this latter conflict that dominated the Christian landscape. Behind the rhetoric and animosity lay real conflicts over doctrine, finances, values, and schools. And it was all embedded in and coloured by rival nationalisms.

Notes

1. See E.R. Norman; R.A. Billington; J.R. Miller, "Anti-Catholicism in Canada: From the British Conquest to the Great War," in Terrence Murphy and Gerald Stortz (eds.), *Creed and Culture* (Montreal: McGill-Queen's University Press, 1993), pp. 25–48; and "Bigotry in the North Atlantic Triangle: Irish, British and American Influences on Canadian Anti-Catholicism, 1850–1900," *Studies in Religion/Sciences Religieuses* 16, 3 (1987): 292–3; "Anti-Catholic Thought in Victorian Canada," *CHR* 66, 4 (December 1985): 487–91.

2. Île-à-la-Crosse, 5 January 1847. *Les Cloches de Saint-Boniface* 32, 1 (January 1933): 24.

3. Île-à-la-Crosse, 3 January 1850. *Les Cloches de Saint-Boniface* 32, 5 (May 1933): 142.

4. Taché to his mother, Île-à-la-Crosse, 4 January 1851. *Les Cloches de Saint-Boniface* 33, 1 (January 1934): 25–6.

5. *Missions OMI* 5, 1866, p. 92.

6. Cited in Dom Benoît, vol. 1, p. 158.

7. N. Laverlochère to Father Léonard, Moose Factory, 15 August 1847. Cited in Gaston Carrière, *Les Missions catholiques dans l'Est du Canada et l'Honorable Compagnie de la Baie d'Hudson (1844–1900)*, p. 41.

8. Cited in Margaret Macleod (ed.), *The Letters of Letitia Hargrave* 28, pp. 34–36. Cited in Sylvia Van Kirk, p. 215.

9. St. Albert, 6 January 1866. *Missions OMI* 7, 1868, p. 232.

10. Cited in C.C. McLaurin, p. 37.

11. *Histoire de l'Église catholique dans l'Ouest canadien...*, p. 202.

12. W.C. Bompas to secretaries of CMS, Fort Simpson, 27 August 1872. MG 17, Class C, C.1/M.9, reel A-80. CMS papers, NAC.

13. W.C. Bompas to secretaries of CMS, Fort Vermilion, 8 April 1868. MG 17, Class C, C.1/M.7, reel A-80. CMS papers, NAC.

14. Ibid., p. 98.

15. W.C. Bompas to secretaries, Fort Chipewyan, 6 July 1871. MG 17, Class C, C.1/M.8, reel A-80, p. 97. CMS papers, NAC.

16. W.C. Bompas to secretary, Peace River, 27 September 1871. MG 17, Class C, C.1/M.8, reel A-80, p. 151. CMS papers, NAC.

17. W.C. Bompas to secretaries, Fort Vermilion, 13 November 1871. MG 17, Class C, C.1/M.8, reel A-80, p. 273. CMS papers, NAC.

18. W.C. Bompas to secretaries, Fort Vermilion, 13 November 1871. MG 17, Class C, C.1/M.8, reel A-80, p. 275. CMS papers, NAC.

19. *Vie de Mgr Taché*, vol. 2, p. 693 and elsewhere.

20. *Histoire de l'Église catholique*, 3 vols., p. 4 and elsewhere.

21. *Vie de Mgr Taché*, vol. 2, p. 693.

22. Ibid., p. 484.

23. *Histoire de l'Église catholique*, vol. 3, p. 4. The identical statement is found in Vital Grandin, "Journal de voyage," *Missions OMI* 19, 1881, p. 198.

24. "Codex historicus de la mission d'Albany," 1883, LCB 3301.A42c 1a, AD.

25. F.-X. Fafard to the Oblate superior general, Fort Albany, 22 December 1893. *Missions OMI* 32, 1894, pp. 52, 65.

26. A. Langevin, "Rapport du vicariat de Saint-Boniface au Chapitre de 1898," *Missions OMI* 36, 1898, p. 269.

27. Ovide Charlebois (1862–1933), the brother of two other Oblates (Guillaume and Charles), became the first apostolic vicar of Keewatin in 1910. He resided at The Pas, Manitoba.

28. É. Bonnald to Oblate assistant general Soullier, Pelican Narrows, 10 November 1891. *Missions OMI* 30, 1892, p. 192.

29. É. Bonnald to Soullier, Pelican Narrows, 29 August 1892. *Missions OMI* 31, 1893, p. 42.

30. É. Bonnald to the director of the *Annales*, Pelican Narrows, 1 November 1894. *Missions OMI* 33, 1895, p. 6.

31. É. Bonnald to [name unknown], Cross Lake, 27 June 1904. *Missions OMI* 42, 1904, p. 407.

32. T. Campeau to Father Camper, Qu'Appelle, 19 January 1890. *Missions OMI* 39, 1891, p. 21.

33. T. Campeau to Oblate superior general, Montagne de Tondre, January, 1895. *Missions OMI* 33, 1895, pp. 279–80.

34. H. Leduc to the Oblate superior general, St. Albert, 22 December 1870. *Missions OMI* 11, 1873, p. 206.

35. *Missions OMI* 11, 1873, p. 351.

36. This is an allusion to Pope Pius IX declaring himself a prisoner of the Vatican in 1870, in protest against the seizure of the Papal States by the government of Italy.

37. H. Leduc to Father Aubert, St. Albert, 29 June 1872. *Missions OMI* 12, 1874, p. 38.

38. H. Leduc to Father De L'Hermite, Calgary, 31 December 1887. *Missions OMI* 26, 1888, p. 153.

39. V. Grandin, *Journal*, 1881. *Missions OMI* 20, 1882, p. 317.

40. H. Leduc to Father De L'Hermite, Calgary, 31 December 1887. *Missions OMI* 26, 1888, p. 158.

41. V. Grandin to Joseph Fabre, St. Albert, 6 April 1889. *Missions OMI* 28, 1890, p. 229.

42. A. Desmarais to I. Clut, Lesser Slave Lake, 8 July 1888. *Missions OMI* 28, 1890, p. 258.

43. I. Clut to Oblate superior general, Fort Yukon, 27 February 1873. *Missions OMI* 12, 1874, p. 283.

44. V. Grandin, *Journal*, Fort Cumberland, 3 August 1880. *Missions OMI* 19, 1881, p. 267.

45. J.-J.-M. Lestanc to Father Aubert, Fort Pitt, 30 July 1879. *Missions OMI* 18, 1880, p. 177.

46. A. Lacombe to Oblate superior general, Winnipeg, 24 December 1877. *Missions OMI* 16, p. 169.

47. V. Fourmond to [name unknown], St. Laurent, 15 December 1879. *Missions OMI* 18, 1880, pp. 258–64.

48. H. Leduc, "Rapport sur le vicariat de Saint-Albert... 1879." *Missions OMI* 17, 1879, p. 446.

49. T. Cahill to a priest, [Rat Portage], n.d. *Missions OMI* 29, p. 30.

50. *À la Baie d'Hudson*, p. 101.

51. Malcolm McLeod, *Peace River: A Canoe Journey* (Ottawa: n.p., 1872), p. 64, cited in A.-G. Morice, *Histoire de l'Église catholique dans l'Ouest canadien*, p. 21.

52. Ibid., vol. 2, p. 386.

53. Ibid., p. 419.

54. C.C. McLaurin, pp. 18–21.

55. "Deux sermons," *Le Manitoba*, 14 August 1884. Cited in *Missions OMI* 22, 1884, p. 401–2.

56. H. Leduc to Father De L'Hermite, Calgary, 31 December 1887. *Missions OMI* 26, 1888, p. 165.

57. É. Grouard to Father De L'Hermite, Dunvegan, 5 December 1883. *Missions OMI* 22, p. 156.

58. É. Bonnald to the director of the *Annales*, Pelican Narrows, 23 November 1897. *Missions OMI* 36, 1898, p. 22.

59. É. Bonnald to the director of the *Annales*, Pelican Narrows, 15 November 1896. *Missions OMI* 35, 1897, pp. 5–23.

CHAPTER IX

OBLATE TACTICS OF CONQUEST

Having scouted, then occupied the immense North and West of Canada after 1845, and while engaged in continual conflict with their Protestant missionary rivals, the Oblates undertook to carry out what had brought them across the Atlantic Ocean, or from Canada through several long weeks of travel across half the North American continent. They set out to convert, or conquer, the native people they encountered, an objective that was achieved by evangelizing and civilizing the Amerindians.

The secular priests who had preceded the Oblates in the region had done little for the native people, their limited numbers barely allowing them to serve the white settlements in the immediate area of Red River and Fort Vancouver. We know that Father Bellecourt was an exception to this rule, Father Thibault another; the same may be said for Father Demers's voyage up the Fraser River in 1841. However, a sustained and consistent effort at evangelizing native people awaited the arrival of the Oblates.

Evangelization required financial resources, and the Oblates had little. How would they manage to conquer such a vast domain, particularly in light of the wealthier Protestant competition? What were their methods and their tactics? These were fundamentally determined by Catholic doctrine, by the bearing of personal Christian witness, and by the establishment and management of churches and schools.

Evangelization also meant civilization, for the nineteenth-century Catholic or Protestant missionary never questioned the superiority of

Euro-Canadian ways, and indeed their necessity for any and all who wished to enter the Kingdom of God. Not that the missionaries could not observe the differences in circumstances and required resources among diverse communities of whites, Indians, and Métis. But all missionaries knew that, willy-nilly, in the end all would have to adapt to Euro-Canadian ways. To conform to the Euro-Canadian model, the Indians had to be taught the white man's language and ways; they had to be assimilated. Only then could they be Christianized. The objective was similar *vis-à-vis* the Métis, the only difference being that these people of mixed race did not have as far to go in order to conform to the ways of the white man.

In terms of the primary objective, conversion through evangelization and civilization, there was no significant difference between the Oblate and Protestant missionaries. Both were assimilationists. However, they did differ in their respective definitions of Christian doctrine, Christian life, and Christian evangelization: in their greater or lesser willingness to endure suffering in the mission field; in the degree of sensitivity and understanding they showed *vis-à-vis* the Indian way of life; in their distance from or *rapprochement* with the latter; in their critical stance before the dominant British culture; and in their clerical roles. Consequently, while the primary objective was the same, Protestant and Catholic tactics and methods differed significantly.

Moreover, the effectiveness of the Oblate missionary methods and tactics were affected by the quality of the Christian witness given by the missionary.

Financing Missions

A recurring weapon in the arsenal of both missionary groups was the accusation that the other was purchasing Indian converts through gifts of tobacco, blankets, clothing, food, beads, medals, or trinkets of one kind or another. Given the avowed official hostility between the camps, and the lack of detailed comparative financial studies of various missions, it is impossible to judge whether such accusations were founded or were merely the result of antipathy or jealousy.

Nevertheless, it would seem that a major inequality between Catholic and Anglican clergymen in Rupert's Land was their respective revenues. Without exception, Church of England clergymen were salaried by one of the Anglican missionary societies or by the Hudson's Bay Company (HBC). For example, in 1854, four of the six Anglican ministers resident in Red River were salaried by one of the three English missionary societies;[1] the two other ministers were in the employ of the HBC as chaplains or teachers.[2] Bishop Anderson lived off the revenue provided by a £10,000 diocesan trust fund, left as an endowment by a retired HBC officer; this was supplemented by a £300 annual salary paid by the HBC. The Church Missionary Society (CMS) minister's annual salary was usually £200 per annum; other grants covering the costs of the mission frequently amounted to some £150 per annum.

Most of the human and financial resources for Church of England missions came from London's CMS. In 1895, the CMS spent £18,000 in support of its Canadian missions, funding the work of forty-nine white clergymen, eleven ordained Indians, and five laymen.

The financing of Catholic missions was different in some ways, but was similarly based in Europe and run from there by an international missionary organization, the Missionary Oblates of Mary Immaculate.

Seventeen Catholic bishops resided and had jurisdiction in Canada's Northwest, British Columbia included, before the year 1900. Five of them were the successive administrators of the diocese of Victoria, covering Vancouver Island; another three directed the destinies of the Catholic Church on the British Columbia mainland. Beginning with Bishop Provencher, the nine others were more or less directly dependent on the diocese of St. Boniface, working either in the archdiocese itself or in its subdivisions that encompassed the prairies and the Mackenzie basin. Eleven of those seventeen bishops were Oblates, the exceptions being the five bishops of Vancouver Island as well as Bishop Provencher. Clearly, therefore, with the sole exception of the diocese of Vancouver Island , the Church of the Canadian Northwest was an Oblate monopoly during the second half of the nineteenth century.

This monopoly was directed by the Oblate superior general and his council residing in Marseilles until 1862, thereafter in Paris. The founder and first superior general of the Oblates, Eugène de Mazenod, was succeeded by Joseph Fabre, who remained in office until his death in 1893, and then by Louis Soullier, who died in 1898.

Just as Church of England missionaries in the Northwest were usually despatched, led, and funded by England's CMS, with some assistance from the Society for the Promotion of Christian Knowledge in the areas of church-building and the provision of prayerbooks and Bibles, Roman Catholic missionaries in the Northwest were with few exceptions sent out, directed, and funded by France's Missionary Oblates of Mary Immaculate. The funding was obtained by Oblate headquarters primarily from the French Société pour la propagation de la foi, a secondary source of funding being the Œuvre de la Sainte Enfance. Oblate headquarters received an annual block grant from the former, the Society for the Propagation of the Faith, and then distributed the money to the various areas of Oblate endeavour, after having deducted whatever costs it felt were applicable to the respective missions. So it was that Bishop Taché received an annual block grant, which he used as necessary. For example, for the twelve months preceding September 1863, Bishop Taché's revenues consisted of 55,000 francs[3] from the Society for the Propagation of the Faith, 3,000 from the Œuvre de la Sainte Enfance, 6,000 in Mass stipends, and 8,500 in investment revenues, a total of 72,500 francs. Taché declared that fully 60,000 of the total was spent on northern missions, while the balance of 12,500 francs was used in Red River to cover the expenses of the bishop's house, the college, the convent, and the parishes.[4]

As would be expected, available funds were never sufficient to meet the demands of all the missionaries, a situation that resulted in protracted disputes and animosity among some Oblates. Bishop Henri Faraud was probably the most cantankerous in this regard. Not only did he accuse Taché of keeping an excessive share of money for himself, but he also spent most of his episcopal years (1865–90) engaged in protracted quarrels with Oblate headquarters over various issues relating to money. For example, Faraud was incensed when he and other missionary bishops were ordered by Oblate headquarters to cease collecting money in France, because the Society for the Propagation of the Faith did not appreciate the competition for the money of the French faithful. Bishop Faraud was also furious in 1882 when Oblate headquarters deducted $2,000 from his grant in order to cover travel expenses for the mentally deranged Émile Petitot. Faraud also felt that the Oblate congregation was taxing him excessively for the costs of training prospective Oblates, and asked that his share of the expenses be reduced. He commented in 1882:

> My request has raised indignation, antipathy, and wrath. To punish me, for the past six years all of my letters have gone unanswered... The ties with the directors of the congregation are already seriously weakened... All my comments and criticisms are met by a silence worse than the most damaging insults... It is self-satisfied absolutism that brooks no discussion.[5]

Faraud continued to complain in subsequent years, always condemning the "false ideas" entertained by the Oblate administrators about the Northwest, ideas resulting in alleged glaring injustices and the ongoing weakening and destruction of Catholic missions.

In this system of funding, Catholic missionaries did not receive salaries from any quarter. In 1854, the annual grant from the Société pour la propagation de la foi to the diocese of St. Boniface amounted to £450. The Catholic bishop used these funds as he saw fit. In fact the Catholic priest had the reputation of being poor, the Presbyterian Alexander Ross writing in 1855 that the typical priest was usually sent out on his missionary journeys equipped with little more than £10 and his bishop's blessing.

It was much more expensive to support a Church of England minister. The total annual grant for the Catholic diocese of St. Boniface was barely more than the cost of keeping the Anglican mission of The Pas, which was staffed by one minister and his family, in addition to a catechist. Associate Governor Eden Colville of the HBC therefore wrote to Governor Simpson in the 1850s as follows:

> I think it is quite out of the question for anyone to think of establishing a Church of England mission in Athabasca or McKenzie River, as they must have in the first place a wife, and in the second place about two boat loads of goods, provisions and luxuries. As an instance of the moderate way in which the Catholic missionaries conduct their affairs, I may observe that at Isle la Crosse last year, the total expenses of the [Catholic] mission amounted to £54, while the allowance of flour was limited to one bag per individual connected with the mission. If you will compare this with the expenses of the Pas [Anglican] mission, and the boat loads of Red River produce and pemmican that are sent there annually, I think you will agree with me that... Church of England clergymen [are not suitable for McKenzie River or Athabasca].[6]

Oblate Missionary Methods and Tactics

Evangelization meant that the Indians were to be taught Catholicism, to memorize the doctrines, to recite the prayers, to perform the rituals, and generally to believe in and abide by the instructions of the missionary. A new world-view was in the offing.

Because of their Roman Catholicism, the Oblates had a decided advantage over their Protestant rivals[7] in the conduct of Indian missions. The most fundamental reason for this advantage is the sacramentalism that is a basic characteristic of Catholic doctrine. Starting from a theology of continuity between nature and the transcendent, Catholics believe that any created object, person, or institution can be the locus and bearer of God's grace. The Catholic thus tends to be much more appreciative of the ways of nature, of the ways of the Indian, including marriages *à la façon du pays*. The seven rites designated by the Church as statutory carriers of God's grace, the sacraments, are the completion, or the perennial ritual fulfilment, of this visible and tangible presence of the gifts of God. These sacraments are baptism, the Eucharist, penance, confirmation, marriage, Holy Orders, and the sacrament of the sick. The administration of the sacraments is usually embedded in liturgical ritual forms that are colourful, aesthetically pleasing or at least dramatic, and unlike any other form of social activity. God can thus be made readily apparent.

The Catholic missionary sought to nurture the Indian towards sanctity by gradually increasing his faith, guided by sermons, the catechism, and the sacraments. After teaching the Indian the rudimentary tenets of Catholic doctrine, the missionary could baptize him, confident that in time, nourished by sacraments, the convert would advance to a more robust Catholic faith. As was the case for the Catholic missionary, the Catholic convert's Christian health depended more upon the gradual nurture by his Church's sacramental teachings and practices than upon his individual history or accomplishments.

For their part, evangelical Protestant missionaries started from a fundamentally different theology, one of discontinuity between nature and the transcendent. Martin Luther and his sixteenth-century followers had taught that the human being is corrupt to the core; only the merits of the atoning Christ, as son of God, could make a man appear just in the eyes of God. God empowered sinners to acknowledge this state of affairs, and to change their ways through conversion, a cathartic personal experience whereby one turned suddenly and miraculously, by the gift of God, from sin to grace. There was nothing gradual about this. It was analogous to passing instantaneously from darkness to light, or to being knocked off your horse by a divine thunderbolt. Here, conversion was a definite and radical step instead of a process. This meant that Indians were expected to show a sudden change of heart, in order to become members of a Protestant church. If they were truly converted, they would have to immediately abandon any and all reprehensible behaviour. The logic of Protestant doctrine made the minister more intolerant of human foibles, for either you were converted or you were not; you either had the grace of God, or you didn't. The same logic also tended to cast a pall over native customs and traditions that were foreign to the Protestant missionary. After all, was sin not all-pervasive?

Sacrament is not as central to Protestant theology as it is to the Catholic. Thus, for the Catholic, baptism immediately removes sin and delivers grace; while, for the Protestant, baptism can be understood as the symbolic recognition of a conversion that has already taken place in the person's heart. Therefore, the Catholic missionary was in more of a hurry to baptize converts, for the very act of baptizing ensured the washing away of sin. Similarly, for the evangelical Protestant the Eucharist was merely a symbol of the communicant's faith; for the Catholic it was the eating of the body of Christ, and the drinking of His blood, which meant a physical and immediate communion with God. Therefore, the priest was determined to celebrate the Eucharist frequently and regularly, while the minister was in less of a hurry.

These basic theological differences resulted in notable differences between Protestant and Catholic missions. John Webster Grant writes:

> There was a difference of atmosphere between a Protestant and a Roman Catholic mission that could not have been missed by the most casual visitor. A Protestant mission was open at least to the more official aspects of Canadian life... A Roman Catholic mission was much more an entity to itself... In a Protestant mission one could observe the makings of a Christian congregation, in its Catholic counterpart those of a Christian band or clan... Priests and nuns were surrounded by a mystique of separateness which the Protestant clergy did not share... Roman Catholics often came close to identifying sanctity with suffering... Protestants were more inclined to think of hardships as obstacles to be overcome... On a Protestant mission there was likely to be greater pressure to conform to European norms and more evidence of the effects of such pressure. Roman Catholics might habitually use the same rhetoric of Christianity and civilization, but acculturation was clearly secondary to catechism. By contrast, Roman Catholics kept a closer check on Indian behaviour and religious practice, whereas a Protestant mission was likely to allow Indians more freedom of action... Indian initiative was more conspicuous around a Protestant mission..., while the ambience of a Catholic community was more recognizably Indian.[8]

Armed with a theology aimed at transforming the natural environment, as opposed to condemning and escaping it, the Oblates adopted missionary methods and tactics that were very similar in the prairies, Athabasca–Mackenzie, and British Columbia. Once among the Indians, the missionary usually followed a standard agenda of daily activity, aimed at creating a local church.

When evangelizing the Métis, Catholic missionaries had no language to learn, for the missionaries were with rare exception French-speaking, as were the Métis. This gave the priests a decided advantage over the Protestant missionaries who were all English-speaking, in a country where the vast majority of HBC workers were Métis or French-Canadian. This was the main reason why Father Thibault was able to reap such a rich reward in souls immediately upon his arrival in the

Edmonton area in 1842, in spite of the fact that the Reverend Rundle had been at work there for the previous two years; and Rundle was no slouch.

In all areas, the first priority was to learn the aboriginal languages, preferably before even setting foot in the mission field.

In fact most Catholic missionaries did learn the Indian languages. In his 1859 report to the Canadian surveyor Dawson, Bishop Taché declared categorically:

> The first thing we do upon arrival amidst a tribe, even before arriv-
> ing if possible, is to learn its language. Not all missionaries are
> equally successful, but all soon manage to do without interpreters,
> and instruct the Indians directly, a condition essential to the suc-
> cess of a mission.[9]

A number of missionaries spent some time with the Sulpician priests in Oka near Montreal, learning the Algonquian language of the Montagnais. Others would learn the language of the Ojibwa from Father Bellecourt in Red River, and others from a variety of other experienced missionaries at Île-à-la-Crosse or elsewhere. In most cases, this was their first duty upon being chosen for the missions.

The Oblates had soon borrowed the Reverend Evans's syllabic script to compose or translate prayerbooks, hymnals, and catechisms into a variety of aboriginal languages; the texts were printed at centres like Lake La Biche and Fort Chipewyan, or in more distant places such as Montreal or Paris.

Taché vigorously denied accusations by detractors that missionaries purchased converts by giving them tobacco and other gifts; on the other hand, several Catholic missionaries accused their rivals of doing just that. In fact, Protestant missionaries had more money, allowing them to make more generous gifts to the Amerindians who frequented their missions. This constantly rankled Catholic missionaries, leading to accusations by the latter.

As a rule, the Catholic missionary was more explorer and builder than theologian. Bishop Taché rushed to the defence of his men when they were accused of being too rough-hewn. He argued that their lives were all too frequently those of workers, swinging an axe, wielding a hoe, snowshoeing, fishing, farming, or building a cabin. Such activities, year in and year out, did not make for sophisticated men of letters or theologians. However, it was such thankless work that had ensured the foundations of most of the Northwest's first Christian communities.

Neither were the Métis boatmen sophisticated or educated people. Nevertheless, many observers testified to their unwavering Christian faith and sincerity. The 1854 observations of Methodist pastor John Ryerson will be seen later. Émile Petitot spoke in similar terms, based on his observations during his voyage on HBC barges from St. Boniface to the upper Saskatchewan in June 1862. Petitot wrote of the boatmen:

> In the evening, we recite the rosary, followed by instructions, prayers, and the singing of a hymn. The piety of these people would shame many Europeans, especially French Christians, and I rejoice in acknowledging it. One never hears them cursing or swearing. After taking their evening meal, they unashamedly drop to their knees to say their prayers; and upon waking in the morning, the first thing they do is cross themselves. What an admirable simplicity and faith among these rough-hewn men... Their life is very hard, and yet they never complain or grumble but always have a ready smile... Bent over their oars until nine or ten o'clock in the evening, they take a short rest, only to begin anew at two o'clock in the morning.[10]

In the missions of British Columbia, a unique system of evangelization was put in place by the Oblates, Father Paul Durieu in particular. After working for five years at the Oblate station on Lake Okanagan (1859–64), and then spending the following year at New Westminster (1864–65), Durieu busied himself with the evangelization of the Indians on the lower Fraser River. Using the Catholic ladder invented by Father François-Norbert Blanchet in 1838 and refined by Albert Lacombe in 1874, Durieu had a clear and simple instrument for teaching Christian doctrine. The "Catholic ladder" was a graphic representation of the history of salvation, showing the human being's progressive peregrination towards salvation, from the time of creation. It would become a standard instrument of Indian evangelization from Lake Superior to the Pacific Ocean. Lacombe's ladder included the innovation that the story of salvation was presented in two paths, good and evil. Needless to say, Protestants were not on the side of the angels.

Father Durieu reinforced his teaching by organizing Indian villages around the Eucharistic rite. The residents were entrusted with the policing of their own villages to ensure that they observed the teachings of the missionaries. When engaged on his missionary tours, a priest, upon arriving in an Indian village, spent the better part of the day instructing the people and baptizing children. In the evening, the inhabitants held a ceremony wherein a village captain, two soldiers, and two policemen were elected to assist the village chief in policing the village, according to the rules laid down by the missionary. Such elections and system of self-government were organized in as many Indian villages as possible. Bishop D'Herbomez felt that it was a very effective system for keeping the Amerindians on the straight and narrow path.[11]

Some missionaries spent most of their time resident at their stations near the fur-trade posts that Indians visited once or twice a year, usually in the early summer and the fall. In these cases they were very busy for the few weeks of the year when the Indians visited; the rest of the time they simply ran their small parish of year-round white and Métis residents. Many itinerant missionaries to aboriginal people travelled at the expense of the HBC, which provided canoe, barge, or horse, in addition to handling the transportation of supplies for the missionary. Once in place in his mission of residence, the missionary frequently travelled in the surrounding area on his own, providing his own dog team or canoe.

On arriving in an Indian village, at times seeing to the election of elders or policemen, the missionary held three meetings a day in his church. The morning meeting consisted of prayers, Mass, and sermon; the midday meeting centred on catechetical instruction; the evening meeting was the occasion for another sermon. In the intervals, the priest met individuals or smaller groups of Indians to teach them catechism or hymns. This was the system that led to the entry of most of the Indians of the Canadian Northwest into the Catholic Church.[12]

The schedule of missionaries working with white people, either along the railroad or in the new white settlements of the prairies, differed somewhat from the above. We have seen that Father Lacombe evangelized the CPR construction gangs in 1880–82. Such practices were typical for all missionaries working along the railroads, be it in northern Ontario, British Columbia, or the prairies. It was also the schedule for itinerant missionaries to white settlements—that is to say, the priest would arrive in the afternoon, gather the people together for prayers in the evening, give catechetical preparation to facilitate the reception of sacraments on the morrow, and hear confessions. At dawn, Mass was celebrated, Communion was distributed, the team of horses was hitched to the buckboard, and the priest headed to his next missionary way station.

We know that Catholic missionaries usually got along well with civil or HBC administrators, be they Protestant or Catholic. There are several cases of noteworthy cooperation and goodwill. One of these occurred when the governor of Vancouver Island registered his daughters in the sisters' school in Victoria in 1858; in the same town seven years later Oblate Father James McGuckin reported on the generosity of the Royal Navy Protestants, chaplain included, when McGuckin collected money for the construction of a chapel in Esquimalt.

Quality of Oblate Christian Witness

One of the most powerful tools of evangelization in any mission is the Christian witness given by the missionary. When the potential convert sees a missionary who truly and sincerely practises what he preaches, the effectiveness of his apostolate is greatly enhanced. Conversely, when the missionary is seen to be a living contradiction of his own words, scepticism, indifference, and hostility ensue. How did the Oblates fare in this regard?

The best laid plans and the skills of church administrators were directly dependent on the number, and especially the quality, of the priests who staffed and oversaw the mission stations. Protestant clergymen, especially those of the Church of England, have not received very favourable comment in recent scholarly studies of the Northwest. As far as Catholic priests are concerned, their story is the same as that for the bishops; most traditional writing about them that does exist is hagiographic. In order to better understand the missionary story, it is useful to examine these men more carefully.

In addition to a score of secular priests, 273 Oblates worked in Canada's greater Northwest between 1845 and 1900, some of them spending most of their adult lives in the territory, others staying for varying lengths of time. The record of these missionaries reveals that most of them were honest men, trying as best they could to bear witness to the Gospel in circumstances that were frequently very difficult. Indeed, the missionaries, particularly the earliest ones, were dealing with a Stone Age civilization, in languages that they had to learn in the field without the benefit of book or guide. Moreover, they performed their spiritual tasks while frequently fending for themselves to ensure adequate shelter, food, and transportation, in a climate that was far from hospitable. Most missionaries led honest, honourable, and generous lives of Christian witness, while showing all the greatness and misery that are the lot of humankind. While ranging in moral quality all the way from the mediocre to the outstanding, some ninety percent of the Catholic missionaries in the Canadian North and West were faithful to their calling.

Some ten percent of all the clergymen active in the Northwest before 1900 were problem cases. These men created serious problems for their colleagues, for the faithful, and for their superiors, and they did so for a variety of reasons. Some simply became insane, in some cases stark-raving mad, having to be removed from the territory in chains and under armed guard. It seems that the total isolation of some missionaries in the more remote stations resulted in a good number losing their senses. Others were misfits who should never have been either ordained or allowed to fill positions of responsibility. Others again proved satisfactory for a few years, and then soured, seeming to have given up on their religious or their Christian ideals. This group of missionaries, perhaps twenty in all over more than half a century, included just about every kind of sinner, ranging from thieves, pedophiles, and fornicators, to liars and generally miserable human beings—lazy, vain, or incapable of living with anyone.[13]

Some of the Oblates who were considered outstanding have been discussed, including Archbishop Taché, Bishop Grandin, fathers Lacombe and Séguin, and Brother Kearney. Some of the more extreme problem cases we have also met, such as Émile Petitot and Henri Grollier. Most of the others fell into the intermediate category, ranging from the very good to the mediocre.

While Protestant clergymen constantly attacked the evils of popery, the perception of the Catholic missionary by Protestants, both clerical and lay, was a most favourable one in the writings of the period. The Catholic priest was admired, respected, and feared by his Protestant adversary. He was also frequently highly praised by sundry clergymen and faithful for his abnegation, zeal, and dedication.

The reputation of the Catholic missionaries outshone that of the Protestants. One expression of this grudging respect was that of Superintendent John Ryerson of the Canadian Methodist Conference, who visited Rupert's Land and commented at length on the Catholic missions he visited. On 3 July 1854, upon visiting the Catholic mission in an Indian village, a mile and a half above Fort William, he was received and treated "with courteous respect" by the resident missionary, probably Jesuit Father Dominique Du Ranquet.[14] Ryerson described the mission station:

> The church is comfortable, and... is a fine building... about 30 by 40 feet in size... and will accommodate from 200 to 300 persons. The parsonage is a neat house, 30 by 36 feet on the ground... The building of these... substantial structures... was accomplished principally by [Du Ranquet's] own hands, and during the same time he performed his ordinary work as priest, besides assisting in the day school, visiting it twice every day, catechising and instructing the children. [Du Ranquet] has only been eight or nine years among the Indians, yet speaks their language fluently, and preaches in it with great ease. His bedroom is also his workshop, study, and sitting-

room. In one corner of the room is the bed, consisting of a pillow and two buffalo skins; in another corner of the room are wide shelves, holding his carpenter and joiner tools, and in another corner is his desk, writing-apparatus, and a few books; in another part of the room a box, stool, and two chairs... I remarked to our brethren, that such laborious and self-denying zeal was worthy of a better cause than the spreading of Popery, and that it was humiliating to ourselves, contrasted with the exertion and success of some of our own missionaries, who seemed to measure out their work, both with regard to kind and extent, with as much care and exactness as a Jew would measure silk velvet. I recollect one missionary, if not more than one, who objected to teaching a day-school on the ground that it was not quite canonical, and was beneath the dignity of the ministerial office;... One thing is certain, that the Roman Catholic missionaries throughout these extensive regions, in zeal, in labour, self-denial, and in success in their work, are much, very much before us, and unless we bestir ourselves with very much more united, earnest, and persevering exertion than what we yet have, this whole country will be overspread and hedged in with the briars, thorns, and hedges of Popery.[15]

John Ryerson continued his tour, describing the gratifying reception reserved for him in the Red River Catholic and Anglican missions. While travelling from Norway House to York Factory in an HBC boat brigade, the Methodist superintendent described the behaviour of the Catholic boatmen on the sabbath, thereby indirectly praising the work of the Catholic missionary. The Métis leader, the guide Bruce, gathered the crews together and "they united in the prayers of the Roman church, in which they apparently engaged with sincerity and earnestness."[16]

Another expression of the esteem felt for Catholic missionaries can be found in the published account of the 1859 visit to the area by a British tourist, the Earl of Southesk. Southesk wrote of the kindness and hospitality shown him at the Lake St. Anne mission run by "perfect gentlemen," fathers Lacombe and Frain. According to Southesk, Rome had a decided advantage in this respect, for the Protestants regularly sent crude and uneducated people to their missions, while Rome sent well-mannered and educated gentlemen who also excelled in the art of winning over the Indians.[17] Southesk spoke in glowing terms of the prosperity and beauty of the Lake St. Anne mission.

Four years later, two other British tourists, Lord Milton and W.B. Cheadle, visited the mission at St. Albert. They wrote:

It must be confessed that the Romish priests far excel their Protestant brethren in missionary enterprise and influence. They have established stations... far out in the wilds, undeterred by danger or hardship..., while the... [Protestants] remain inert enjoying the ease and comfort of the Red River settlement, or at most make an occasional summer's visit to some of the nearest posts.[18]

Although there is no denying the courage and abnegation of some Protestant missionaries—George McDougall, for example—in the 1860s their reputation was not the best. While several observers, such as Ross, Southesk, and Milton noted the ministers' propensity to stay within the confines of the trading posts, over the years the character, personality, and activities of several Protestant missionaries had been impugned by Governor Simpson and other HBC officers. The most famous case had been the recall of James Evans from Norway House in 1846, at the request of Governor Simpson; although formally cleared of charges, a cloud hung over Evans due to the nature of the accusations against him. He had been suspected of killing his assistant, Thomas Hassall, in 1844, in order to avail himself of Hassall's wife. He was also accused by Rossville residents of sexually exploiting young Indian women who lived in his residence. The charges were never proven, but the innuendo was devastating.

In 1862–63, a more clear-cut case occurred when a Church of England clergyman at Red River, Griffiths Owen Corbett, was imprisoned and officially charged with attempting, no fewer than five times, to induce a miscarriage in the sixteen-year-old Maria Thomas, who was carrying his child. The sensational trial was held in February 1863, and Corbett was found guilty, imprisoned, and then liberated (May 1863) by a mob of country-born followers whom he had impressed with his anti-Catholic and anti-French oratory. For the next year, in spite of having been suspended by Bishop Anderson, Corbett reassumed command of his parish at Headingley, which he had founded ten years earlier.

Such events were bound to impress any observer, and to cause considerable scepticism about the integrity of the Protestant clergy. In reaction, many praised the Catholic missionaries, in some cases making them larger than life.

The Oblates of Mary Immaculate were the cutting edge of the Catholic ultramontane conquest of Canada's Northwest. Their apostolic methods were fundamentally determined by their Catholic doctrine and theology, which in turn determined specific policies, methods, and tactics in relation to Indians, their evangelization, and their conversion to Christianity.

However, in the eyes of the Oblates, two other avenues of endeavour were almost as important as the Church in the successful conquest and conversion of the greater Northwest. These were the settlement of the West by Francophone Catholics, and the establishment of Catholic schools. This was where nationalisms clashed.

Notes

1. The Church Missionary Society (CMS), the Society for the Propagation of the Gospel (SPG), and the Colonial and Continental Church Society (CCCS).

2. William Howard Brooks, p. 100. John Ryerson, p. 71.

3. The franc had been the legal currency of France since the Revolution. Since its value fluctuated considerably over the years, it is difficult to establish its equivalent value in English pounds sterling, the legal currency in Canada until 1850 and in the Northwest until it became part of Canada. The value of the franc was strengthened in 1960 when one *new franc* was declared to be worth 100 old francs. In 1850, the English pound was worth twenty shillings, each shilling in turn being worth twelve pence.

4. A. Taché to H. Faraud, Red River, 16 September 1863. Taché papers, AG.

5. H. Faraud to I. Clut, Lake La Biche, 18 November 1882. Faraud papers, AG.

6. Cited in E.E. Rich (ed.), *London Correspondence from Eden Colville, 1849–52*, p. 225, cited in F.A. Peake, "The Achievements and Frustrations of James Hunter," p. 155.

7. In comparing Catholic and Protestant missionary methods, the author has been influenced by a large number of studies. Particularly useful in their perceptive analyses are John Webster Grant, *Moon of Wintertime*, and Howard L. Harrod.

8. John Webster Grant, *Moon of Wintertime*, pp. 227–8.

9. Red River, 7 February 1859. *Missions OMI* 2, 1863, p. 177.

10. Portage la Loche, 23 July 1862. *Missions OMI* 2, 1863, p. 215.

11. New Westminster, 28 November 1868. *Missions OMI* 9, 1870, p. 101.

12. In 1899 the Department of Indian Affairs enumerated 100,000 Indians in Canada of whom three quarters were Christian. The 1971 census enumerated 313,000 native people in Canada, some 300,000 of whom were Christian. Of these Christians, 174,000 were Catholic, 69,000 Anglican, and 32,000 United Church. (See John Webster Grant, *Moon of Wintertime*, p. 242.) The census of Canada for 1991 reported that 401,000 of Canada's aboriginal population of 471,000 claimed to be Christian, fully eighty-five percent of the total. (Statistics Canada, *Religions in Canada: The Nation*, Catalogue 93–319.)

13. In studying the missionary record, the reader must be cautious, for the isolation of many mission stations frequently led missionaries to the edge of depression and consequent exaggeration of their difficulties; in other words, they tended to make mountains out of molehills.

14. The Fort William mission was staffed by Jesuit Father Jean-Pierre Chôné between 1847 and 1852, and then by Jesuit Father Dominique Du Ranquet from 1852 to 1877. Ryerson does not mention the missionary's name.

15. John Ryerson, pp. 18–19.

16. Ibid., p. 93.

17. Earl of Southesk, *Saskatchewan and the Rocky Mountains* (Edinburg: n.p., 1875), pp. 167–68. Cited in A.-G. Morice, *Histoire de l'Église catholique*, vol. 2, p. 105.

18. Cited in Katherine Hughes, p. 96.

CHAPTER X

A CLASH OF NATIONALISMS

One striking characteristic of the Oblate conquering regiment was that it was made up, almost to a man, of troops of French ethnic origin, from either France or Canada. Needless to say, their adversaries, the ministers of the Church of England's Church Missionary Society (CMS) and of the Methodist denomination, were just as overwhelmingly of British ethnic origin.

Few writers have commented on this, despite its manifest evidence. The reason they have not is that the theologies of neither the Catholics nor the Protestants made allowance for ethnic, cultural, or linguistic considerations. All people, whatever their ethnocultural roots, were supposed to be dealt with equally by the missionaries, for the Gospel was one, for any and all. While one cannot quarrel with this belief from a Christian theological perspective, what it meant in fact was that the churches and their missionaries were not conscious of the extent or depth to which their own religious stance was coloured by their own cultural attachments. Such cultural peculiarities become apparent in many areas of missionary history in the Northwest, in the rivalry between French and French-Canadian Oblates, and most obviously in the ethnocultural homogeneity of the opposing Catholic and Protestant regiments. They are also apparent in the French-Canadian Oblates' efforts to promote francophone settlement in the West, and in the manifold and conflictual endeavours of both parties in the area of schooling.

In fact, the 1870s proved to be the undoing of the Northwest's French-speaking Catholic community—a decade before the law would be changed to reflect the Anglo-Protestant dominance. In 1871, there was still hope for the West's francophones, who, in spite of the hounding of Riel, were busy establishing newspapers[1]; in 1877 they affiliated their St. Boniface College with the newly created University of Manitoba.

In Manitoba and Saskatchewan, the cry of "French domination" reverberated throughout the late nineteenth and early twentieth centuries, as it had done regularly in Canada since the Conquest. The francophobia was based on the same general fear of any and all who were different from, and therefore inferior to, the Anglo-Protestant governing elite. However, in the eyes of the latter, the French were especially dangerous, not only because of their power base in eastern Canada, and consequently in the Parliament of Canada, but also because they enjoyed full constitutional equality in the Manitoba Act and the Northwest Territories Act. French schools existed alongside English ones and, with few exceptions, all the Catholic clergymen, missionaries, and sisters who staffed hospitals and schools from Red River to British Columbia were francophone, a network constituting a real power base for the Catholics. Moreover, French was understood to be synonymous with Catholic. What better adversary for an Anglo-Protestant bigot? In legislating against all things French, the bigot could slay both French and Catholic dragons with one stroke of his Protestant pen. The "man of sin," the "Whore of Babylon," and the "Antichrist" would be lain to rest alongside the unworthy remnants of the Plains of Abraham.

St. Boniface College, erected in 1855.

In fact, by the latter part of the nineteenth century religious faith and ethnocultural feelings were intimately interwoven in the minds of most, anglophone or francophone. Bishop Grandin wrote in his personal notes:

> I am led to believe that several laypersons who support Protestantism fervently, even fanatically, do so primarily out of patriotism. The Indians call Catholicism the French religion and Protestantism the English religion. It is the truth for many of the public figures with whom I have had dealings; religion is for them more a matter of nationality than of conviction... To be a true English subject, one must be Protestant... [These people] favoured the ministers while telling me that they despised them, and opposed us more out of a sense of nationality than because of religious spirit. Many, I believe, are such.[2]

French and Canadian Oblates

By 1871, the year after the province of Manitoba had been created, the year of the founding of the Catholic diocese of St. Albert, and the year of British Columbia's entry into Confederation, a total of ninety-four Oblates had come to the greater Northwest. Fully eighty-two of these men were still there in 1871. Of the thirteen who were not, three had died in the country, three had left the Oblate congregation, and seven had gone to other areas of Oblate activity. Altogether, by the time of their deaths, these ninety-four men had averaged 36.6 years each in the missions of the Northwest.[3]

During the last thirty years of the century, the number of Oblates sent into the missions of the greater Northwest increased even more. In fact, by the year 1900 a total of 273 had been stationed in the region since 1845.

While the overwhelming majority of the first generation of Oblate missionaries were from France, only a few, like Alexandre Taché and Albert Lacombe, coming from Canada, during the latter part of the century the proportion of Canadians, mostly from Quebec, increased dramatically. Indeed, Superior General de Mazenod had constantly berated his colleagues in Canada for the few Oblate vocations the country was producing during the 1850s.[4] This changed rapidly in subsequent years so that by the turn of the century Canada was producing the lion's share of Oblate missionaries to the West and North.

As table 5 shows, the vast majority of Oblates came from France and Canada, and with few exceptions the Canadians were francophones from Quebec. Moreover, when one adds the Belgians and the

Table 5
Number and Country of Origin of Oblates in the Northwest, 1845–1900

COUNTRY OF ORIGIN	PRIESTS	BROTHERS	TOTAL
France	90	48	138
Canada	63	19	82
Germany	13	6	19
Belgium	5	1	6
Ireland	7	9	16
Other	6	6	12
TOTAL	184	89	273

Source: Archives of the Missionary Oblates of Mary Immaculate, St. Joseph's Provincial House, Montreal.

Germans, many of whom were from German lands adjacent to France, it is clear that the Oblates were an overwhelmingly francophone regiment. Oblate missionaries of British origin, like Joseph Patrick Kearney, Constantine Scollen, and James McGuckin, were unusual in the nineteenth century.

But francophone did not necessarily mean like-minded. These men belonged to the same church, worked under the same bishop, belonged to the same religious congregation under the same superior general, but did not necessarily see eye to eye on a wide range of issues. Upon conquering Canada in 1760, the British had discovered that a Canadian was not a Frenchman, each having forged his own distinct national identity. This would become just as apparent in the Northwest, among the Oblates in particular.

The seeds of ethnic and nationalistic division came to the dioceses of the North and West with the settlers and missionaries themselves. So it was that in the wake of the arrival of the Oblates in the Northwest, Bishop Provencher frequently reminded Bishop Bourget of Montreal that Canadian missionaries would be preferable to Frenchmen in the Northwest; they would be better liked by the Indians because of their more amenable personalities, their greater facility in undertaking long and difficult voyages, and their greater resistance to the cold.[5] Both Provencher and Bourget were Canadian. Much to Provencher's regret, a majority of European, particularly French, Oblates would be sent to the Northwest by Oblate headquarters in France, and all of the Oblate bishops would be Frenchmen. The sole exception would be Taché, who was chosen by the Canadian Provencher when another Canadian, Father Laflèche, could not accept the appointment. While none of these men would have confessed to nationalistic bias, all were convinced that the best episcopal candidates belonged to their ethnic group. It is therefore not surprising that animosities soon surfaced between French and Canadian Oblates.

Young Bishop Alexandre Taché first bore the brunt of this animosity. In 1851 Taché left Île-à-la-Crosse for Europe, where he was consecrated coadjutor bishop to Provencher on 23 November. Upon his return to his mission station in 1852, Taché discovered that his Oblate colleagues who had remained at Île-à-la-Crosse during his absence, fathers Jean Tissot and Augustin Maisonneuve, held a very low opinion of him; they were of the view that it would have been preferable to give the man a head instead of a mitre. It seems that the French Oblates wanted one of their own, Father François-Xavier Bermond of Red River, to be appointed coadjutor bishop. They refused to accept Taché's appointment and proceeded to make life as unbearable as possible for him, in the hope of forcing him to abandon the place. Bishop Taché described how he was treated like a fool, an animal, a detestable being with whom it was impossible to get along. In October 1852, when Taché held the Oblates' annual retreat at Île-à-la-Crosse, he also decreed that henceforth the mission's Oblates were to cease their disorderly lifestyle and follow Oblate rules. Thereupon, fathers Tissot and Maisonneuve went on strike, refusing to lift a finger around the mission and leaving the bishop to do all the chores, arguing that Taché had rendered them prisoners. Taché pretended not to be affected, performing all the chores himself with the assistance of the Oblate brother and the three hired men at the post. This ludicrous situation continued for several months, Taché writing in January 1853 that the Oblate Fathers of Île-à-la-Crosse were divided into two enemy camps.[6]

In the fall of 1854, upon Taché's departing Île-à-la-Crosse to take over the episcopal see of St. Boniface, the cabal by the French Oblates against their Canadian bishop was in full swing. Bishop Taché even accused his friend and colleague Henri Faraud of displaying the same pro-French and anti-Canadian sentiments in letters to the Oblate superior general, thereby contributing to Taché's discredit. While Taché vehemently denied any pro-Canadian bias, his Oblate colleagues had hatched the plan to have the French Oblate Father François-Xavier Bermond appointed as Taché's coadjutor, allegedly in order to prevent Taché from appointing a Canadian coadjutor. It was hoped that Taché would then remain in the wilds of Île-à-la-Crosse while Bermond handled the administration of the diocese and of the Oblates from St. Boniface. In fact, Taché later accused Bermond of being the prime agent of a long-standing plot to get rid of him, and had him recalled to France in 1856. However, Bermond continued agitating against Taché and managed to make him appear suspect in the eyes of Oblate headquarters.

Bishop de Mazenod resisted these feelings of mistrust, which would become full-blown under Father Fabre's administration. This in turn resulted in Taché's long-standing resentment over the machinations of Paris.[7]

The mutual suspicion between French and Canadian Oblates was then compounded for Taché by an administrative regulation adopted by Oblate headquarters on the recommendation of Visitor[8] Florent Vandenberghe on the occasion of his visit to the Northwest missions in 1865. The regulation established an Oblate bursar in St. Boniface, in the person of Father Joseph Lestanc. Lestanc was to control all Oblate finances in the Northwest, supplanting Bishop Taché, who had been performing these services. Taché considered the decision a slap in the face, a vote of non-confidence; he was profoundly hurt and humiliated. His feeling that, as a Canadian, he did not enjoy the full trust of his French colleagues and superiors was confirmed.

White Anglo-Protestantism

English was, of course, the common language of all British Protestants in the Northwest. Any other British language—those of the Scots or the Irish, for example, which were on the wane in the nineteenth century—was in fact disappearing from the areas of Canada where it had gained a toehold. Although there were some tensions and animosities between Scots, English, and Irish, these ethnic groups usually found themselves gathered in distinct churches that reflected their particular ethnocultural traits. While denominational divisions may have been a weakness of the Protestants in some respects, it did allow them to avoid the worst tensions of ethnocultural rivalry within the same church. So it was that Red River Presbyterian Alexander Ross enjoyed taking pot-shots at the Church of England clergy, the favourite scapegoats of many critics because of their close identification with the English ruling class in Red River. Methodists being just as English as the Church of England whence they sprung, both denominations usually got along very well; indeed, they frequently collaborated.

While the Oblate conquerors were challenging Protestants, they were simultaneously confronting English-speaking people, be they English, Scots, or Irish—that is, people of a distinct and common linguistic group, many of whose ancestors had been fighting the French for centuries.

During the last quarter of the nineteenth century, an ideology of imperialism was well rooted among English-speaking people, "a psychology which stressed the superiority of one 'race' over another, and attributed 'missions' and 'burdens' to the white man's nations."[9] The young British politician Joseph Chamberlain addressed a Toronto audience in 1887 on "the greatness and importance of the destiny which is reserved for the Anglo-Saxon race... infallibly predestined to be the predominating force in the future history and civilization of the world."[10] In Canada, this Anglo-Saxon imperialism put on the mask of British-Canadian nationalist sentiment and was primarily driven by Anglo-Protestant millennialism and identification of the Dominion of Canada with the Kingdom of God.

By 1867, the year of Confederation, the fragmented Protestantism of the early nineteenth century had evolved into a slowly coalescing common front of Protestant churches in Canada. The older tensions and outright conflicts among established Protestant churches on the one hand and dissenting Protestant churches on the other, the traditional struggle between a religion of order and a religion of experience, had largely dissipated by 1867.[11] In its place stood a progressively more distinct coalition of Canadian Anglo-Protestants. The late historian N. Keith Clifford has written:

> The inner dynamic of Protestantism in Canada during the first two thirds of the century following Confederation was provided by a vision of the nation as "His Dominion." This Canadian version of the Kingdom of God had significant nationalistic and millennial overtones, and sufficient symbolic power to provide the basis for the formation of a broad Protestant consensus and coalition. Not only the major Protestant denominations but also a host of Protestant-oriented organizations such as temperance societies, missionary societies, Bible societies, the Lord's Day Alliance, the YMCAs and YWCAs utilized this vision as a framework for defining their task within the nation, for shaping their conceptions of the ideal society, and for determining those elements which posed a threat to the realization of their purposes.[12]

Immigrant groups from northwestern Europe were generally well received in the Canadian Northwest; these included Norwegians, Icelanders, Danes, Swedes, Swiss, and Dutch. However, any and all groups that issued from farther afield, and that did not share this ideal of an Anglo-Protestant Kingdom of God, were suspect, for they constituted a threat to the norm. In the Northwest this included Mennonites, Mormons, Chinese, Ukrainians, Doukhobors, Catholics, French Canadians, and aboriginal people. Indeed, as Howard Palmer has written:

> The desirability to Canada of particular immigrant groups varied almost directly with their physical and cultural distance from London, England, and the degree to which their skin pigmentation conformed to Anglo-Saxon white.[13]

Given the centuries-old No-Popery in the Protestant tradition, its fusion with Anglo-Protestant nationalism and ethnic prejudice could prove to be an explosive recipe. The fact that many Slavs or Eastern and southern European immigrants were either Orthodox or Catholic seemed to confirm the fears of the Anglo-Protestant leaders, who feared any and all who were different from themselves. Since the leaders of the Protestant Social Gospel movement of the early twentieth century were Anglo-Protestant, this reform movement and the related prohibitionist and feminist crusades proved to be equally fearful of differences. They became agencies for assimilation and homogenization. This fear of the immigrant, the Catholic, the different, eventually led, after World War I, to the emergence of several Protestant fundamentalist sects and the Ku Klux Klan. Anglo-Protestant leaders in the Northwest were insecure, yet convinced of their superiority. Any cultural, ethnic, or linguistic variety was considered a threat to their very existence.

Another factor in the rise of this chauvinism was that in the latter third of the nineteenth century the balance of French and English in the Northwest was shifting decisively. As early as 1874, the originally evenly balanced number of electoral ridings in Manitoba was changed to fourteen English ridings and ten French. Manitoba's Board of Education was likewise changed to twelve Protestant members and nine Catholic. In January 1873, Archbishop Taché was complaining that of the eighty administrative appointees to the Northwest by the government of Canada a mere five were Métis while only twelve had French names. The Northwest's Métis and francophone population was being swamped by a flood of white Anglo-Protestant migrants from Ontario, a people who all too often detested anyone who differed from them in any significant way. The story of Louis Riel has enshrined these facts in our history.

Francophone Colonization

The white Anglo-Protestant juggernaut that began in the 1870s and 1880s provoked Archbishop Taché into fighting back. Indeed during most of his episcopal career Taché tried to attract French-speaking settlers to the West, in order to counterbalance the tide of English-speaking immigration. In fact, other ethnic groups were migrating to the West—Icelanders (1875) and German-speaking Mennonites (1874), for example—but the overwhelming majority were English-speaking Ontarians; those who spoke other languages soon assimilated into the English-speaking mainstream. Of the 42,000 immigrants to Manitoba in the 1870s, only some 2,200 were French-speaking.[14]

Archbishop Taché's foremost agent of francophone immigration was Oblate Father Albert Lacombe, who was also a salaried immigration agent of the government of Canada. In 1872, when Taché sent Lacombe on the first of his several voyages to Europe, Quebec, and the United States to recruit francophones for the West, there was still hope of reversing the tide of English-speaking immigration. Father Lacombe visited various bishops and pastors in Quebec, preaching and lobbying in favour of increased French-Canadian migration to the Northwest. When an 1874 order-in-council reserved land for repatriated French Canadians and more than 2,000 came from New England and Quebec (1875–78), Taché and Lacombe were encouraged; their elation was short-lived, however. In spite of the fact that Canadian immigration policy was the responsibility of the Minister of Agriculture, a French Canadian whose deputy minister was Archbishop Taché's brother, francophones soon ceased coming West while the English-speaking immigration continued unabated. Father Lacombe continued his efforts into the 1880s. He enjoyed some success, because a series of French-language colonies did appear during these decades in various parts of the prairies. They were usually small settlements: Végreville, Beaumont, Morinville, Legal, Bellegarde, Zenon Park, Gravelbourg, St. Brieuc, Fannystelle, and a series of others. These French, Belgian, or French-Canadian settlements were frequently led by priests. However, for those who hoped to sustain the important place of French in the Northwest, they were too little, too late.

Faith, Language, and Schools in Manitoba

Whether French or Canadian, however, the Oblate rose to the defence of the French language, which was increasingly under attack in the schools and public life of western Canada towards the end of the nineteenth century. Here, the two national groups could find common ground in the belief that the French language served as a moat protecting the French Catholic minority of the West against Protestantization by the growing anglophone majority.

Among these Oblates, however, only the Canadians felt strongly enough to expend the energy, resources, and time required to engage in sustained, bitter, and prolonged fighting to protect their French school rights. While the Frenchman Grandin acknowledged the need to protect French Catholic interests through language,[15] the Canadian Oblates, like Taché, Lacombe, Adélard Langevin, and Ovide Charlebois, were ready to do battle to protect the French fact in western Canada. In fact the schools debate was the prime arena for the defence of

French-Canadian interests in the Northwest, as it was in Ontario. And the leaders of the fight were clergymen, usually Oblates.

These Canadian Oblate leaders resisted the Anglo-Protestant urge to homogenize western Canada, transforming it into their own image and likeness. Protestant churches and clergymen became leading agents of Anglo-Canadian repression of the French minority, of their schools in particular. British Columbia had never had tax-supported confessional schools for whites; the battles therefore would take place in Manitoba and the Northwest Territories, comprising what would become the provinces of Alberta and Saskatchewan.

In Manitoba, the controversy over confessional schools began when Tory Member of Parliament Dalton McCarthy, founder of the Equal Rights Association, and one of Ontario's foremost contributions to bigotry and prejudice, visited Red River in August 1889. Fresh from his crusading against the French Catholic forces of evil in Quebec, McCarthy suggested that the Plains of Abraham had sealed the fate of the French in Canada and that any attempt to use French outside Quebec was an act of aggression, indeed of treason. This incendiary rhetoric fell on willing ears in Canada's Northwest. McCarthy provided a banner under which could rally the fearful nativists of the Northwest.

Methodists, Presbyterians, Baptists, Anglicans, and English-speaking Catholics all rallied to the cause. They closed ranks in spite of long-standing denominational differences. They did so in the name of "progress," righteousness, sanctification, and the Kingdom of God; French and all languages other than English were to be banned from God's "new Jerusalem" in the Northwest. The greatness of Canada required homogeneity and conformity to the Anglo-Protestant model. Assimilation was to be effected primarily through the schools. After 1885, the necessity of the Protestant faith, the British flag, and the uniform public school were unassailable dogmas of the nativist's creed.

In Manitoba, in spite of earlier attacks on the dual-confessional system of schools (1876), and on the official use of French (1879), peaceful coexistence had been the norm until 1889. In May of that year the *Brandon Sun* began a campaign to abolish Manitoba's dual system, soon to be followed by other newspapers. On 1 August, members of the province's Executive Council, spurred on by the position of the superintendent of Protestant schools, announced that the government intended to abolish the system of confessional schools. Within days (5 August 1889), Dalton McCarthy delivered a rousing speech in Portage la Prairie, prompting his co-speaker, Attorney General Joseph Martin, to pledge himself, and by implication the government, to abolish not only the dual system of schooling, but also the official status of

French in Manitoba. By the following March, the necessary legislation had been adopted; Manitoba's schools were henceforth to be non-denominational, while French was abolished as an official language in the legislature and the courts.

In some respects and for a variety of reasons, the reaction of the Catholics and francophones to this curtailment of their constitutional rights was neither as swift nor as decisive as would be expected. One reason for this was the diminishing numbers of Catholics; in 1890, they numbered only 20,000, or thirteen percent of a provincial population of 150,000. In 1870, they had represented more than fifty percent of the province's 12,000 people. Moreover, only one quarter, 5,000 of the 20,000 Catholics, were non-francophone; in fact, the French-speaking majority of Catholics were largely unaffected by the 1890 school legislation, because of the rural location and the homogeneous nature of their communities—where schools continued to operate much as they had before 1890, whatever their official classification.

It was the English-speaking Catholics who were most directly affected by the abolition of Catholic public schools in 1890. They tended to reside in cities like Winnipeg and Brandon where the new public, allegedly non-denominational school boards were in fact Protestant schools in disguise, because the majority of rate-payers were Protestant. In these urban centres, the Catholics were required to pay taxes to the public schools; if they wanted Catholic schools, they had to create private ones at their own expense, and were not excused from paying taxes for the public schools. In sum, despite the 1890 school act, French Catholic Manitobans outside the cities continued to enjoy French Catholic schools, at least until 1894 when another piece of provincial legislation was intended to prevent any circumvention of the law.

Within days of the royal assent given to the Manitoba legislation of 1890, the province's defunct Catholic section of the Board of Education, on which sat Archbishop Taché, petitioned the federal government (7 April 1890) asking for disallowance, a constitutional procedure that had to be requested within twelve months; meanwhile, Archbishop Taché orchestrated a series of petitions from Catholics, Franco-Manitobans, and Canadian bishops, denouncing the new education law. John A. Macdonald's government chose not to disallow the law, instead leaving it to the courts to decide whether the Parliament of Canada was authorized to intervene. Having failed to obtain federal disallowance of the law, Taché and Manitoba Catholics took a second constitutional recourse, a petition to the Governor General in Council requesting remedial legislation. These petitions were filed in September

1892, but again the federal government referred the matter to the courts (the Brophy case).

Meanwhile, another Manitoba Catholic, J.K. Barrett, went before the courts in November 1890, arguing that it was unconstitutional for the government of Manitoba to require him to pay public school taxes while Barrett was supporting a Catholic school in Winnipeg. After two reversals, the case was resolved in July 1892, when the Judicial Committee of the British Privy Council rejected the Barrett appeal and upheld the right of the government of Manitoba to legislate as it did in the matter of schools. Then came the Brophy case, filed in 1893 and consisting primarily of six questions put by the government of Canada. The decision of January 1895 acknowledged that the Catholics of Manitoba had a legitimate grievance and could have recourse to the government of Canada for redress. In addition, while again reversing the decision of the Supreme Court of Canada, the Judicial Committee declared that the government of Canada was indeed empowered to take remedial action against the government of Manitoba in this matter. To use W.L. Morton's phrase, the "poisoned chalice" had been returned to Canada.[16]

There followed a federal remedial order issued on 21 March 1895, aimed at effecting the restoration of Manitoba's Catholic school rights. In May 1894, Canada's bishops had already asked for disallowance of both the Northwest Territories' ordinance of 1892 (discussed later in this chapter) and the Manitoba statute of 1894 compelling municipalities to enforce the provincial education law. The federal government chose not to disallow either measure. The government of Manitoba then informed Ottawa, in October 1895, that it had no intention of complying with Ottawa's remedial order to amend its school legislation. Instead, Manitoba held a general election wherein Greenway's Liberals were returned with a resounding vote of confidence. Canada's governing Conservative party, reeling from crisis to crisis since the death of John A. Macdonald in 1891, found itself damned if it intervened and damned if it didn't. The new prime minister, Sir Charles Tupper, who took office in January 1896, introduced remedial legislation in the House of Commons as early as February 1896. Faced with the sustained opposition of Wilfrid Laurier's Liberal party, the legislation died on the order paper upon expiration of Parliament's five-year term in the spring of 1896. The subsequent election of 23 June resulted in the ousting of the Conservatives, and the election of Laurier's Liberals.

Laurier had promised to solve the Manitoba school imbroglio through friendly negotiation with Greenway's government. So it was that shortly after the election of 1896 the new prime minister despatched two friends and colleagues, Israel Tarte and Henri Bourassa, to Winnipeg, with orders to strike a deal. The resulting agreement of

November 1896 held that in Manitoba's public schools religious teaching would be permitted for half an hour at the end of each school day; that urban schools with forty or more Catholic pupils, and rural ones with twenty-five or more, were entitled to Catholic teachers; and finally:

> When ten of the pupils in any school speak the French language or any language other than English, as their native language, the teaching of such pupils shall be conducted in French, or such other language, and English upon the bilingual system.[17]

This "Laurier–Greenway compromise" was enacted into provincial law in the spring of 1897.

The school law of 1890 had been silent on the matter of languages of instruction; this meant that French or English could be employed in any Manitoba public or private school with equal justification. The amended legislation of 1897 extended language rights by enshrining a bilingual system of schools for any number of language pairs. The new policy served to reinforce Manitoba's multi-ethnic mosaic, particularly when huge numbers of immigrants poured into the region in the fifteen years preceding World War I. This latter phenomenon, coupled with white Anglo-Protestant xenophobia and messianic zeal, would spell the end of language tolerance in Manitoba in 1916, when the bilingual school system of 1897 was abolished in favour of uniform English schools.

In the matter of school legislation, the degree of satisfaction of Protestant clerics was in direct correlation with the intransigence of the law. The more restrictive provincial law proved to other-than-English languages and other-than-Protestant denominations, the more satisfied were Protestant clerics. For their part, Manitoba's Catholic clerics fought the restrictive legislation that had abolished their confessional schools. Archbishop Taché led the fight until his death in 1894; his successor, Adélard Langevin, continued in the same vein.

Beginning in September 1896, while negotiating his school deal with Premier Greenway, Prime Minister Laurier also lobbied the Pope in order to secure his flanks. Between September 1896 and November 1897, Laurier sent to Rome a series of representatives, including his friend Father Jean-Baptiste Proulx (September 1896), pastor of the parish of St. Lin in Quebec, Solicitor General Charles Fitzpatrick (January 1897), and party stalwart Charles Russell (October 1897). Laurier himself met the Pope on 12 August 1897. The bishops of Canada also had their representative in the Eternal City—the Canadian Dominican priest Dominique-Ceslas Gonthier, who was active in Rome between June 1897 and March 1898.

Through these spokesmen, Laurier and the bishops struggled to win the Pope over to their side in the Manitoba school dispute. In late 1896, archbishops Louis-Nazaire Bégin (Quebec) and Adélard Langevin (St. Boniface) and bishops Elphège Gravel (Nicolet) and Paul-Stanislas Larocque (Sherbrooke) visited Rome, and they secured a papal promise to issue an encyclical letter supportive of the bishops' position. In January 1897, when the letter was about to be circulated, Laurier got wind of it and sent Charles Fitzpatrick to obtain a stay of publication and the appointment of a special papal delegate to Canada. Archbishop Merry de Val arrived in Canada on 30 March 1897 and left the following July. The bishops of Canada were concerned at his conciliatory attitude; they felt that he had somehow been suborned by Laurier. The see-saw rivalry for papal favour continued until the encyclical *Affari Vos* was finally published in December 1897. In a nutshell, Pope Leo XIII declared that, while not ideal, the Manitoba school legislation that had resulted from the Laurier–Greenway compromise was to be accepted by Catholics, at least until the dawn of a better day. Prime Minister Laurier had managed to avoid a politically explosive papal condemnation, while Archbishop Langevin felt that he had been betrayed by his own leader.

Faith, Language, and Schools in the Northwest Territories

In these same latter decades of the nineteenth century, a similar spoliation of Catholic and francophone constitutional rights was being perpetrated in the Northwest Territories by a like-minded bigoted and intolerant white Anglo-Protestant majority. Here, too, it was French Canadians, rather than Frenchmen, who rose to the defence.

The Northwest Territories Act of 1875 empowered the territory's government to establish confessional schools. The law followed the early Ontario model whereby the majority in a given district established a public school, while the confessional minority, Catholic or Protestant, remained free to establish an alternate confessional public school; the latter was the separate school. A council ordinance of 1884 implemented the legislation. A board of education, divided into Catholic and Protestant sections, was established; each section enjoyed quasi-autonomy in all important matters such as hiring and firing, curricula, textbooks, examinations, and the certification of teachers. In short, the Northwest Territories established a dual confessional school system, similar to those of Quebec and Manitoba. As was the case in Manitoba, there was no mention of languages of instruction in the schools, each school remaining free to teach in the language of its choice. In fact, all members of the Catholic section of the Territories' Board of Education were French-speaking, while their Protestant colleagues were just as unanimously English-speaking.

Beginning in 1886, a series of ordinances and regulations gradually eroded this confessional and linguistic harmony. As was the case in Ontario, Manitoba, and elsewhere, white Anglo-Protestant intolerance was rearing its ugly head. The veteran missionary Albert Lacombe predicted the onslaught. On 27 October 1887 he wrote to Archbishop Taché:

> I do not pretend to be a prophet, but it seems to me that a big storm is brewing on the horizon. The English element, with all its fanaticism and its usual brutality, will attempt to find out whether now would not be the time to attack us frontally, with a chance of success. I expect the unleashing of the storm, both among the members of our legislature and in the press.[18]

In fact the anti-French tirades began appearing in a chain of western newspapers in early 1888, the *Regina Journal* taking the lead. The groundswell of feeling stood for the elimination of the French-Canadian identity and culture. Within a year the Assembly of the Northwest Territories asked Ottawa to repeal section 110 of the Northwest Territories Act (1877), the section that made French an official language. When Dalton McCarthy put forth a similar motion in the House of Commons on 23 January 1890, the Macdonald government responded by granting the territorial Assembly the power to so decide. Subsequent to the territorial elections of November 1891, the Assembly adopted such ordinances in 1892. Although Lieutenant-Governor Joseph Royal never signed the ordinances into law, in fact French was no longer an official language in the Northwest Territories; English became the required language of communication in schools, with the exception of a primary course that could still be taught in French. Although the length of this primary course was not defined, it was usually understood to be limited to the first three years of elementary schooling.

It was also by an ordinance of 1892 that the dual confessional school system was abolished in the Northwest Territories. Although separate schools continued to exist, they were subject to identical policies, regulations, and administration as the Territories' public schools. Separate schools differed from public schools in name only; even religious instruction was authorized for only thirty minutes, after regular school hours. In effect, Catholic schools had disappeared along with the official status of the French language. However, due to white Anglo-Protestant determination to assimilate all new Canadians, an ordinance of 1901 authorized the teaching of French, as a subject of study, for one hour per day. When the provinces of Alberta and Saskatchewan were carved out of the Northwest Territories in 1905, the school legislation was retained. Catholic schools continued to be separate in name only, while French could be used as a language of instruction only during the first three years of primary school. The elite had managed to transform the Northwest Territories into an image of itself. In British Columbia, the same homogeneity had prevailed from the outset, that province never having funded confessional schools.

By the turn of the century, the rapidly developing Northwest was very different from what it had been in 1870. British Columbia, Manitoba, the Northwest Territories, and the Yukon Territory had all become overwhelmingly English-speaking and Protestant in their population, government, and social and political philosophy. The linguistic and confessional duality so fundamental in the Manitoba and the Northwest Territories of 1870 had been swept aside by an aggressive and intolerant governing elite, supported by a growing Anglo-Protestant majority. An Anglo-Protestant Kingdom of God was emerging in the new Jerusalem of the Canadian Northwest. The concomitant jubilation among Protestant clergy was accompanied by growing fear and resentment among Catholics.

Indian Schools

From the outset, upon the establishment of Indian missions both Protestant and Catholic missionaries hurried to open schools as quickly as possible. The schoolchildren were sometimes taught by the missionary himself, more frequently by missionaries' auxiliaries like the minister's wife, or teachers hired specifically to do so. Both the CMS and the Oblates recruited teachers for their mission schools. CMS recruits were usually Englishmen sent out as teachers, Indian boys trained in the Red River academy founded in the 1830s, or the wives of clergymen working in the mission. The Oblates' first choice usually fell upon a religious congregation of sisters, preferably the Sisters of Charity of Montreal.

These early mission schools were private, funded by the churches themselves, the Hudson's Bay Company (HBC) having little role to play.

This changed in the wake of the purchase of the HBC lands by the Dominion of Canada in 1870. Thereafter, in fulfilling its constitutional responsibilities as guardian and supervisor of Indian interests, the Crown sought to regulate and control Indian life, schools included.[19]

The Indian policy that was implemented was that which had been developed in Upper Canada since the 1830s. Through a process of acculturation, the government of Canada sought to change the Indian's language, culture, and way of life—in a word, to assimilate the Indian into the Anglo-Canadian way, for he was considered to have become an obstacle to the white man's development in Canada. Contrary to what had been the case in the seventeenth and eighteenth centuries, in the nineteenth century the Canadian Indian was needed neither as a military ally nor as a partner in the fur trade.[20]

Education was a key instrument for the implementation of this policy, as was the displacement of Indians onto land reservations. The creation of reservations allowed the government to remove the Indians from the path of the growing number of white settlers moving into the country, first into Upper Canada, then into the Northwest. Given that Christian missionaries were in place among the Indians, had already established schools among them, and were in fundamental agreement with the government policy of assimilation of the Indians into Euro-Canadian ways, the government of Canada decided to co-opt the churches in its campaign to complete this process.[21]

Churches, usually Roman Catholic, Anglican, Methodist, and Presbyterian, were entrusted with running the Indian schools that were funded to a greater or lesser extent by the government. These schools were located either on or near the reservations, and were thus day schools; when located at considerable distance from the Indians' place of residence they were residential schools. Although supposedly founded to serve the needs of the itinerant Indians, the residential schools of the Canadian churches, Catholic and Protestant, were intended as key instruments in the assimilation, for they served to remove the Indian child from his home environment.

Residential schools existed in two forms, the *boarding school* and the *industrial school.* Industrial schools were simply a chain of better-funded residential schools, established by the government of Canada after 1883 but administered by the churches just as the boarding schools were. Both sought to enrol Indian children at the tender age of six or seven. They had similar academic programmes whereby half the day was devoted to learning the three Rs, half to learning a trade, usually working the farm that belonged to the school. Both systematically endeavoured to remove the Indian from the child, by condemning the use of native languages, native dress, native customs, and of course native religions. These policies were enforced even at the cost of Indian goodwill. Of course, the primary objective of all church-run schools was the conversion of the Indians, an objective taken to be largely synonymous with assimilation into Euro-Canadian culture. In 1902, the Department of Indian Affairs reported a total of 283 Indian schools in Canada, 221 day schools, 40 boarding schools, and 22 industrial schools. Of the total, 100 were Catholic schools, 87 Anglican, 41 Methodist, 14 Presbyterian, and 41 non-denominational.[22]

Indian schools were most definitely stages for the display of Christian denominational rivalries, each trying to better the other in number of pupils recruited, number of converts listed—even in the number of religious vocations developed. The correspondence of the various missionaries is replete with anecdotes in this regard. They were not, however, stages for the continuation of francophone internecine nationalistic bickering. Just about all Catholic Indian schools in the Northwest used English rather than French, in spite of the fact that their staff was almost all of French ethnocultural origin. The main reason for this was the growing prevalence of English throughout the Northwest, and the consequent strongly expressed desire of the Indians to learn English in order to survive the white onslaught. Given that Protestant schools answered this need for the English language, Catholic schools realized that they had to do likewise; otherwise they would lose their Catholic Indians to the Protestant schools. So it was that Bishop Grandin wrote about the Catholic industrial school in Calgary in 1888:

> To my knowledge, French is not taught [there]... I don't believe that it is forbidden by any written regulation, but...the directors of the school have understood that they should not teach it... I know that in several circumstances it was insisted that teachers speak only English to the children. Bookkeeping and correspondence must be done in English.[23]

Even while fighting tooth and nail in defence of French schools in white areas of the West, French-Canadian patriots like Alexandre Taché and Albert Lacombe were required to bite the bullet and support Indian schools that were anglicizing Indian children. What made the pill more bitter was that these schools were their own.

The Oblate regiment that assaulted Canada's Northwest was not only Catholic but both French and French-Canadian. Its adversaries were not only Protestants, but anglophone nationalists. The Oblates were bound together, sometimes very unhappily, by their Catholicism and their membership in the congregation, while their rivals were bound together by their common English and Protestant ancestry. In the latter half of the nineteenth century, the religious identities that had been at the forefront of these conflicting identities since at least the beginning of the century were gradually but inexorably ceding pride of place to ethnic and cultural factors. By the turn of the century, linguistic and ethnocultural considerations replaced religious ones as the primary elements in the identities of each. Then Canadian Catholicism fragmented into French, French-Canadian, and Irish strains, to name only a few ethnic groups. Simultaneously, white Anglo-Protestants played down the denominational differences that had been so important a century earlier, and banded together in a linguistic and cultural common front whose common programme was the assimilation of any and all into British—that is to say, Anglo-Canadian—ways. The French, the Catholics, the Indians, the Ukrainians, the Mennonites—all were expected to fall into line.

In Canada's Northwest, the Oblates stood on both sides of this issue. While all Oblates could honestly claim to be fighting for the preservation of the Catholic faith and Catholic schools, for some, like Bishop Grandin, this was the overriding motive for his actions. Grandin defended French not because of pro-French nationalistic convictions, but because he thought the language was a useful barrier to anglicization, and hence Protestantization or religious indifference. However, for French-Canadian Oblates like Lacombe, Taché, and Langevin, the battle for French survival in the West was not only a tactical one aimed at the protection of Catholicism. It *was* that, but it was also a French-Canadian nationalist fight for *la survivance* against the English. These men were therefore in strong disagreement with their French Oblate colleagues, as the Oblate cabal against Taché's episcopal appointment demonstrated. Simply put, French Oblates were ready and willing to accept anglicization, providing the Catholic faith was protected. French-Canadian Oblates were not. They were just as committed to Catholicism as were their French colleagues, but they felt that to accept anglicization was to engage on the slippery slope that inevitably led to apostasy, or at least to Protestantization. The irony was that in Indian schooling even the French-Canadian Oblates had to engage in the anglicization of their pupils.

Notes

1. *Le Métis*, the first French newspaper in Red River, began appearing in St. Boniface in 1871, only twelve years after the founding of the English *Nor'Wester* in 1859. *Le Métis* was renamed *Le Manitoba* in 1881. Surprisingly enough, the first French newspaper in the West was founded in Victoria in 1856; *Le Courrier de la Nouvelle-Calédonie* lasted only three weeks.

2. V. Grandin, "Notes intimes sur les commencements du diocèse de Saint-Albert," cited in Claude Champagne, p. 196.

3. Donat Levasseur, *Les Oblats de Marie Immaculée dans l'ouest et le nord du Canada*, pp. 207–8.

4. There are several letters that strike that note in E. de Mazenod, *Lettres aux correspondants d'Amérique*, vols. 1 and 2.

5. St. Boniface, 30 December 1845 and 2 August 1848. ACAM copy, 71.220, 1007, APA.

6. A. Taché to H. Faraud, Île-à-la-Crosse, 17 January 1853. Faraud papers, AG.

7. V. Grandin, *Souvenirs* (St. Albert: n.p., n.d.), 84.400, 1006, APA.

8. A Visitor in the Oblate congregation is a very powerful representative of the Oblate superior general. A Visitor is usually sent into a region to settle particularly thorny problems.

9. Robert Craig Brown and Ramsay Cook, *Canada*, p. 26.

10. Cited ibid.

11. On the history of this phenomenon in nineteenth-century Ontario, see William Westfall.

12. "His Dominion," *SR* 2, 4 (1973): 315.

13. Howard Palmer, "Strangers and Stereotypes: The Rise of Nativism, 1880–1920," in Francis and Palmer, p. 312.

14. See Robert Painchaud, *Un rêve français dans le peuplement de la prairie.*

15. Vital Grandin wrote to Bishop James Rogers of Chatham, N.B., on 26 April 1891: "I attach much greater importance to separate schools than to the official conservation of the French language." (Cited in Claude Champagne, p. 203.)

16. W.L. Morton, p. 270.

17. Cited in Robert Craig Brown and Ramsay Cook, *Canada*, p. 13.

18. Cited in Keith Alwyn McLeod, "Education and the Assimilation of the New Canadians in the North-West Territories and Saskatchewan, 1885–1934," unpublished Ph.D. dissertation, University of Toronto, 1975, p. 39.

19. The British North America Act of 1867 gave to the government of Canada the powers and responsibilities originally entrusted to the British Crown.

20. This case is made eloquently by Miller, *Skyscrapers Hide the Heavens.*

21. Studies of Canadian Indian schools are numerous, and are becoming more so year by year. For a summary presentation of their relationship to Christian missions see John Webster Grant, *Moon of Wintertime.* For a more complete, yet summary review see J.R. Miller, *Skyscrapers Hide the Heavens.* Some of the more specialized studies are E. Brian Titley, "Indian Industrial Schools in Western Canada," in Nancy M. Sheehan et al. (eds.), *Schools in the West: Essays in Canadian Educational History* (Calgary: Detselig, 1986), pp. 133–53; E. Brian Titley, *A Narrow Vision*, pp. 75–93; Jacqueline Gresko, "White 'Rites' and Indian 'Rites,'" pp. 163–81.

22. Statistics cited in John Webster Grant, *Moon of Wintertime*, p. 177.

23. V. Grandin to F.-X.-A. Trudel, 26 October 1888, cited in Claude Champagne, *Les débuts de la mission dans le Nord-Ouest canadien*, p. 198.

CHAPTER XI

THE LEGACY
OF THE OBLATE CONQUEST

By the turn of the century, the Missionary Oblates of Mary Immaculate had largely succeeded in conquering the northern half of the North American continent for the Gospel in its ultramontane Catholic form. Most of the Indians were Christian, indeed Roman Catholic, the Anglican and Protestant rival had more often than not been checked, and the conquering Anglo-Protestant empire had suffered a partial setback. The Kingdom of God, in its ultramontane Catholic form, was well on the way to being realized in Canada's Northwest. God's forces were fighting the good fight in defending the new Jerusalem against the forces of modern and Protestant evil, those of that other Jerusalem.

The Oblate Assault: The Military Analogy

The Oblate conquest of the Northwest was a regional implementation of the international plan of battle put together by the Roman Catholic Church in the mid-nineteenth century. The military analogy is appropriate: in its reaction to the perceived evil forces of modernity and liberalism issuing forth from the revolutions of the eighteenth century, the Roman Catholic Church developed the theology of ultramontanism, a theology whose most characteristic traits appear in Pope Pius IX's *Syllabus of errors* of 1864, reinforced by the declarations of Vatican Council I in 1870.

According to ultramontane thinking, which would prevail in Catholicism for the next hundred years, the modern world was the devil's playground, where the Catholic saints were called to do battle on a continual basis against a wide and diversified array of enemy forces, including liberals, Protestants, modernists, public school supporters, Freemasons, and secularists of all stripes. In fact the enemy legions included any and all who disagreed with official ultramontane teaching, be they within the Roman Catholic Church or without. These forces and many others threatened this last remnant of God's people.

Catholics had therefore to gird their loins and to field an army of soldiers to do battle. The clergy was that legion, its numbers growing by leaps and bounds after 1840. These men and women needed to be inculcated with a form of teaching that prized obedience above all—that is, obedience to the Church, to the Pope, to the bishop, to the pastor, indeed to any Church spokesman. In the training of these soldiers, theology, even an emasculated one, was of secondary concern at the best of times, in spite of declarations to the contrary. Critical theology was out of the question. These troops were to wear their frequently outlandish uniforms at all times, a measure that also assured Church control over their minds and their behaviour. The Oblates were the chosen regiment in Canada's North and West.

The tactics adopted by the Oblate regiment reflected the theology that prevailed in their Church. As many Indians as possible were to be baptized, consistent with the rule that at least a minimum of catechetical instruction was a prerequisite. The entire Indian community was to be transformed by the effects of Church, sacrament, and priest, its members being gradually nurtured into a heightened level of Christian living.

Because of the Catholic theology of continuity between this world and the next, between the natural and supernatural orders, Indian or natural customs were perceived as less foreign to God's law, more amenable to Christianization, than they were in the eyes of the Protestant missionaries. In some instances, all that was required to become a Christian was to participate in an existing custom to its fullest significance. The Catholic missionary was therefore inclined to be less negative than his Protestant rival in his initial judgement of native customs and beliefs.

In sum, the Missionary Oblates of Mary Immaculate were organized along military lines, trained to value obedience and discipline above all, and were sent into Canada's Northwest as soldiers of the faith bent on conquest of the land in the name of Jesus Christ. Their doctrine, plan of battle, and logistical support came from Oblate headquarters in France and Rome. The overall objective was nothing less than conquest of the world for the Catholic faith. Their understanding of evangelization, a perennial Christian concern, was a very aggressive one. They would counter, fight, remove, or crush any and all opposition.

The Clash with the Anglo-Protestant Opposition

In carrying out this aggressive campaign in Canada's Northwest the Oblates ran headlong into the Church of England's Church Missionary Society (CMS), an organization very different from the Oblate institution in some respects but very similar in others.

As an evangelical Protestant society, the CMS viewed as repugnant anything that smacked of Catholicism. At first glance, the accusations hurled at Catholics by Protestant missionaries in the Northwest pertained to the usual panoply of traditional Protestant anti-Catholicism: auricular confession, medals, holy water, the Virgin, clerical celibacy, the crucifix, and the Pope. Catholic missionaries countered these accusations by labelling their Protestant rivals false prophets, apostles of error, poor misguided souls who in their ignorance represented heresy.

Most Protestant missionaries sent to the Northwest were of evangelical persuasion, as was their patron, the CMS. Therefore, they were convinced that the Catholic, the priest in particular, was an agent of the Whore of Babylon, the Roman harlot, Romanism, and popery, which was by definition a system of lies and superstition. In fact, the Catholic was not even Christian. Although the intensity and depth of these convictions varied from one minister to another, according to personality, character, and training, by and large these beliefs stood for all CMS missionaries.

For their part, Catholic priests, products of the growing ultramontane school of theology, truly believed that outside the Church there was no salvation. Therefore, anyone who denied the authority of the Church of Rome was headed straight to Hell.

On the face of it, then, doctrinal differences were at the root of Catholic–Protestant differences in the Northwest. Catholics held to the series of beliefs and practices that were reprehensible to Protestants because the Roman Catholic Church defined these customs and beliefs as part of the Christian religion, and the authority of the Church was unquestioned in the ultramontane school of thought. Protestants instinctively rejected these beliefs because they found little evidence of them in the Bible, God's Word, their sole rule of faith. It would seem, therefore, that no reconciliation was possible between the two camps, short of one party abandoning its position.

The theologies that fuelled both the Catholics and the Protestants were intransigent and uncompromising. From the mid-nineteenth century, ultramontanism was the dominant theology in the Roman Catholic Church; and ultramontane Catholics truly believed that outside the Church there was no salvation. Catholic missionaries worked with the firm purpose of converting all people to Catholicism. In the eyes of the Catholic missionary, there was no other option for the Protestant short of damnation. The Protestant missionary, meanwhile, just as earnestly proclaimed God's Word, the sole avenue of liberation from the papist cage. The two parties closely resembled each other, in conviction, determination, arrogance, zeal, and intransigence. They differed only in their theologies or ideologies, and usually in their language and culture.

Strangely enough, in spite of these doctrinal and theological differences, and the accusations they engendered, several instances of strong mutual respect, indeed friendship, developed between Catholics and Protestants. We have seen that such tended to be the norm in the relations between the Anglo-Protestant Hudson's Bay Company (HBC) officers and Franco-Catholic missionaries and that several such cases could be found among Catholic and Protestant missionaries, be it the Reverend Rundle's friendship with fathers de Smet and Bourassa, or Father Petitot's praise for his travelling companion, Robert McDonald, or the Reverend Ryerson's admiration for the Catholic missionary at Fort William, or Father Étienne Bonnald's positive experience in this regard in northern Manitoba and Saskatchewan. All indications are that these instances of mutual assistance, respect, and friendship occurred in spite of doctrinal, theological, and ecclesiastical pressures to the contrary. In other words, in order to bear witness to Christian charity, both Catholic and Protestant missionaries had to forget for the time being the policies of their respective churches. These same missionaries would then return to uttering their condemnations, in spite of knowing full well that such condemnations had little bearing on reality.

Reasonableness was also shown by Catholic and Protestant church leaders, in spite of their official duty to condemn their confessional rivals. So it was that Bishop Taché reprimanded Father Grollier for his fanaticism *vis-à-vis* Protestants, while Anglican Bishop Machray never became identified with Protestant fanaticism. Another factor in peaceful coexistence was the mutual isolation of most Catholic and Protestant missions. The isolation was virtually total, even in

Red River in the earlier decades of the nineteenth century. It was continued in most of the Northwest throughout the century, the only exceptions being a handful of centres such as Victoria or New Westminster where both groups of clergymen had a presence. Even in these few towns, however, there was little contact between Catholic and Protestant clergymen, the little information they learned about each other being frequently hearsay or gleaned from newspaper accounts. There were several reasons for this isolation: one was the HBC policy of not allowing rival denominations in the same region; another was the tendency among many Indian nations to favour one "religion" or another; a third was the constituency served by each. Indeed, while an HBC officer usually belonged to either the Church of England or the Presbyterian Church, the vast majority of Métis boatmen and other HBC employees were Catholic.

This isolation had a bearing on Catholic–Protestant relations, not only because it is difficult to fight with an absent adversary, but also because information about one's rivals became even more sketchy. So it was that the several cases of moral scandal that besmirched the good names of several Protestant and Catholic clergymen were rarely, if at all, the subject of any comment in the correspondence or journals of their confessional rivals. One possible explanation of this silence is that the clergymen were practising Christian charity; a more probable explanation is that they simply did not know that the scandal had occurred.

It has been noted that as a general rule Catholic missionaries had a much better reputation in the Northwest than their Protestant rivals, not only among HBC officers but also in public opinion, which was largely dominated by Anglo-Protestants. The reasons for this are not easy to elucidate. Spokesmen tended to point to the cultural refinement of the French Catholic missionary, to his frugality and abstinence from worldly comforts, to his greater willingness to follow the Indians in their wanderings in the bush, to his willingness to learn and greater facility in Indian languages, and to the Catholic missionary's policy of not meddling in commercial and political affairs. It is also likely that the leaders of public opinion appreciated the greater discipline of the Catholic clergymen, who did not appear as fractious as some Protestant ministers. We know that such qualities were not the badge of distinction of each and every Catholic missionary, but as a general rule they seem to be valid.

The observation regarding the degree of cultural refinement seems to pertain to education. The level of theological education was not impressive among Catholic missionaries, as tended to be the rule among Catholic clergymen generally until the mid-nineteenth century. Bishops Provencher and Grandin bitterly complained of the shortcomings of their men in this regard. Nevertheless, leaving theological education aside, it would seem that the typical Catholic priest had a superior general education to his typical Protestant counterpart in the Northwest.

Since the Indian community was an integral element in the evangelization process, Oblate missionaries gave great importance to learning Indian languages; linguistic skills were considered a *sine qua non* condition for the success of the mission. A priest who did not learn the language of his flock was considered for the most part useless by Catholic bishops. While many priests arrived in the Northwest knowing only French, most Oblates soon learned English in addition to one or more Indian languages, for Oblate leaders insisted that the missionaries learn the languages spoken in a given country.

In contrast, most Protestant missionaries arrived and left the country knowing only English, for most felt that it would be demeaning for them to learn other languages. They expected others to learn English, to adjust to their ways, because they belonged to the dominant social, cultural, political, and economic group. Moreover, many Protestant ministers, like Catholic secular priests before them, came to the Northwest for a limited period of time, fully intending to return to England or elsewhere after a few years. Most Protestant ministers, therefore, in order to minister to Indians, had to avail themselves of the services of an interpreter, never being sure of how the interpreter rendered their message. Therefore, too, the Protestant minister, like most of the handful of Catholic secular clergy, by necessity remained more distant from his potential converts.

The high regard in which the Catholic missionary was held was also a result of the peculiar lifestyle adopted by the Oblates, a lifestyle which gave them a decided advantage. The Oblate vows of poverty and chastity allowed them to live at a remote mission station with very little material support, a fact that was not lost on the HBC officers who had to transport their supplies. Indeed, the more supplies a mission station required, the more it cost the HBC in dollars, work, or lost space on the barges. With few exceptions, Oblate missionaries lived more frugally than the most frugal of HBC officers. The vow of chastity meant that the missionary had no wife—that is to say, no white woman to disturb the often precarious social equilibrium of a remote and tiny trading post. The Oblate vow of obedience meant that the religious superior had full control over each one of his missionaries, thus enabling ecclesiastical superiors to remove the man at will or to transfer him to another station.

Numerous testimonies by HBC officers, among others, certify that the Oblates were willing to accept much more difficult living conditions than Protestant missionaries. There are several reasons for this: the priest was celibate, while most Protestant clergymen had a wife and children, and it was much more expensive to raise a family than to support the bachelor lifestyle of an Oblate missionary. Also, as members of a religious congregation Oblates took a vow of poverty; conditions of life in the Northwest missions therefore seemed a providential testing ground for their religious calling. These men had freely chosen a life of poverty as a way of bearing witness to Jesus Christ; indeed the motto of the Missionary Oblates of Mary Immaculate was *Evangelizare pauperibus misit me* (He sent me to evangelize the poor). Moreover, they belonged to a congregation that provided them with personal security, undertaking to care for them in illness or in old age. Therefore, the Oblate was unconcerned with financial security. As Bishop Provencher had noted in the late 1840s, it was necessary to obtain the services of a religious congregation if the Northwest missions were to be provided with adequate personnel. Indeed the collective organization and pooling of resources of a religious congregation, coupled with the strong authority structure of the Catholic Church, made the distant and costly missions of the Northwest possible. When Catholic

From left to right: Father Albert Lacombe (1827–1916), Bishop Émile Legal (1849–1920), Bishop Émile Grouard (1840–1931), Bishop Gabriel Breynat (1867–1954), and Father Auguste Husson (1849–1928).

missions were not so organized, prior to 1845, it is not at all clear that Catholic missionaries had any significant advantage over the Protestants.

Another advantage that observers saw in Catholic missionaries was a tendency to seek greater *rapprochement* with the Indian people. This included the Oblates' greater willingness to learn native languages, their greater inclination to travel beyond white trading posts in order to minister to Indians, their greater perseverance in remaining in isolated mission stations for several years, for a lifetime in several cases. This observation is confirmed by the historical record. Again, there was little difference between Protestant and Catholic secular clergy in this regard. We have seen that of the dozen secular priests who came to Red River before the arrival of the Oblates, only two (Thibault and Bellecourt), in addition to Provencher, devoted their careers to the region, a proportion similar to that for Church of England ministers.

However, the record of Oblate missionaries when compared to that of their Protestant counterparts shows a much higher proportion who devoted their entire lives to the Northwest missions. Of the first hundred Oblates to work in the Northwest after 1845, the average duration of stay in the region was nearly forty years. There is no question that Oblates were there for the long haul. This group included not only leaders like Alexandre Taché, Henri Faraud, Vital Grandin, Isidore Clut, Émile Grouard, and Paul Durieu, but ordinary missionaries like Jean Séguin, Joseph Patrick Kearney, Albert Lacombe, Nicolas Coccola, and Hippolyte Leduc. Numerous others served in the region for two or three decades before returning to France or eastern Canada broken in body, mind, or both. The problem cases we have discussed should not allow us to forget that most missionaries worked faithfully and generously. Having decided to stay permanently in their missions, these men necessarily identified much more closely with their Indian and Métis flocks than would a clergyman who knew that he was on temporary assignment. This is still true today. This observer has been struck by the fierce loyalty and dedication of several contemporary Oblate missionaries in the North and West. They instinctively defend their people, some would say with bias and partisanship, all would say with vigour and conviction.

Part of the *rapprochement* with Indian people involved protracted and difficult voyages. Much has been made of this colourful aspect of the missionary record in the Canadian North and West. A few Protestant missionaries travelled as much as any Oblate, Bishop William Carpenter Bompas for one. Indeed it was difficult to keep Bompas in any one place for any length of time; he flitted from one station to another, always seeking to be further removed from society. However, he was an exception to the rule. Most stayed in place in white trading posts.

Many Oblate missionaries not only travelled phenomenal distances, but took pride in doing so. For example, upon returning to the Northwest in 1860 after being consecrated as coadjutor bishop of St. Boniface, Vital Grandin undertook a three-year voyage throughout his vast diocese in order to visit every mission station. Believing that the Yukon was beckoning as virgin missionary territory, Bishop Isidore Clut spent more than a year travelling throughout the lower Mackenzie, Peel River, and the Porcupine and Yukon rivers, which he descended as far as the Bering Sea. Émile Petitot was frequently on the move throughout the Northwest Territories from his base at Good Hope; he not only founded and visited a mission on Great Bear Lake, but travelled far and wide from Great Slave Lake to the Arctic Sea, discovering and naming numerous geographical features of the land. Father Albert Lacombe also loved to be on the road, visiting various Indian and Métis camps in Alberta. To these record-breaking travellers, one would need to add the names of several missionaries who were also frequently moving about, such as Alexandre Taché, Jean-Baptiste Thibault, George-Antoine Bellecourt, Paul Durieu, Jean Séguin, Joseph Bourassa, and Alexis André.

Why did they travel so much? Without exception they would answer to better minister to their widely scattered flocks. This is undoubtedly true for most cases, for frequently the only real opportunity to evangelize the Indians and Métis were those occasions when they all came together at certain key trading posts in the early and late summer. Given the shortage of missionaries, the Oblates had to serve several stations, and consequently to travel a great deal.

There were also, however, other reasons for travelling, at least for some missionaries. Some seem to have had itchy feet, finding it difficult to stay in one place. This was the case with the Church of England's Bompas; it was also true for Albert Lacombe, Isidore Clut, and most certainly Émile Petitot. In some instances, the missionary preferred to be on the move with his dog team or canoe and a hired man or boy than back at the mission station with a colleague or sisters who may have been difficult company, or with chores that were the only relief from the boredom of long winter nights. Such a situation is obvious in the case of Petitot, who was unhappy in Good Hope, under the watchful eye of an Oblate colleague—a supervision he could escape with the freedom of the trail; the fact that the temperature might be minus forty degrees Celsius in blizzard conditions was of secondary consideration. Moreover, some of these missionaries had chosen the life precisely because they were adventurous explorers, impatient with the constraints of white society, particularly in an isolated missionary post.

Last but not least, both a cause and an effect of this Catholic missionary *rapprochement* with Indian people was the greater sympathy they seemed to show their charges. Several observers, including the Reverend William W. Kirkby, who cannot be suspected of harbouring Catholic partisanship, noted the affinity between Catholic priest and Indian. Given that in Kirkby's case he was observing Father Grollier, who was by all other accounts a most unpleasant character, one must consider what this affinity rested on.

The affinity may well have rested on an unconscious cultural alliance between the Franco-Catholic missionary and the Canadian Indian against an established, powerful, and ruling Anglo-Protestant power so willingly represented in the region by both the HBC and the Church of England. With few exceptions, Catholic missionaries came from either France or French Canada, two regions that rarely produced worshippers for England's temple. Moreover, not only were they subject to the rule of the HBC, they were largely dependent on the HBC for transportation and supplies. While grateful for all the assistance they received, on several occasions Catholic missionaries expressed resentment at what they felt were excessive demands of the HBC, either in the fees it charged for transporting supplies or in the attitudes of some HBC trading post directors. Such resentment could easily evolve into accusations, the missionaries holding the company responsible for all difficulties in the territory, in much the way that people tend to blame their government for all that is wrong in society.

Given the close alliance between the Church of England and the HBC, Indians may well have seen Protestant ministers first and foremost as representatives of the English Crown. In other words, Protestant ministers could much more readily be suspect of being in league with the HBC, which they were, than could the Catholic priests who were so different in dress, language, ritual, religion, and behaviour. Although such a situation could work in favour of the ministers, it could backfire on them whenever Indian people harboured resentment against the HBC.

More important, however, was the cultural arrogance of the Anglo-Protestant ministers. While each ethno-cultural group had its own biases and prejudices, the difference was that the French and Canadian Catholics were used to being in a minority position linguistically, culturally, and religiously. None could realistically hope to dominate in the Northwest. Their best hope was to survive with as few losses as possible. In this fundamental respect, they were very close to the Indian people.

Needless to say, the Anglo-Protestants held a completely different attitude in this regard. In tune with their culture and their times, Anglo-Protestant clergymen truly believed that they were destined by God and progress to dominate the world, because of their inherent superiority. Therefore, when Anglo-Protestant ministers moved into the Northwest, they simply took up station at a trading post, having brought along with them as much of England as they could, and waited for Indians to come to them—in order to reap all the benefits of English religion and civilization. Inevitably this implied that they look down upon all who differed from them—Métis, Indian, French, Canadian, and Catholic. They could not understand why it was that most Indians shied away from them.

So it was that Church of England missions succeeded best where Indian catechists and ministers worked, places like The Pas, Lake La Ronge, and forts McPherson and Yukon. Metlakatla was a case apart. In all those mission stations it was men like Henry Budd and Robert McDonald who laid the foundations of the CMS missions that would develop into the strongest Protestant ones in the area. Similarly, the most successful Methodist mission was at Rossville near Norway House, a post developed by the Reverend Evans with the strong support of native clergymen. It is noteworthy that Evans was one of the few Protestant ministers to learn native languages. Another was the Reverend Hunter, who developed the CMS mission at The Pas after it had been nurtured for four years by native catechist Henry Budd.

Finally, one cannot help noting the fact that for both Catholic and Protestant missionaries policies were being set in Europe, far removed from any contact with the actual inhabitants of the Northwest, be they Indian or white, Catholic or Protestant, clergyman or layman. The result was a kind of ecclesiastical schizophrenia whereby missionaries of both churches uttered condemnations of clerical adversaries fuelled by ideologies imported from Europe. The same missionaries would then lay down their vitriolic pens, silence their venomous tongues and, by necessity, learn to cooperate with their Protestant or Catholic rival. Indeed, the field experience of neither Catholic nor Protestant missionaries ever managed to overpower bigoted theologies of European origin in setting of the policy of the churches.

The Indians: Liberated or Subjugated?

It has become commonplace in recent literature, scholarly or otherwise, to hold Christian missionaries among the foremost agents of the destruction of Indian cultures and identities. One leading historian of native Americans writes:

> The Native American encounter with Christianity seems to be a rather one-sided affair, one in which native religions have not only been ignored, but also suppressed; one in which Christianity has been the measure and the only acceptable religious presence. It has been a history of oppression, insensitivity, arrogance, and misunderstanding. Certainly from the native point of view, the encounter with Christianity has often been unhappy and frustrating.[1]

Christian missionaries, Catholic and Protestant, were simultaneously evangelists seeking to replace Indian animist spiritualities with Christian faith and agents of white Euro-Canadian civilization. There is no doubt that from either perspective, and from both, they judged the Indian ways primitive, savage, backward, and wrong; Indian ways needed to be replaced by Euro-Canadian Christian ways. In their "civilizing" motivation, the missionaries were no different from the traders, merchants, soldiers, or teachers.

In their "Christianizing" motivation, however, there were distinct differences. The most obvious is the fact that few white people in the Northwest, other than the missionaries, cared a whit about evangelizing the Indians. And the missionary thrust to evangelize was based on a theology of Christian charity, loving all people in the name of Jesus Christ, working towards the salvation—that is to say, the liberation—of all people, in this instance the Indian people. Had this not been the case, the missionaries would simply not have been there, for they could not aspire to make a fortune as did the HBC, nor were they driven by the need to govern the region as were later government agents. One may quibble or quarrel with the specific theologies, methods, or tactics of the various missionaries, but there is no doubting the fact that the fundamental reason these missionaries were there was Christian concern for evangelization.

While the trader was in the country to make money, and while the settler came to take the land for himself, the missionary had disinterested motives. He or she truly and honestly believed they were there solely in the interests of the Indians. And they were, if one considers that Christian evangelization can work in the interests of the Indians, knowing that at that time Christian evangelization implied the replacement of native spiritualities, and the heavy baggage of Euro-Canadian culture. The missionaries to Canada's Northwest therefore had two motives, a religious one—to liberate the people—and a cultural one that sought to crush the Indian cultures.

How does one evaluate the effects of such a mission? John Webster Grant has written:

> Estimates of the effects of Christian missions on Indian life are likely to depend, in the final analysis, on whether they are distinguished from the total impact of the European presence or included as an integral part of it. If reckoned as a distinct entity, they may well be seen as mitigating some of its harmful effects. If lumped in, they will almost certainly be condemned for their complicity in undermining the bases of Indian society. Since the missionaries were at once emissaries of Christ and associates of Caesar, there is no basis on which one can make an unambiguous judgment between these alternatives.[2]

This is no doubt true, given that no gesture or action can be purely religious—that is, totally defined by the transcendent; it always carries some cultural elements. Canada's Indians therefore experienced the Christian Church as an enemy of their native cultures.

This being said, it remains nevertheless true that since the turn of the century a strong majority of Canada's Indians consider themselves Christian; and while some Indians have harshly criticized the Christian churches for their actions in this regard, others rise to defend these same churches. This may well be because the latter realize that although the churches are unquestionably guilty of having worked to crush Indian cultures, they are also the only Euro-Canadian institutions to have also worked—generously, honestly, and heroically in many instances—for the liberation of Indian people. In other words, despite the fact that the mission churches and schools were agencies of cultural assimilation, these same churches and schools gave Indian people the wherewithal to survive in the alien but conquering Euro-Canadian culture.

There is a middle ground between the two opposing evaluations of the Christian missionary effort, that charging the Christian Church with thoroughgoing exploitation and oppression, and that lauding its missionary work as a heroic undertaking. Given the obvious technological disadvantage of the aboriginal nations of the Northwest when meeting Euro-Canadian civilization, and given the fact that in unequal encounters the weaker party, if it is to survive, must adjust to the conditions decreed by the stronger party, did the Catholic missionaries assist or hinder the aboriginal people in their inevitable adjustment to the conquering culture? Did the French and Canadian Catholic missionaries make the cultural trauma caused by Euro-Amerindian contact more or less endurable for the cultural underdogs in the conflict for domination? Assuming that the technologically more powerful Euro-Canadian culture would inevitably dominate the weaker Indian cultures, was the Christian Gospel used by the missionaries an instrument of liberation or of oppression?[3]

In the nineteenth-century Northwest, the Oblates played the role that the Jesuits had played in New France. Both were agents of European cultural change, and both were the leading agents in the repression of the religions of the Indian people, religions they considered false.

Yet in both cases missionaries frequently proved to be the best allies the Indian people had among the white men. Many missionaries, both Jesuit and Oblate, devoted their entire adult careers to their Indian charges, developing lasting friendships and ties of love and affection that were severed only in death, and not even then in the eyes of the devout. Frequently, the same missionaries who sought to crush and eradicate native religions lobbied and worked tirelessly for the economic, social, and communal welfare of their aboriginal flock. The French Catholic missionary frequently became a trusted adviser, leader, and friend to the Indian people of the Northwest. That trust rested on long years, and in many cases lifetimes, of disinterested devotion and service by the missionaries. These missionaries of both seventeenth-century New France and nineteenth-century Canada had committed themselves to the best interests of their aboriginal flock, as they saw them.

As had been the case in earlier times, few and far between were the other white people who could make a similar claim. The difference was that the missionaries, Catholic and Protestant, were endeavouring to preach the Gospel.

In the end the Missionary Oblates of Mary Immaculate served to liberate the Indian people of Canada, but did so within a context of ethnocultural subjugation of the Indians driven by the Euro-Canadian conquest of Canada's North and West. Only in the latter part of the twentieth century would the Euro-Canadians put sufficient critical distance between their own culture and religion to realize that the evangelization of Canada's Indian people need not have been the bearer of such heavy cultural baggage.

But a different missionary policy would have presupposed a different Euro-Canadian culture, English and French, European and Canadian. And Oblates and CMS missionaries were men of their time, an era when the Euro-Canadian way was considered *the* way. The only disputes and disagreements pertained to less fundamental questions such as whether the French or the British, the Catholics or the Protestants, the liberals or the ultramontanes, the evangelicals or the Anglo-

Catholics, were to emerge victorious in the power stuggles that permeated God's fractured Kingdom.

Notes

1. Sam Gill, "Native American Religions," in Lippy and Williams, *Encyclopedia of the American Religious Experience*, vol. 1, p. 149.

2. John Webster Grant, *Moon of Wintertime*, p. 258.

3. I wrote of a similar situation in colonial New France in Lippy, Choquette, and Poole, *Christianity Comes to the Americas*, p. 189.

BIBLIOGRAPHY

ABEL, Kerry. *Drum Songs. Glimpses of Dene History.* Montreal and Kingston: McGill-Queen's University Press, 1993.

AIRHART, Phyllis D. *Serving the Present Age.* Montreal and Kingston: McGill-Queen's University Press, 1992.

ALEXANDER, Hartley Burr. *The World's Rim: Great Mysteries of the North American Indians.* Lincoln, Neb.: University of Nebraska Press, 1953.

BAILEY, Alfred Boldsworthy. *The Conflict of European and Eastern Algonkian Cultures, 1504–1700: A Study in Canadian Civilization.* Toronto: University of Toronto Press, 1969.

BAILLARGEON, Noël. *Le Séminaire de Québec de 1760 à 1800.* Québec: Les Presses de l'Université Laval, 1981.

BALLANTYNE, Robert M. *Hudson's Bay.* Edmonton: Hurtig Publishers, 1972.

BARMAN, Jean, Yvonne HÉBERT, and Don MCCASKILL, eds. *Indian Education in Canada.* Vol. 1, *The Legacy*; vol. 2, *The Challenge.* Vancouver: University of British Columbia Press, 1986, 1987.

BAUDRILLART, Alfred. "Le renouvellement du clergé de France au 19e siècle." *Science et Religion.* Paris: Librairie Bloud et Cie., 1903.

BEAUDOIN, Y. *Le Grand Séminaire de Marseille et scolasticat oblat sous la direction des Oblats de Marie Immaculée.* Ottawa: Éditions des Études oblates, 1966.

BEBBINGTON, D.W. *Evangelicalism in Modern Britain.* London: Unwin Hyman, 1989.

BENOÎT, Dom. *Vie de Mgr Taché.* 2 vols. Montreal: Beauchemin, 1904.

BERKHOFER, Robert F. *Salvation and the Savage: An Analysis of Protestant Missions and American Indian Response, 1787–1862.* Lexington: University of Kentucky Press, 1965.

BILLINGTON, Ray Allen. *The Protestant Crusade, 1800–1860: A Study of the Origins of American Nativism.* Chicago: Quadrangle Books, 1938, 1964.

BLANCHET, F.-N., et al. *Notices and Voyages of the Famed Quebec Mission to the Pacific Northwest, 1838–1847.* Portland: Oregon Historical Society, 1956.

BOLT, Christine. *Victorian Attitudes to Race.* London: Routledge and Kegan Paul, 1971.

BOON, Thomas C.B. *The Anglican Church from the Bay to the Rockies.* Toronto: Ryerson Press, 1952.

—. "William West Kirkby, First Anglican Missionary to the Loucheux." *The Beaver* (Spring 1965): 36–43.

—. "The Archdeacon and the Governor: William Cockran and George Simpson at the Red River Colony, 1825–65." *The Beaver* (Spring 1968): 41–49.

BOWDEN, Henry Warner. *American Indians and Christian Missions: Studies in Cultural Conflict.* Chicago: University of Chicago Press, 1981.

BRABANT, A.J. *Mission to Nootka, 1874–1900: Reminiscences of the West Coast of Vancouver Island.* Sydney, B.C.: Gray's Publishing, 1900, 1977.

BRETON, Paul-Émile. *Vital Grandin: La merveilleuse aventure de l'Évêque des Prairies et du Grand Nord.* Paris: Arthème Fayard, 1960.

BREYNAT, Gabriel. *Cinquante ans au Pays des Neiges.* Montreal: Fides, 1945.

BROOKS, William Howard. "Methodism in the Canadian West in the Nineteenth Century." Ph.D. diss., University of Manitoba, 1972.

—. "The Uniqueness of Western Canadian Methodism, 1840–1925." *Journal of the Canadian Church Historical Society* 19, 1–2 (1977): 57–74.

BROWN, G., and R. MAGUIRE. *Indian Treaties in Historical Perspective.* Ottawa: Research Branch, Department of Indian and Northern Affairs, 1979.

BROWN, Jennifer S.H. *Strangers in Blood: Fur Trade Company Families in Indian Country.* Vancouver: University of British Columbia Press, 1980.

BROWN, Robert Craig, and Ramsay COOK. *Canada, 1896–1921: A Nation Transformed.* Toronto: McClelland and Stuart, 1974.

BULIARD, Roger. *Inuk.* Paris: Éditions Saint-Germain et Pères Oblats, 1949.

BUTCHER, Dennis L., et al., eds. *Prairie Spirit: Perspectives on the Heritage of the United Church of Canada in the West.* Winnipeg: University of Manitoba Press, 1985.

CADIEUX, Lorenzo, ed. *Lettres des nouvelles missions du Canada, 1843–1852.* Montreal: Bellarmin, 1973.

CAMPBELL, Marjorie Wilkins. *The Northwest Company.* Vancouver and Toronto: Douglas and McIntyre, 1957, 1983.

CANADA. "Rapport du Comité spécial sur les causes des troubles du Territoire du Nord-Ouest, en 1869–70." *Journaux de la Chambre des Communes du Canada.* Vol. 8, appendix 6 (1874): 1–108.

CANADIAN CONFERENCE OF CATHOLIC BISHOPS, National Steering Committee. "Some Observations on the Residential School Experience and Its Implication for the Church in Canada." Ottawa: CCCB (September 1992).

CARRIÈRE, Gaston. *Les Missions catholiques dans l'Est du Canada et l'Honorable Compagnie de la Baie d'Hudson (1844–1900).* Ottawa: Éditions de l'Université d'Ottawa, 1957.

—. *Histoire documentaire de la congrégation des missionnaires Oblats de Marie-Immaculée dans l'Est du Canada.* 12 vols. Ottawa: Éditions de l'Université d'Ottawa, 1957–75.

—. "L'affaire de Blackfoot Crossing." *Revue de l'Université d'Ottawa* 17 (1967): 519–28.

—. "Le Père Albert Lacombe, o.m.i., et le Pacifique Canadien." *Revue de l'Université d'Ottawa* 18 (1968): 114–18.

—. "Mgr Provencher à la recherche d'un coadjuteur." *Sessions d'Étude* 36 (1970): 71–93.

—. "Fondation et développement des missions catholiques dans la Terre de Rupert et les Territoires du Nord-Ouest (1845–1861)." *Revue de l'Université d'Ottawa* 41 (1971): 253–81, 397–427.

—. "Le Père Pascal Ricard, évêque en Orégon?" *Études Oblates* (1971): 241–68.

—. "Les relations amicales du Père Lacombe et de Lord et Lady Aberdeen." *Études Oblates* (1971): 16–34.

—. "Les évêques oblats de l'Ouest canadien et les ruthènes (1893–1903)." *Études Oblates* (1974): 95–119.

—. *Dictionnaire biographique des Oblats de Marie-Immaculée au Canada.* 3 vols. Ottawa: Éditions de l'Université d'Ottawa, 1976, 1977, 1979.

—. "The Early Efforts of the Oblate Missionaries in Western Canada." *Prairie Forum* 4, 1 (Spring 1979): 1–26.

CARTER, Sarah. "The Missionaries' Indian: The Publications of John McDougall, John Maclean and Egerton Ryerson Young." *Prairie Forum* 9 (Spring 1984): 27–44.

CERRUTI, Pietro. "Il Padre Emile Petitot e le sue relazioni sui nord-ouest Canadese." Master's thesis, University of Genoa, 1973.

CHADWICK, Owen. *The Victorian Church: An Ecclesiastical History of England.* London: Adam and Charles Black, 1966.

CHAMPAGNE, Claude. *Les débuts de la mission dans le Nord-Ouest canadien.* Ottawa: Éditions de l'Université Saint-Paul and Éditions de l'Université d'Ottawa, 1983.

CHAMPAGNE, Joseph-Étienne. "Aux origines de la mission de la Rivière Rouge (1818–1845)." *Études Oblates* (1945): 37–59.

—. "Nos premières missions dans l'Ouest canadien (1845–1853)." *Études Oblates* (1945): 149–73.

—. "Les méthodes missionnaires des Oblats dans l'Ouest canadien (1845–1875)." *Études Oblates* (1946): 143–60.

CHARLAND, Thomas. *Le Père Gonthier et les écoles du Manitoba: Sa mission secrète en 1897–1898.* Montreal: Fides, 1979.

COCCOLA, Nicolas. "Pioneer Days in Okanagan and Kootenay. The 'Memoirs' of Father Nicolas Coccola, o.m.i., 1883–1890." *Études Oblates* (1976): 21–49.

—. "Oblate Work in Southern British Columbia (1891–1905)." *Études Oblates* (1980): 145–165.

CODY, H.A. *An Apostle of the North: Memoirs of the Right Reverend William Carpenter Bompas, D.D.* Toronto: Musson Book Co., 1908.

COLVILLE, Eden. *Letters.* Toronto: The Champlain Society, 1956.

CRONIN, Kay. *Cross in the Wilderness.* Toronto: Mission Press, 1960.

CROSBY, Thomas. *Up and Down the Pacific Coast by Canoe and Mission Ship.* Toronto: Missionary Society of the Methodist Church, 1914.

CRUNICAN, Paul. *Priests and Politicians: Manitoba Schools and the Election of 1896.* Toronto: University of Toronto Press, 1974.

DANYLEWYCZ, Marta. *Taking the Veil in Montreal, 1840–1920: An Alternative to Marriage, Motherhood and Spinsterhood.* Ph.D. diss., University of Toronto, 1981.

DAVID, L.-O. *Mgr Ignace Bourget et Mgr Alexandre Taché.* Montreal: Beauchemin, 1924.

DELACROIX, S., et al. *Histoire universelle des missions catholiques.* 3 vols. Vol. 3, *Les missions contemporaines, 1800–1957.* Paris: Librairie Grund, 1957.

DeMOISSAC, Elisabeth. "Les femmes de l'Ouest: Leur rôle dans l'histoire." Master's thesis, University of Ottawa, 1945.

—. "Les sœurs Grises et les événements de 1869–1870." SCHEC *Sessions d'Étude,* 36 (1970): 215–228.

DEMPSEY, Hugh A., ed. *The Rundle Journals, 1840–1848.* Calgary: Historical Society of Alberta, 1977.

DENAULT, Bernard, and Benoît LÉVESQUE. *Éléments pour une sociologie des communautés religieuses au Québec.* Sherbrooke and Montreal: Université de Sherbrooke and Presses de l'Université de Montréal, 1975.

D'ESCHAMBAULT, Antoine. "La Compagnie de la Baie d'Hudson et l'effort missionnaire." SCHEC *Rapport* (1944–45): 83–99.

Dictionary of Canadian Biography/Dictionnaire biographique du Canada. Ed. Francis G. Halpenny. Vols. 5 to 12 (1800–1900). Toronto and Quebec: University of Toronto Press and Les Presses de l'Université Laval, –1990.

DOWN, M.M. *A Century of Service, 1858–1958: A History of the Sisters of Saint Ann and Their Contribution to Education in British Columbia, the Yukon and Alaska.* Victoria: Sisters of Saint Ann, 1966.

DROUIN, Eméric. "The Beginnings and Development of the Catholic Church in the Edmonton Area and the Contribution of the Oblate Fathers and Brothers." *Vie Oblate* (1981): 209–250.

DUCHAUSSOIS, Pierre. *Les Soeurs Grises dans l'Extrême-Nord.* Montreal: Les Sœurs Grises, 1917.

—. *Apôtres inconnus.* Paris: Spes, 1924, 1931.

DUGAS, Georges. *Mgr Provencher et les missions de la Rivière-Rouge.* Montreal: Beauchemin, 1889.

—. *Histoire de l'Ouest canadien de 1822 à 1869.* Montreal: Beauchemin, 1906.

DUPASQUIER, Maurice. *Dom Paul Benoît et le Nouveau Monde, 1850–1915.* Ph.D. diss., Université Laval, 1970.

—. "Quelques aspects de l'œuvre de Paul Benoît au Nouveau Monde, 1891–1915." *SCHEC Sessions d'Étude* 36 (1970): 111–144.

EMERY, George Neil. "Methodism on the Canadian Prairies, 1896–1914: The Dynamics of an Institution in a New Environment." Ph.D. diss., University of British Columbia, 1970.

FARAUD, Henri. *Dix-huit ans chez les sauvages.* Paris: Régis Ruffet, 1866, 1966.

FERGUSON, Bruce, ed. *The Anglican Church and the World of Western Canada, 1820–1970.* Regina: Canadian Plains Research Centre, University of Regina, 1991.

FISHER, Robin. *Contact and Conflict: Indian–European Relations in British Columbia, 1774–1890.* Vancouver: University of British Columbia Press, 1977.

FLANAGAN, T. *Louis "David" Riel: Prophet of the New World.* Toronto: University of Toronto Press, 1979.

—. *Louis Riel and the Rebellion: 1885 Reconsidered.* Saskatoon: Western Producer Prairie Books, 1983.

FOSTER, John, ed. "Program for the Red River Mission: The Anglican Clergy, 1820–1826." *Histoire sociale/Social History* 4 (November 1969): 49–75.

—. *The Developing West.* Edmonton: University of Alberta Press, 1983.

FRANCIS, Douglas R., and Howard PALMER, eds. *The Prairie West: Historical Readings.* Edmonton: University of Alberta Press, 1984.

FRIESEN, G. *The Canadian Prairies: A History.* Toronto: University of Toronto Press, 1984.

FUMOLEAU, R. *As Long as This Land Shall Last: A History of Treaty 8 and Treaty 11, 1870–1939.* Toronto: McClelland and Stewart, n.d.

GAUVREAU, Michael. "History and Faith: A Study of the Evangelical Temper in Canada, 1820–1940." Ph D. diss., University of Toronto, 1985.

—. *The Evangelical Century.* Montreal and Kingston: McGill-Queen's University Press, 1991.

GETTY, Ian A.L. "The Failure of the Native Church Policy of the CMS in the North-West." In *Religion and Society in the Prairie West...*, ed. Richard Allen. N.p.: n.p., 1974, pp.19–34.

GILL, Sam. *Native American Religions.* Belmont, Calif.: Wadsworth Publishing Company, 1982.

GIRAUD, Marcel. *Le Métis canadien, son rôle dans l'histoire des provinces de l'Ouest.* Paris: n.p., 1945.

GORDON, Charles W. *The Life of James Robertson, Missionary Superintendent in Western Canada.* Toronto: Westminster Company, 1908.

GOWEN, Herbert H. *Church Work in British Columbia Being a Memoir of the Episcopate of Acton Windeyer Sillitoe..., First Bishop of New Westminster.* New York: Longmans, Green and Co., 1899.

GRAHAM, Elizabeth. *Medicine Man to Missionary: Missionaries as Agents of Change among the Indians of Southern Ontario, 1784–1867.* Toronto: Peter Martin Associates, 1975.

GRANT, John Webster. "Indian Missions as European Enclaves." *Studies in Religion* 7 (1978): 263–275.

—. "Missionaries and Messiahs in the Northwest." *Studies in Religion* 9 (1980): 125–136.

—. *Moon of Wintertime.* Toronto: University of Toronto Press, 1984.

—. *A Profusion of Spires.* Toronto: University of Toronto Press, 1988.

GRESKO, Jacqueline. "Missionary Acculturation Programs in British Columbia." *Études Oblates* 32 (1973): 145–58.

—. "White 'Rites' and Indian 'Rites': Indian Education and Native Responses in the West, 1870–1910." In *Western Canada Past and Present,* ed. A.W. Rasporich. Calgary: McClelland and Stewart West, 1975.

—. "Roman Catholic Missions to the Indians of British Columbia: A Reappraisal of the Lemert Thesis." *Journal of the Canadian Church Historical Society* 24 (1982): 51–62.

—. "Creating Little Dominions within the Dominion: Early Catholic Indian Schools in Saskatchewan and British Columbia." In *Indian Education in Canada,* ed. Jean Barman et al. Vol. 1, *The Legacy.* Vancouver: University of British Columbia Press, 1986, pp. 88–109.

HAIG, Alan. *The Victorian Clergy.* London: Croom Helm, 1984.

HALLIDAY, W.M. *Potlach and Totem: The Recollections of an Indian Agent.* Toronto: J.M. Dent, 1935.

HAMELIN, Jean, and Nicole GAGNON. *Histoire du catholicisme québécois.* Vol. 3. Montreal: Boréal Express, 1984.

HAMELIN, Louis-Edmond. "Évolution numérique séculaire du clergé catholique dans le Québec." *Recherches Sociographiques* 2, 2 (1961): 189–242.

HARGRAVE, Letitia. *Letters.* Toronto: Champlain Society, 1947.

HARROD, Howard L. *Mission among the Blackfeet.* Norman: University of Oklahoma Press, 1971.

HEENEY, Brian. *A Different Kind of Gentleman: Parish Clergy as Professional Men in Early and Mid-Victorian England.* Springfield, Ohio: Archon Books, 1976.

HOCEDEZ, Edgar. *Histoire de la théologie au 19ᵉ siècle.* Paris: Desclée de Brouwer, 1952.

HORNER, Norman A. *Cross and Crucifix in Mission.* New York: Abingdon Press, 1965.

HOSTIE, Raymond. *Vie et mort des ordres religieux.* Paris: Desclée de Brouwer, 1972.

HUEL, Raymond. "*La Survivance* in Saskatchewan: Schools, Politics and the Nativist Crusade for Cultural Conformity." Ph.D. diss., University of Alberta, 1975.

—. "The Public School as a Guardian of Anglo-Saxon Traditions: The Saskatchewan Experience, 1913–1918." In *Ethnic Canadians...,* ed. Martin L. Kovacs. Canadian Plains Studies 8, Regina, 1978.

—. "J.J. Maloney: How the West Was Saved from Rome, Quebec, and the Liberals." In *The Developing West,* ed. John Foster. Edmonton: University of Alberta Press, 1983, pp. 221–241.

—, ed. *Western Oblate Studies 1/Études Oblates de l'Ouest 1.* Edmonton: Western Canadian Publishers, 1990.

—, ed. *Western Oblate Studies 2/Études Oblates de l'Ouest 2.* Lewiston, Queenston, N.Y.: Edwin Mellen Press, 1992.

—, ed. *Western Oblate Studies 3/Études Oblates de l'Ouest 3.* Edmonton: Western Canadian Publishers, 1994.

HUGHES, Katherine. *Father Lacombe: The Black-Robe Voyageur.* New York: Moffat, Yard and Company, 1911.

HUTCHINSON, Gerald. "British Methodists and the Hudson's Bay Company, 1840–1854." In *Prairie Spirit,* ed. Butcher et al.

JAENEN, Cornelius J. "The Manitoba School Question: An Ethnic Interpretation." In *Ethnic Canadians: Culture and Education,* ed. Martin L. Kovacs. Regina: Plains Research Centre, 1978.

JENNESS, Diamond. *The Indians of Canada.* Ottawa: National Museum of Canada, 1960.

JENNINGS, Francis. *The Invasion of America: Indians, Colonialism, and the Cant of Conquest.* Chapel Hill: University of North Carolina Press, 1975.

JONQUET, E. *Mgr Grandin.* Montreal: n.p., 1903.

KAPSNER, Oliver R. *Catholic Religious Orders Listing Conventional and Full Names in English, Foreign Languages, and Latin. Also Abbreviations, Dates and Country of Origin and Founders.* Collegeville, Minn.: St. John's Abbey Press, 1948, 1957.

KENNEDY [GRESKO], Jacqueline. *Roman Catholic Missionary Effort and Indian Acculturation in the Fraser Valley, 1860–1900.* Essay, University of British Columbia, 1969.

—. "Qu'Appelle Industrial School: White 'Rites' for the Indians of the Old North-West." Master's thesis, Carleton University, 1970.

KOWALSKY, Nikolaus. "Mgr de Mazenod et l'œuvre de la Propagation de la Foi." *Études Oblates* 11 (1952): 239–60.

LAFLÈCHE, L.-F. "Mission de la Rivière-Rouge." *Rapport sur les Missions du diocèse de Québec* 11 (March 1855): 118–37.

LAMIRANDE, Émilien. "Unpublished Academic Literature Concerning the Oblate Missions of the Pacific Coast." *Études Oblates* (1957): 360–79.

—. "L'implantation de l'Église catholique en Colombie-Britannique, 1838–1848." *Revue de l'Université d'Ottawa* 28 (1958): 213–25, 323–63, 453–89.

—. "Le centenaire des *Missions*." *Études Oblates* (1962): 274–9.

—. "Traditions orales du XIXe siècle sur la présence de prêtres espagnols en Colombie-Britannique." *Revue de l'Université d'Ottawa* 47 (1977): 393–412.

—. "L'établissement espagnol de Nootka (1789–1795) et ses aspects religieux." *Revue de l'Université d'Ottawa* 48 (1978): 212–31.

—. "Le P. A. Trudeau, O.M.I., et son refus de l'épiscopat." *Vie Oblate* (1985): 157–81.

—. "Le rayonnement intellectuel, social et pastoral du Scolasticat Saint-Joseph." *Vie Oblate* 45 (1986): 49–78.

—. "Les Oblats et la coadjutorerie de Mgr M. Demers Ile de Vancouver (1861–1865)." *Vie Oblate* (1986): 370ff.

—. "L'Université pontificale d'Ottawa (1889–1890)." *Église et Théologie* 20 (1989): 439–69.

LANDON, Fred. "Selections from the Papers of James Evans, Missionary to the Indians." Ontario Historical Society Papers and Records, 26, 1930.

LANGLOIS, Claude. *Le catholicisme au féminin.* Paris: Les Éditions du Cerf, 1984.

LASCELLES, Thomas A. "Leon Fouquet and the Kootenay Indians, 1874–87." Master's thesis, Simon Fraser University, 1987.

—. *Roman Catholic Indian Residential Schools in British Columbia.* Vancouver: Order of OMI in B.C., 1990.

LE CHEVALLIER, Jules. *Batoche: Les missionnaires du Nord-Ouest pendant les troubles de 1885.* Montreal: L'œuvre de presse dominicaine, 1941.

LECOMPTE, R.P. *Les Anciennes Missions de la Compagnie de Jésus dans la Nouvelle-France (1611–1800)*. Montreal: Imprimerie du Messager, 1925.

—. *Les Missions modernes de la Compagnie de Jésus au Canada (1842–1924)*. Montreal: Imprimerie du Messager, 1925.

LEFLON, Jean. *Eugene de Mazenod*. 3 vols. New York: Fordham University Press, 1961.

—. "Les grands séminaires de France au XIXe siècle." *Études* (November 1963): 175–86.

LEIGHTON, J. Douglas. "The Development of Federal Indian Policy in Canada, 1840–1890." Ph.D. diss., University of Western Ontario, 1975.

—. "A Victorian Civil Servant at Work: Lawrence Vankoughnet and the Canadian Indian Department, 1874–1893." In *As Long as the Sun Shines and Water Flows*, ed. I.A.L. Getty and A.S. Lussier. Vancouver: University of British Columbia Press, 1983.

LEMERT, Edwin M. "The Life and Death of an Indian State." *Human Organization* 13 (1954).

LEMIEUX, Lucien. "Mgr Provencher et la pastorale missionnaire des évêques de Québec." *Sessions d'Étude* 37 (1970): 31–49.

—. *Les années difficiles (1760–1839)*. Montreal: Boréal Express, 1989.

LESAGE, Germain. "Début de l'évangélisation au Keewatin (1670–1846)." *Études Oblates* (1956): 50–67.

LESLIE, J., and R. MAGUIRE, eds. *The Historical Development of the Indian Act*. 2nd ed. Ottawa: Department of Indian Affairs, 1978.

LEVASSEUR, Donat. *Histoire des Missionnaires Oblats de Marie Immaculée. Essai de synthèse*. 2 vols. Montreal: Maison provinciale des OMI, 1983.

—. *Les Oblats de Marie Immaculée dans l'ouest et le nord du Canada, 1845–1967*. Manuscript. Edmonton: Western Canadian Publishers, 1993.

LEWIS, Arthur. *The Life and Work of the Rev. E.J. Peck among the Eskimos*. London: Hodder and Stoughton, 1904.

LIPPY, Charles H., Robert CHOQUETTE, and Stafford POOLE. *Christianity Comes to the Americas, 1492–1776*. New York: Paragon House, 1992.

LIPPY Charles H., and Peter W. WILLIAMS, eds. *Encyclopedia of the American Religious Experience*. New York: Charles Scribner's Sons, 1988.

LOFTHOUSE J. *A Thousand Miles from a Post Office or, Twenty Years' Life and Travel in the Hudson's Bay Regions*. London: SPCK, 1922.

LOOY, A.J. "The Indian Agent and His Role in the Administration of the North-West Superintendency, 1876–1893." Ph.D. diss., Queen's University, 1977.

LOWER, J. Arthur. *Western Canada: An Outline History*. Vancouver and Toronto: Douglas and McIntyre, 1983.

MACDONALD, Catherine. "James Robertson and Presbyterian Church Extension in Manitoba and the North West, 1866–1902." In *Prairie Spirit*, ed. Butcher et al.

MACDONALD, W., ed. *Guide to the Holdings of the Archives of the Ecclesiastical Province of Rupert's Land*. Winnipeg: [Archives of Rupert's Land], 1986.

MACGREGOR, James C. *Father Lacombe*. Edmonton: Hurtig Publishers, 1975.

MACHRAY, Robert. *Life of Robert Machray*. Toronto: Macmillan, 1909.

MACLEOD, M.A., ed. *The Letters of Letitia Hargrave*. Toronto: Champlain Society, 1947.

MAKINDISA, Isaac K. "The Praying Man: The Life and Times of Henry Bird Steinhauer." Ph.D. diss. University of Alberta, 1984.

MANLEY, Philip M. "Father Lacombe's Ladder." *Études Oblates* (1973): 82–99.

MARIE-JEAN DE PATMOS, Sœur. *Les Sœurs de Sainte-Anne: Un siècle d'histoire*. Lachine: Les Sœurs de Sainte-Anne, 1950.

MAZENOD, Eugène de. *Lettres aux correspondants d'Amérique, 1841–1850*. Écrits oblats, 1. Rome: Oblate General House, 1977.

—. *Lettres aux correspondants d'Amérique, 1851–1860*. Écrits oblats, 2. Rome: Oblate General House, 1977.

McCARTHY, Martha. "The Missions of the Oblates of Mary Immaculate to the Athapaskans, 1846–1870: Theory, Structure and Method." Ph.D. diss., University of Manitoba, 1981.

—. *To Evangelize the Nations: Roman Catholic Missions in Manitoba, 1818–1870*. Papers in Manitoba History, Report Number 2. Winnipeg: Manitoba Culture Heritage and Recreation Historic Resources, 1990.

McLAURIN, C.C. *Pioneering in Western Canada: A Story of the Baptists*. Calgary: Author, 1939.

MEYER, Patricia, ed. *Honoré-Timothée Lempfrit, O.M.I.: His Oregon Trail Journal and Letters from the Pacific Northwest, 1848–1853*. Fairfield, Washington: Ye Galleon Press, 1985.

MILLER, J.R., *Skyscrapers Hide the Heavens*. Revised edition. Toronto: University of Toronto Press, 1989.

MORICE, Adrien-Gabriel. *The History of the Northern Interior of British Columbia*. Toronto: William Briggs, 1904.

—. "The Roman Catholic Church West of the Great Lakes." In *Canada and Its Provinces*, ed. Adam Shortt and Arthur G. Doughty. Toronto: Edinburgh University Press, 1914, pp. 113–96.

—. *Histoire de l'Église catholique dans l'ouest canadien (1659–1915)*. 4 vols. Saint-Boniface and Montreal: Author and Granger Frères, 1921.

—. *M. Darveau: Martyr du Manitoba*. Winnipeg: Author, 1934.

MORTON, Arthur S. *A History of the Canadian West to 1870–71*. 2nd ed. Toronto: University of Toronto Press, 1939, 1973.

MORTON, W.L. *Manitoba: A History.* Toronto: University of Toronto Press, 1967.

MULHALL, David. *Will to Power: The Missionary Career of Father A.G. Morice.* Vancouver: University of British Columbia Press, 1986.

MURRAY, Peter. *The Devil and Mr Duncan: A History of the Two Metlakatlas.* Vancouver: Sono Nis Press, 1988.

NEWMAN, Peter C. *Company of Adventurers.* Markham: Penguin Books, 1985.

—. *Caesars of the Wilderness.* Markham: Penguin Books, 1987.

NICHOLS, M. Leona. *The Mantle of Elias: The Story of Fathers Blanchet and Demers in Early Oregon.* Portland, Ore.: Binfords and Mort, 1941. This includes 255 pages of text and eighty pages (256–337) of reprints of church records of the local parishes of the period.

NIX, James Ernest. *Mission among the Buffalo: The Labours of the Reverends George M. and John C. McDougall in the Canadian Northwest, 1860–1876.* Toronto: Ryerson Press, 1960.

NOCK, David. *A Victorian Missionary and Canadian Indian Policy: Cultural Synthesis vs. Cultural Replacement.* Waterloo: Wilfrid Laurier University Press, 1988.

NORMAN, E.R. *Anti-Catholicism in Victorian England.* New York: Barnes and Noble, 1968.

NORMANDEAU, L., et al. *Les populations amérindiennes et inuit du Canada: Aperçu démographique.* Montreal: Presses de l'Université de Montréal, 1984.

NUTE, Grace Lee. *Documents Relating to Northwest Missions, 1815–1827.* St. Paul: Minnesota Historical Society, 1942.

O'BRIEN, Conor Cruise. *God Land: Reflections on Religion and Nationalism.* Cambridge, Mass.: Harvard University Press, 1988.

ORMSBY, Margaret A. *British Columbia: A History.* Toronto: Macmillan, 1958.

ORTOLAN, T. *Les Oblats de Marie Immaculée dans le premier siècle de leur existence.* 4 vols. Paris: Lethielleux, 1914.

OWRAM, Douglas. "The Myth of Louis Riel." In *The Prairie West,* ed. Francis and Palmer.

PAINCHAUD, Robert. "Les exigences linguistiques dans le recrutement d'un clergé pour l'Ouest canadien, 1818–1920." SCHEC *Rapport* (1975): 43–64.

—. *Un rêve français dans le peuplement de la prairie.* Saint-Boniface, Man.: Éditions des Plaines, 1986.

PALMER, Howard. *Patterns of Prejudice: A History of Nativism in Alberta.* Toronto: McClelland and Stewart, 1982.

PANNEKOEK, Frits. "Protestant Agricultural Missions in the Canadian West to 1870." Master's thesis, University of Alberta, 1970.

—. "The Historiography of the Red River Settlement, 1830–1868." *Prairie Forum* 6 (Spring 1981): 75–85.

—. *A Snug Little Flock: The Social Origins of the Riel Resistance of 1869–70.* Winnipeg: Watson and Dwyer, 1991.

PAUL-ÉMILE, Soeur. *La Baie James: Trois cents ans d'histoire.* Ottawa and Montreal: Éditions Oblates and Maison-mère des SGC, 1952.

PAYTON, W.F. *An Historical Sketch of the Diocese of Saskatchewan of the Anglican Church of Canada.* Prince Albert: [Diocese of Saskatchewan], 1974.

PEAKE, F.A. *The Anglican Church in British Columbia.* Vancouver: Mitchell Press, 1959.

—. *The Bishop Who Ate His Boots: A Biography of Isaac O. Stringer.* Toronto: Anglican Church of Canada, 1966.

—. "Fur Traders and Missionaries: Some Reflections on the Attitude of the Hudson's Bay Company towards Missionary Work among the Indians." *Western Canadian Journal of Anthropology* 3 (1972): 72ff.

—. "Robert McDonald (1829–1913): The Great Unknown Missionary of the Northwest." *JCCHS* 17 (September 1975): 54–72.

—. "The Achievements and Frustrations of James Hunter." *JCCHS* 19 (July–December 1977).

—. "David Anderson...." *JCCHS* 24 (April 1982): 3–46.

—. "Anglicanism on the Prairies: Continuity and Flexibility." In *Visions of the New Jerusalem,* ed. Benjamin G. Smillie, 1983.

—. "From the Red River to the Arctic." Full issue of *Journal of the Canadian Church Historical Society (JCCHS)* 21 (October 1989).

PETTIPAS, Katherine, ed. *The Diary of the Reverend Henry Budd 1870–1875.* Winnipeg: Manitoba Record Society Publications, 1974.

PIOLET, J.-B. *Les Missions Catholiques Françaises au XIXe siècle.* Vol. 6, *Missions d'Amérique.* Paris: Librairie Armand Colin, 1903.

POULIOT, Léon. "Mgr Bourget et la mission de la Rivière-Rouge." *Sessions d'Étude* 37 (1970): 17–30.

PRUD'HOMME, L.A. *Monseigneur Noël-Joseph Ritchot.* Winnipeg: n.p., 1928.

RAWLYK, George A., ed. *The Canadian Protestant Experience, 1760–1990.* Burlington, Ont.: Welch Publishing Co., 1990.

REARDON, James Michael. *George Anthony Belcourt: Pioneer Catholic Missionary of the North West, 1803–1874.* St. Paul, Minn.: North Central Publishing Co., 1955.

RICH, E.E., ed. *London Correspondence from Eden Colville, 1849–1852.* London: Hudson's Bay Record Society, 1956.

—. *The Fur Trade and the Northwest to 1857.* The Canadian Centenary Series 11. Toronto: McClelland and Stewart, 1967.

RIDDELL, J.H. *Methodism in the Middle West.* Toronto: Ryerson Press, 1946.

ROCHE, Claude. *Monseigneur du grand nord.* N.P.: Éditions Ouest-France, 1989.

ROSS, Alexander. *The Red River Settlement.* Edmonton: Hurtig Publishers, 1972.

ROY, David. "Monseigneur Provencher et son clergé séculier." *Sessions d'Étude* 37 (1970): 1–16.

RYERSON, John. *Hudson's Bay, or A Missionary Tour.* Toronto: G.R. Sanderson, 1855.

SAGE, Walter. "The Early Days of the Church of England on the Pacific Slope 1579–1879." *JCCHS* 2 (June 1953).

SCHOENBERG, Wilfred P. *Paths to the Northwest: A Jesuit History of the Oregon Province.* Chicago: Loyola University Press, 1982.

SHEA, John Gilmary. *Catholic Missions among the Indian Tribes of the United States.* New York: Arno Press and *The New York Times,* [1883] 1969.

SILVER, A.I. "French Canada and the Prairie Frontier, 1770–1890." In *The Prairie West,* ed. Francis and Palmer, pp. 140–162.

SIMONSON, Gayle. "The Prayer Man: Ojibwa Henry Bird Steinhauer Brought Religion to the Cree." *The Beaver* (October–November 1988): 28–33.

SMILLIE, Benjamin. *Visions of the New Jerusalem: Religious Settlement on the Prairies.* Edmonton: NeWest Press, 1983.

—. "The Woodsworths: James and J.S.—Father and Son." In *Prairie Spirit,* ed. Butcher et al.

SŒUR DE LA PROVIDENCE. *Le Père Lacombe... d'après ses mémoires et souvenirs.* Montreal: *Le Devoir,* 1916.

SPRY, I. "The Métis and Mixed-Bloods of Rupert's Land before 1870." In *The New Peoples: Being and Becoming Métis in North America,* ed. J. Peterson and J.S.H. Brown. Winnipeg: University of Manitoba Press, 1985, pp. 95–118.

STANLEY, George F.G. *The Birth of Western Canada: A History of the Riel Rebellions.* Toronto: University of Toronto Press, 1936, 1963.

STOCK, Eugene. *The History of the Church Missionary Society: Its Environment, Its Men and Its Work.* 4 vols. London: CMS, 1899.

STOGRE, Michael. *That the World May Believe: The Development of Papal Social Thought on Aboriginal Rights.* Sherbrooke: Éditions Paulines, 1992.

SYLVAIN, Philippe, and Nive VOISINE. *Histoire du catholicisme québécois.* Vol. 2, 2. *Réveil et consolidation.* Montreal: Boréal Express, 1991.

TACHÉ, Alexandre. "Vingt années de missions." *Missions OMI* 5 (1866): 342–75.

THÉRIAULT, Michel. *The Institutes of Consecrated Life in Canada from the Beginning of New France up to the Present: Historical Notes and References.* Ottawa: National Library of Canada, 1980.

THOMAS, Lewis Gwynne. "The Church of England and Higher Education in the Prairie West before 1914," *JCCHS* 13, 1 (January 1956): 1–11.

THOMPSON, Arthur N. "The Expansion of the Church of England in Rupert's Land from 1820–39 under the Hudson's Bay Company and the Church Missionary Society." Ph.D. diss., University of Cambridge, 1962.

—. "The Wife of the Missionary." *JCCHS* 15 (1973): 35–44.

THOMPSON, Margaret E. *The Baptist Story in Western Canada.* Calgary: Baptist Union of Western Canada, [1975].

TIMS, John W. "Anglican Beginnings in Southern Alberta." *JCCHS* 9, 2 (June 1967): 28–40.

TITLEY, E. Brian. *A Narrow Vision: Duncan Campbell Scott and the Administration of Indian Affairs in Canada.* Vancouver: University of British Columbia Press, 1986.

—. "Indian Industrial Schools in Western Canada." In *Schools in the West: Essays in Canadian Educational History,* ed. N. Sheehan, D. Jones, and J.D. Wilson. Calgary: Detselig, 1986.

—. "Religion, Culture and Power: The School Question in Manitoba." In *Canadian Education: Historical Themes and Contemporary Issues,* ed. E. Brian Titley. Calgary: Detselig, 1990, pp. 45–77.

TUCKER, S. *The Rainbow in the North: A Short Account of the Establishment of Christianity in Rupertsland by the Church Missionary Society.* London: James Nisbet and Co., 1858.

USHER, Jean. "Apostles and Aborigines: The Social Theory of the Church Missionary Society." *Histoire sociale/Social History* 7 (April 1971): 28–52.

—. *William Duncan of Metlakatla: A Victorian Missionary in British Columbia.* Ottawa: National Museums of Canada, 1974.

VAN KIRK, Sylvia. *Many Tender Ties: Woman in Fur-Trade Society in Western Canada 1670–1870.* Winnipeg: Watson and Dyer Publishing, 1980.

VOISINE, Nive. "L'abbé Louis-François Laflèche, missionnaire dans l'Ouest." *Sessions d'Étude* 36 (1970): 61–9.

VOISINE, Nive, and Jean HAMELIN, eds. *Les ultramontains canadiens-français.* Montreal: Boréal Express, 1985.

WESTFALL, William. *Two Worlds: The Protestant Culture of Nineteenth-Century Ontario.* Kingston and Montreal: McGill-Queen's University Press, 1989.

WHITEHEAD, Margaret. *The Cariboo Mission: A History of the Oblates.* Victoria: Sono Nis Press, 1981.

—, ed. *They Call Me Father: Memoirs of Father Nicolas Coccola.* Vancouver: University of British Columbia Press, 1988.

WILLIAMS, C. Peter. "'Not Quite Gentlemen': An Examination of 'Middling Class' Protestant Missionaries from Britain, c. 1850–1900." *Journal of Ecclesiastical History* 31, 3 (July 1980): 301–15.

—. *The Ideal of the Self-governing Church: A Study in Victorian Missionary Strategy.* Leiden and New York: E.J. Brill, 1990.

WILSON, J. Donald. "No Blanket to Be Worn in School: The Education of Indians in Nineteenth-Century Ontario." In *Indian Education in Canada,* ed. Jean Barman et al. Vol. 1, *The Legacy.* Vancouver: University of British Columbia Press, 1986, pp. 64–87. The article originally appeared in *Histoire sociale/Social History* 7, 14 (November 1974): 292–305.

WILSON, Keith. *William Carpenter Bompas.* Winnipeg: Faculty of Education, University of Manitoba, n.d.

ZASLOW, Morris. "The Missionary as Social Reformer: The Case of William Duncan." *JCCHS* 8 (September 1966): 52–69.

—. *The Opening of the Canadian North, 1870–1914.* The Canadian Centenary Series. Toronto: McClelland and Stewart, 1971.

ZIMMER, Ronald P. "Early Oblate Attempts for Indian and Métis Priests in Canada." *Études Oblates* 32 (1973): 276–91.

INDEX OF NAMES